Foundations in Accountancy/ACCA

Applied Knowledge

Business and technology (FBT/BT)

Workbook

For exams from 1st September 2022 to 31st August 2023

BPP LEARNING MEDIA

First edition 2020

Second edition 2022

ISBN: 9781-5097-4556-2

Previous ISBN: 9781-5097-3761-1

ISBN (for internal use only): 9781-5097-4553-1

e-ISBN: 9781-5097-4602-6

British Library Cataloguing-in-Publication Data

A catalogue record for this book is available from the British Library

Published by

BPP Learning Media Ltd

BPP House, Aldine Place

142–144 Uxbridge Road

London W12 8AA

www.bpp.com/learningmedia

Printed in the United Kingdom

Note. Your learning materials, published by BPP Learning Media Ltd, are printed on paper obtained from traceable sustainable sources.

Contains public sector information licensed under the Open Government Licence v3.0

We are grateful to the Association of Chartered Certified Accountants for permission to reproduce past examination questions and extracts from the syllabus. The suggested solutions in the further question practice bank have been prepared by BPP Learning Media Ltd, except where otherwise stated.

Contents

Helping you to pass

BPP Learning Media – ACCA Approved Content Provider

As an ACCA Approved Content Provider, BPP Learning Media gives you the opportunity to use study materials reviewed by the ACCA examining team. By incorporating the examining team's comments and suggestions regarding the depth and breadth of syllabus coverage, the BPP Learning Media Workbook provides excellent, ACCA-approved support for your studies.

These materials are reviewed by the ACCA examining team. The objective of the review is to ensure that the material properly covers the syllabus and study guide outcomes, used by the examining team in setting the exams, in the appropriate breadth and depth. The review does not ensure that every eventuality, combination or application of examinable topics is addressed by the ACCA Approved Content. Nor does the review comprise a detailed technical check of the content as the Approved Content Provider has its own quality assurance processes in place in this respect.

BPP Learning Media do everything possible to ensure the material is accurate and up to date when sending to print. In the event that any errors are found after the print date, they are uploaded to the following website: www.bpp.com/learningmedia/Errata.

The PER alert

Before you can qualify as an ACCA member, you not only have to pass all your exams but also fulfil a three-year practical experience requirement (PER). To help you to recognise areas of the syllabus that you might be able to apply in the workplace to achieve different performance objectives, we have introduced the 'PER alert' feature (see the next section). You will find this feature throughout the Workbook to remind you that what you are learning to pass your ACCA exams is equally useful to the fulfilment of the PER requirement. Your achievement of the PER should be recorded in your online My Experience record.

Chapter features

Studying can be a daunting prospect, particularly when you have lots of other commitments. This Workbook is full of useful features, explained in the key below, designed to help you to get the most out of your studies and maximise your chances of exam success.

Key term

Central concepts are highlighted and clearly defined in the Key terms feature. Key terms are also listed in bold in the Index, for quick and easy reference.

Formula to learn

This boxed feature will highlight important formula which you need to learn for your exam.

PER alert

This feature identifies when something you are reading will also be useful for your PER requirement (see 'The PER alert' section above for more details).

Real world examples

These will give real examples to help demonstrate the concepts you are reading about.

Illustration

Illustrations walk through how to apply key knowledge and techniques step by step.

Activity

Activities give you essential practice of techniques covered in the chapter.

Essential reading

Links to the Essential reading are given throughout the chapter. The Essential reading is included in the free eBook, accessed via the Exam Success Site (see inside cover for details on how to access this).

At the end of each chapter you will find a Knowledge diagnostic, which is a summary of the main learning points from the chapter to allow you to check you have understood the key concepts. You will also find a Further study guidance which contains suggestions for ways in which you can continue your learning and enhance your understanding. This can include: recommendations for question practice from the Further question practice and solutions (available in the digital edition of the Workbook), to test your understanding of the topics in the Chapter; suggestions for further reading which can be done, such as technical articles, and ideas for your own research.

Introduction to the Essential reading

The electronic version of the Workbook contains additional content, selected to enhance your studies. Consisting of revision materials and further explanations of complex areas (including illustrations and activities), it is designed to aid your understanding of key topics which are covered in the main printed chapters of the Workbook.

A summary of the content of the Essential reading is given below.

Chapter		Summary of Essential reading content
1	Business organisations and stakeholders	• Types of business organisation, providing more detail on the various different types of organisation
2	The business environment	• Environmental factors • Social and demographic changes • Cultural trends • Competitive advantage - Porter's five forces model
3	The legal framework	• Termination of employment
4	The macro-economic environment	• Government policies and obligations • Unemployment
5	Micro-economic factors	• Markets and competition • Supply • Elasticity • Long-run and short-run cost curves
6	Business organisation structure	• Organisational structure - includes important information including outsourcing and offshoring.
7	Organisational culture and committees	• The marketing function - includes more detail about the marketing mix • The finance function - an important area
8	Corporate governance and social responsibility	• Principles of corporate governance • Developments in corporate governance • Corporate governance regulations • Committees
9	Role of accounting	• What is accounting? • International Accounting Standards Board • Financial systems and controls

10	Control, security and audit	• Other classifications of internal control procedures
		  - Internal checks
		  - Internal audit and internal control systems
		  - Systems integrity issues for PCs and networks
		  - Further information on Fintech
		  - Distributed ledger technology

11	Identifying and preventing fraud	• Fraud controls • Evolving control systems
12	Leading and managing	• Leading and managing - further details about the role of managers, including project management

Chapter		Summary of Essential reading content
		• The process of management • Management theory • Contingency theories
13	Recruitment and selection	• Recruitment and job design • Interviews
14	Individuals, groups and teams	• Individuals
15	Motivating individuals and groups	• Job design as a motivator
16	Training and development	• Training needs and objectives • Training methods
17	Performance appraisal	• Purpose of performance appraisal • The process of performance appraisal
18	Personal effectiveness and communication	• Personal development • Managing conflict
19	Ethical considerations	• The ethical environment • Ethical threats

Introduction to Business Technology (FBT)

Overall aim of the syllabus

To introduce knowledge and understanding of the business and its environment and the influence this has on how organisations are structured and on the role of the accounting and other key business functions in contributing to the efficient, effective and ethical management and development of an organisation and its people and their interaction with technology, data and information systems.

Brought forward knowledge

There is no brought forward knowledge for this paper.

The syllabus

The broad syllabus headings are:

A	The business organisation, its stakeholders and the external environment
B	Business organisational structure, functions and governance
C	Accounting and reporting systems, compliance, control, technology and security
D	Leading and managing individuals and teams
E	Personal effectiveness and communication in business
F	Professional ethics in accounting and business

Main capabilities

On successful completion of this exam, you should be able to:

A	Understand the purpose and types of businesses and how they interact with key stakeholders and the external environment.
B	Understand business organisation structure, functions and the role of corporate governance.
C	Recognise the functions, systems and new technologies in accountancy and audit in communicating, reporting and assuring financial information, including the effective compliance, internal control and security of financial and other data.
D	Recognise the principles of authority and leadership and how teams and individuals are recruited, managed, motivated and developed.
E	Understand the importance of personal effectiveness as the basis for effective team and organisational behaviour.
F	Recognise that all aspects of business and finance should be conducted in a manner which complies with and is in the spirit of accepted professional ethics and professional values.

Links to other exams

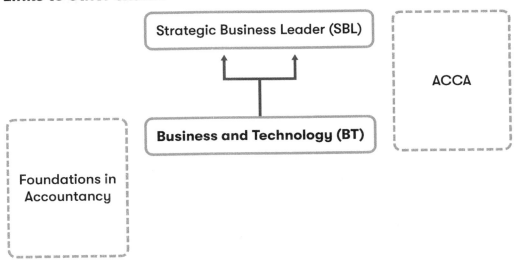

This diagram shows where direct (solid line arrows) and indirect (dashed line arrows) links exist between this exam and others that may precede or follow it.

The FBT syllabus assumes auditing knowledge acquired in FBT.

Achieving ACCA's Study Guide Outcomes

This BPP Workbook covers all the FBT syllabus learning outcomes. The tables below show in which chapter(s) each area of the syllabus is covered.

A	The business organisation, its stakeholders and the external environment	
A1	The purpose and types of business organisation	Chapter 1
A2	Stakeholders in business organisations	Chapter 1
A3	Political and legal factors affecting business	Chapters 2 & 3
A4	Macro-economic factors	Chapter 4
A5	Micro-economic factors	Chapter 5
A6	Social and demographic factors	Chapter 2
A7	Technological factors	Chapter 2
A8	Environmental factors	Chapter 2
A9	Competitive factors	Chapter 2

B	Business organisations structure, functions and governance	
B1	The formal and informal business organisation	Chapter 6
B2	Business organisation structure and design	Chapters 6 & 7
B3	Organisational culture in business	Chapters 2 & 3
B4	Committees in business organisations	Chapter 7
B5	Governance and social responsibility in business	Chapter 8

C		Accounting and reporting systems, compliance, control, technology and security
C1	The relationship between accounting and other business functions	Chapter 6
C2	Accounting and finance functions within business organisations	Chapters 7, 9 & 10
C3	Principles of law and regulation governing accounting and audit	Chapter 9
C4	The sources and purpose of internal and external financial information, provided by business	Chapter 9
C5	Financial systems, procedures and related IT applications	Chapters 9 & 10
C6	Internal controls, authorisation, security of data and compliance within business	Chapter 10
C7	Fraud and fraudulent behaviour and their prevention in business, including money laundering	Chapter 11
C8	The impact of Financial Technology (Fintech) on accounting and systems	Chapter 10

D		Leading and managing individuals and teams
D1	Leadership, management and supervision	Chapter 12
D2	Recruitment and selection of employees	Chapter 13
D3	Individual and group behaviour in business organisations	Chapter 14
D4	Team formation, development and management	Chapter 14
D5	Motivating individuals and groups	Chapter 15
D6	Leading and training at work	Chapter 17
D7	Review and appraisal of individual performance	Chapter 16

E		Personal effectiveness and communication in business
E1	Personal effectiveness techniques	Chapter 18
E2	Consequences of ineffectiveness at work	Chapter 18
E3	Competence frameworks and personal development	Chapter 18
E4	Sources of conflicts and techniques for conflict resolution and referral	Chapter 18
E5	Communicating in business	Chapter 18

F	Professional ethics in accounting and business	
F1	Fundamental principles of ethical behaviour	Chapter 19
F2	The role of regulatory and professional bodies in promoting ethical and professional standards in the accountancy profession	Chapter 19
F3	Corporate codes of ethics	Chapter 19
F4	Ethical conflicts and dilemmas	Chapter 19

The complete syllabus and study guide can be found by visiting the exam resource finder on the ACCA website: www.accaglobal.com/gb/en.html.

The exam

Computer-based exams

Computer-based examinations (CBEs) are available for all of the Foundations in Accountancy exams. The CBE exams for the first seven modules can be taken at any time; these are referred to as 'exams on demand'. The Option exams can be sat in June and December of each year; these are referred to as 'exams on sitting'. For more information on CBE exams and to access Specimen exams in the CBE software, please visit the ACCA website.

How do CBEs work?

- Questions are displayed on a monitor.
- Candidates enter their answer directly onto the computer.
- Candidates have two hours to complete the examination.
- Candidates sitting exams on demand are provided with a Provisional Result Notification showing their results before leaving the examination room.
- The CBE Licensed Centre uploads the results to the ACCA (as proof of the candidate's performance) within 72 hours.
- Candidates sitting the Option exams will receive their results approximately five weeks after the exam sitting once they have been expert marked.
- Candidates can check their exam status on the ACCA website by logging into myACCA.

Benefits

- Flexibility – the first seven modules, exams on demand can be sat at any time.
- Resits for the first seven modules can also be taken at any time and there is no restriction on the number of times a candidate can sit a CBE.
- Instant feedback for the exams on demand as the computer displays the results at the end of the CBE.

For more information on computer-based exams, visit the ACCA website.

www.accaglobal.com/gb/en/student/exam-entry-and-administration/computer-based-exams.html

Essential skills areas to be successful in Business Technology (FBT)

We think there are three areas you should develop in order to achieve exam success in FBT:

(a) Knowledge application

(b) Specific FBT skills

(c) Exam success skills

These are shown in the diagram below.

Specific FBT skills

These are the skills specific to FBT that we think you need to develop in order to pass the exam.

In this Workbook, there are five **Skills Checkpoints** which define each skill and show how it is applied in answering a question. A brief summary of each skill is given below.

Skill 1: Approaching objective test questions

All questions in the BT/FBT exam are OT questions, using a number of different formats.

BPP recommends a step-by-step technique for approaching objective test questions:

Step 1	Answer the easier questions first.
Step 2	Answer all questions.
Step 3	Start each question by reading the requirement.
Step 4	Apply your technical knowledge to the data in the question.

Skills checkpoint 1 covers this technique in detail through application to an exam-standard question.

Skill 2: Learning the models

There are many models in the BT/FBT syllabus that you need to know for the exam. This Skills Checkpoint provides you with advice on how to learn the models.

Step 1	Look at the chapter overview to see the context in which the model belongs.
Step 2	Read through the technical section on the model quickly.
Step 3	Read the technical section again more slowly reflecting on what the model is saying and understanding it.
Step 4	Close your book and write a summary of as much of the model as you can remember.
Step 5	Write some notes, using the memory techniques detailed in the Skill.
Step 6	Attempt the questions in the further question practice to test your knowledge.

Skills checkpoint 2 covers this technique in detail through application to an exam-standard question.

Skill 3: Approaching corporate governance questions

Corporate governance questions involving application of knowledge are not done well according to the examiner's reports. Some techniques are introduced in this Skills Checkpoint to help you succeed better. While the skills are focussed at corporate governance questions, they can be applied to many other application questions in the BT/FBT exam.

BPP recommends a step-by-step technique for approaching corporate governance questions:

Step 1	Read the requirement of the question carefully.
Step 2	Read the scenario. Think about: • Why does the situation present a threat to good corporate governance? • What should/ could be done to reduce the threat?
Step 3	Read the options provided in the question. Eliminate those options which are obviously incorrect. Rank the remaining options and choose the most relevant/ likely option (s).

Skills checkpoint 3 covers this technique in detail through application to an exam-standard question.

Skill 4: Approaching multi-task questions

Section B of the exam contains six multi-task questions of four marks each. In this section you have to answer many different types of OT question, and details of the different types of question are given in this skills point.

The questions can be challenging because they tend to contain longer scenarios than the Section A questions, so you need to manage more information.

BPP recommends a step-by-step technique for approaching multi-task questions:

Step 1	Read the requirements of all tasks
Step 2	Recall any relevant technical theory.
Step 3	Read the scenario
Step 4	Answer each task in turn, doing the easiest task first.

Skills checkpoint 4 covers this technique in detail through application to an exam-standard question.

BPP LEARNING MEDIA

Skill 5: Approaching ethics questions

Questions on ethics are likely to feature highly in your exam. Ethics questions are difficult as they often require some judgement rather than being black and white.

A step-by-step technique for attempting these questions is outlined below. It is similar to the structure we have seen for our other Skills.

Step 1	Read the requirements of the question
Step 2	Read through the scenario. Think about: • Whose ethics are under discussion (the company, and employee etc.) • What should they do/ what should they have done if they are behaving ethically
Step 3	Read the options in the question: • Eliminate any options that are obviously not correct • Choose from the remaining options based on which are most likely/ most relevant.

Skills checkpoint 5 covers this technique in detail through application to an exam-standard question.

Exam success skills

Passing the FBT exam requires more than applying syllabus knowledge and demonstrating the specific FBT skills; it also requires the development of excellent exam technique through question practice.

We consider the following six skills to be vital for exam success. The Skills Checkpoints show how each of these skills can be applied specifically to the FBT exam.

Exam success skill 1

Managing information

You will not have to deal with large amounts of information in each individual question in FBT.

Some of the questions in the exam will present you with a short scenario, particularly in the Section B questions. The skill is how you handle this information while working under time pressure.

You must take an active approach to reading each scenario. Focus on the requirement first, underlining/ highlighting key instructions, including words like "NOT" . Then think about any technical knowledge that is relevant before reading the scenario for the question. Doing this means that your mind will be focussed as you read the scenario, which means you will take in the information better.

Exam success skill 2

Correct interpretation of the requirements

It is important to note the requirement carefully. Look out for the number of options you have to choose, as not all questions require only one option. Also, beware of tricks, such as the information being presented in one particular order in the scenario, but being presented in a different order in the options.

Exam success skill 3

This skill is not so relevant for the skills exams.

Exam success skill 4

Efficient numerical analysis

While there could be a small number of numerical questions on topics such as elasticity of demand, the majority of questions in BT/ FBT are qualitative in nature so this skills is not as important as in some of the other ACCA exams.

An important tip in numerical questions is not to look at the options until you have completed the calculation as you think it should be done. The reason for this is that the "wrong answers" are chosen carefully to look very realistic, and you may be tempted to choose one of these if you don't do the calculation first.

Exam success skill 5

Effective writing and presentation

This skill is not relevant for BT/FBT as all the questions are objective test questions so you will not have to write.

Exam success skill 6

Good time management

The exam is 2 hours long. You should therefore spend 1.2 minutes per mark. It is best to work through Section A first, which should take you 91 minutes, before spending the remaining 29 minutes on Section B.

Don't get stuck on difficult questions - if a particular question does appear difficult, move on, and come back to it after you have answered all the easier questions.

Don't time yourself for each question, but do check every half hour that you have answered 25 marks worth of questions.

Two minutes before the end of your time for Section A, go back and answer all outstanding questions, even if you have to guess. There is no harm in guessing as there is no negative marking in ACCA exams, so the worst that can happen is you don't gain two marks for the question.

If you find that this approach doesn't work for you, don't worry – you can develop your own technique.

Question practice

Question practice is a core part of learning new topic areas. When you practice questions, you should focus on improving the Exam success skills – personal to your needs – by obtaining feedback or through a process of self-assessment.

1

Business organisations and their stakeholders

Learning outcomes

On completion of this chapter you should be able to:

	Syllabus reference no.
Define 'business organisations' and explain why they are formed.	A1 (a)
Describe common features of business organisations.	A1 (b)
Outline how business organisations differ.	A1 (c)
List the industrial and commercial sectors in which business organisations operate.	A1 (d)
Identify the different types of business organisation and their main characteristics: (a) Commercial (b) Not-for-profit (c) Public sector (d) Non-governmental organisations (e) Co-operatives	A1 (e)
Define stakeholders and explain the agency relationship in business and how it may vary in different types of business organisation.	A2 (a)
Define internal, connected and external stakeholders and explain their impact on the organisation.	A2 (b)
Identify the main stakeholder groups and the objectives of each group.	A2 (c)
Explain how the different stakeholder groups interact and how their objectives may conflict with one another.	A2 (d)
Compare the power and influence of various stakeholder groups and how their needs should be accounted for, such as under the Mendelow framework.	A2 (e)

Exam context

This chapter lays the foundation for an understanding of what organisations are and how they are controlled. According to the Study Guide, it is not sufficient to simply understand these topics – you must also be able to **apply** your knowledge. It is highly examinable, as shown by the fact that six marks out of 100 in the pilot paper test knowledge from this chapter.

Chapter overview

1 Purpose of business organisations

> **Organisation:** A **social arrangement** which pursues collective **goals**, **controls** its own performance and has a **boundary** separating it from its environment.

1.1 What all organisations have in common

The common characteristics of organisations are as follows:

(a) They pursue a **variety of objectives** and goals.

(b) Different people do different things or specialise in one activity.

(c) Organisations are keen to achieve good **performance**, and meeting or improving their standards.

(d) Organisations contain formal, documented **systems and procedures** which enable them to control what they do.

(e) Most organisations obtain **inputs** (eg materials), and **process** them into **outputs** (eg for others to buy).

1.2 Why organisations exist

Organisations can achieve results which individuals cannot achieve by themselves.

Activity 1: Reason organisations exist

List ways in which organisations can achieve results that individuals cannot achieve by themselves.

Solution

1.3 How organisations differ

The common elements of organisations were described earlier, but organisations also differ in many ways. Here are some areas of difference:

- **Ownership:** private sector vs public sector
- **Control:** owners vs managers
- **Activity:** manufacturing vs services
- **Profit vs non-profit orientation**
- **Legal form:** limited company vs partnership,
- **Size:** small family business vs small and medium sized enterprise vs multinational
- **Sources of finance:** shares, banks, government funding
- **Technology:** use of technology, complexity of production

1.4 Sectors in which business organisations operate

Organisations work in many different business sectors.

Here is a list of the broad categorisation of industry sectors:

Industry	Activity
Agriculture	Producing and processing food
Manufacturing	Acquiring raw materials and, by the application of labour and technology, turning them into a product (eg a car)
Extractive/raw materials	Extracting and refining raw materials (eg mining)
Energy	Converting one resource (eg coal) into another (eg electricity)
Retailing/distribution	Delivering goods to the end consumer
Intellectual production	Producing **intellectual property** (eg software, publishing, films, music)
Service industries	Including retailing, distribution, transport, banking, various business services (eg accountancy, advertising) and public services such as education, medicine
Information technology	Hardware, software and communications links

1.5 Types of business organisation

The key categories of business organisation are:

- Commercial
- Not for profit
- Public sector
- Charities
- Trade unions
- Local authorities
- Non-governmental organisations(NGOs)
- Co-operative societies and mutual associations

Activity 2: Types of business organisation

Identify one 'real-world' example of each of the above categories of organisation.

Solution

1.6 Key sources of differences between profit and not for profit organisations:

- Owner and other stakeholders
- Sources of funding (eg revenue vs. donations)
- Goals (Primary goal of profit orientated business is maximising shareholder wealth while not for profit is the provision of goods/services)
- How they measure performance: profit focus vs value for money/efficiency
- Use of technology (eg Apple Inc vs news agency or social club)

1.7 Public sector organisations

Organisations owned or run by the government (local or national) or government agencies are described as being in the **public sector**. All other organisations are classified as **private sector**.

Activity 3: Public sector organisations

Identify the advantages and disadvantages of using public sector organisations to provide services such as the armed forces or the health service.

Solution

1.8 Limited liability companies

Limited liability companies (denoted by X Ltd or X plc in the UK) are a separate legal entity from their owners (shareholders). The key advantage is that the shareholder's liability is limited to the amount they have invested into that company.

Other notable advantages of a Ltd/plc company are:

- More money available for investment from shareholders
- Easier to raise capital from banks and other lenders
- Ownership and control are legally separated, investors need not run the company

Notable disadvantages would include

- Greater administrative burden and cost, especially for listed entities
- Lack of privacy as anyone can download the financial statements and other public data

In the UK, limited companies come in two types: private limited companies (eg X Limited) and public limited companies (X plc):

- Private companies are usually owned by a small number of people (family members), and their shares are not easily transferable usually.
- Shares of public companies (plcs) will usually be traded on a Stock Exchange. The directors of a public company are less likely to hold a significant shareholding in the company.

Activity 4: Legal form

Florence Nightingale runs a successful and growing small business as a sole trader. She wishes to expand the business and has acquired Scutari Ltd, a small private limited company in the same line. After the acquisition, she runs the two businesses as if they were one operation, making no distinction between them.

Required

What is the legal form of the business she is running?

1.9 Co-operative societies and mutual associations

Co-operatives are businesses owned by their workers or customers, who share the profits. Here are some of the features they have in common.

- Open membership
- Democratic control (one member, one vote)
- Distribution of the surplus in proportion to purchases
- Promotion of education
- Social goals

Although limited companies also have some measure of democratic control, this is on the basis of one share, one vote. So one shareholder could dominate a company if they hold a majority of shares. This would not happen in a co-operative.

Mutual associations are organisations that exist for the mutual benefit of their members. Examples include savings and loan organisations (building societies in the UK) where the members are the savers who deposit their savings in the organisation. Since there are no external shareholders to pay dividends to, the profits of the organisation are enjoyed by members in the form of more favourable interest rates.

Real life example

The best example of a co-operative in the UK is the *Co-operative Foodstores Ltd*. Another example is the *Co-operative Funeral Services Ltd*

Essential reading

See Chapter 1 Sections 1 and 2 of the Essential reading for more on types of business organisation.

The Essential reading is available as an Appendix of the digital edition of the Workbook.

2 Stakeholders

KEY TERM

Stakeholder: A person or group of persons who have a stake in the organisation.

PER alert

In order to fulfil performance objective 2, you must demonstrate that you can identify the key stakeholders that an organisation has, and understand their needs. You can apply the knowledge you obtain from this chapter to help demonstrate this competence.

2.1 Stakeholders and agency

An organisation's managers act as **agents** for the stakeholders, whose influence varies from organisation to organisation. The **agency relationship** in a company therefore refers to the separation between an organisation's owners (the shareholders) as the 'principal', and those managing the organisation on their behalf (the company directors) as their 'agents'.

2.1.1 Main stakeholder groups

Primary

Stakeholders in a business	What is at stake?	What do they typically expect of the business?
Shareholders (or partners or proprietor)	Money invested	A return on their investment so that their wealth increases: • Steady, growing profits paid out by the business • Growth in capital value of their share of the business

Secondary

Stakeholders in a business	What is at stake?	What do they typically expect of the business?
Directors/managers Employees and trade unions	Livelihoods, careers and reputations	Fair and growing remuneration Career progression Safe working environment Training, Pension
Customers	Their custom	Products/services that are of good quality and value Fair terms of trade, Continuity of supply
Suppliers and other business partners	The items they supply	Fair terms of trade, Prompt payment Continuity of custom
Lenders	Money lent	A return on their investment: • Interest • Repayment of capital
Government and its agencies	National infrastructure used by business The welfare of employees Tax revenue	Reasonable employment and other business practices Steady or rising stream of tax revenue
The local community and the public at large	National infrastructure used by business The welfare of employees	Reasonable employment and other business practices
The natural environment	The environment shared by all	Reasonable environmental and other business practices

2.2 Internal, connected and external stakeholders

Johnson and Scholes (2005) identified three types of stakeholder: ICE

(a) **Internal:**

Corporate management

Employees

(b) **Connected:**

Shareholders

Debt holders (eg bank)

Intermediate (business) and final (consumer) customers

Suppliers

(c) **External:**

Immediate community/society at large

Competitors

Special interest groups

Government

2.3 Stakeholder conflict

Since their interests may be widely different, **conflict between stakeholders** can be quite common. Managers must take the potential for such conflict into account when setting policy and be prepared to deal with it if it arises in a form that affects the organisation.

A relationship in which **conflict** between stakeholders is vividly characterised is that between **managers and shareholders.** The relationship can run into trouble when the managers' decisions focus on maintaining the corporation as a **vehicle for their managerial skills** while the shareholders wish to see radical changes so as to enhance their **dividend stream and increase the value of their shares.** The shareholders may feel that the business is a **managerial corporation** run for the benefit of managers and employees without regard for the objectives of the owners. The conflict in this case can be seriously detrimental to the company's stability.

(a) Shareholders may **force resignations and divestments of businesses**, while managers may seek to preserve their empire and provide growth at the same time by undertaking risky policies.

(b) In most cases, however, managers cannot but acknowledge that the shareholders have the **major stake** as owners of the company and its assets. Most companies therefore focus on making profits and increasing the market value of the company's shares, sometimes at the expense of the long-term benefit of the company. Hence long-term strategic plans may be 'hijacked' by the need to make a sizeable profit in one particular year; planning horizons are reduced and investment in long-term business prospects may be shelved.

Clearly, each stakeholder group considers itself in some way **a client of the organisation**, thus broadening the debate about organisation effectiveness.

2.4 Mendelow's Matrix

Stakeholders can be mapped on Mendelow's Matrix in terms of:

- How **interested** they are in the company's strategy (would they **want** to resist it)
- How much **power** they have over the company's strategy (would they be **able** to resist it)

The matrix can be used to:

- **Track the changing influences** between **different stakeholder** groups over time. This can act as a trigger to change strategy as necessary; and
- **Assess the likely impact that a strategy** will have on different stakeholder groups.

Its aim is to assess:

- Whether stakeholders' resistance is likely to inhibit the success of the strategy; and
- What policies or actions may ease the acceptance of the strategy.

		Level of interest	
		Low	High
Power	Low	A eg Casual labour Action: **Minimal Effort**	B eg Core employees Action: **Keep Informed**
	High	C eg Institutional shareholder Action: **Keep Satisfied**	D eg Main suppliers Action: **Key Players**

An organisation can make strategic gains from effectively managing its stakeholder relationships and it needs to **measure levels of satisfaction** amongst its stakeholders. Measurement will not be easy but ideally a combination of qualitative and quantitative measures needs to be established.

Chapter summary

Business organisations and their shareholders

Purpose of business organisations

What all business organisations have in common
- Organisations are social arrangements which pursue collective goals
- Most are preoccupied with performance
- Organisations allow people to specialise

Why organisations exist
- Organisations can achieve results which individuals cannot achieve by themselves

How organisations differ
- Organisations differ in many ways including profit vs non profit and legal form

Sectors in which business organisations operate
- Agriculture
- Manufacturing
- Extractive/raw materials
- Energy
- Retail/distribution
- Intellectual production
- Service industries

Types of business organisation
- Commercial
- Not for profit
- Public sector
- Charities
- Trades unions
- Local authorities
- Non-governmental organisations
- Co-operatives

Key differences between profit and not for profit organisations
- Owners and other stakeholders
- Goals
- Performance measurement

Public sector organisations
- Owned or run by local or national government

Limited liability companies
- Separate legal entity
- Private (ltd) or public limited companies (plcs)

Stakeholders

Shareholders and agency
- Stakeholders are persons who have a stake in an organisation
- Managers act as agents on behalf of the owners of the organisation (the principals)

Main stakeholder groups
- Shareholders
- Directors/managers
- Customers
- Suppliers
- Lenders
- Government and its agencies
- Public
- Natural environment

Internal, connected and external stakeholders
- Internal – management and employees
- Connected – shareholders, customers, suppliers, lenders
- External – competitors, government, society

Stakeholder conflict
- Managers vs shareholders
- Stakeholders are clients of the organisation

Mendelow's Matrix
- Stakeholder classified by power and level of interest

Information for control purposes
- Control is achieved through feedback

Knowledge diagnostic

1. Why do organisations exist?

Organisations can achieve results which individuals cannot achieve themselves.

2. Types of organisation

Key types of organisation include commercial, not for profit, public sector and non-governmental organisations (NGOs).

3. Limited liability companies

Limited liability companies are separate legal entities from their owners.

4. Stakeholders and agency

Stakeholders are persons who have a stake in an organisation.

5. Stakeholder conflict

Managers must take into account the stakeholder's power and interest, and focus on balancing the needs of the different stakeholder when making strategy.

Further study guidance

Question practice

Now try the following from the Further question practice bank [available in the digital edition of the Workbook]:

Number	Level	Marks	Approximate time
Q1	Exam Section A	1	1 min
Q2	Exam Section B	1	1 min
Q3	Exam Section C	2	2 mins
Q4	Exam Section D	4	5 mins

Further reading

There are three articles on the ACCA website entitled "Communicating core values and mission", "Not-for-profit organisations I" and "Not-for-profit organisations II" that are relevant to material in this chapter. You are strongly advised to read these articles in full as part of your preparation for the FBT exam.

Activity answers

Activity 1: Reason organisations exist

Ways organisations can achieve results:

(1) Organisations **overcome people's individual limitations**, whether physical or intellectual.

(2) Organisations **enable people to specialise** in what they do best.

(3) Organisations **save time**, because people can work together or do two aspects of a different task at the same time.

(4) Organisations **accumulate** and share **knowledge**.

(5) Organisations enable **synergy**: by bringing **together** two individuals their combined output will exceed their output if they continued working separately.

Activity 2: Types of business organisation

Here are some examples, but clearly this is not an exhaustive list:

- Commercial: *BPP*
- Not for profit: *BUPA*
- Public sector: *The National Health Service*
- Charities: *Cancer Research*
- Trade unions: *GMB Trade Union*
- Local authorities: *North Yorkshire County Council*
- Non-governmental organisations (NGO) *Red Cross*
- Co-operatives: The Co-operative Group Ltd

Activity 3: Public sector organisations

Advantages:

- Economies of scale
- Fill the gap left by the private sector
- Cheaper service so available to a significant proportion of society

Disadvantages:

- Government influence
  - On funding
  - On running
- Inefficiencies are not addressed

Activity 4: Legal form

This is quite a tricky question. For example, if suppliers have contracts with Scutari Ltd, the contract is with the company; Florence is not legally liable for the company's debts. If their contracts are with Florence, they are dealing with her personally. Florence has to make a choice.

(1) She can run the entire business as a sole trader, in which case Scutari Ltd's assets must be transferred to her.

(2) She can run her entire business as a limited company, in which case she would contribute the assets of her business as capital to the company.

(3) She can ensure that the two businesses are legally distinct in their assets, liabilities, income and expenditure.

 BPP LEARNING MEDIA

2

Business Environment

Learning outcomes

On completion of this chapter you should be able to:

	Syllabus reference no.
Explain how the political system and government policy affect the organisation.	A3 (a)
Explain the medium and long-term effects of social and demographic trends on business outcomes and the economy.	A6 (a)
Describe the impact of changes in social structure, values, attitudes and tastes on the organisation.	A6 (b)
Identify and explain the measures that governments may take in response to the medium and long-term impact of demographic change.	A6 (c)
Explain the potential effects of technological change on the organisation structure and strategy: (a) Downsizing (b) Delayering (c) Outsourcing	A7 (a)
Describe the impact of information technology and information systems development on business processes and the changing role of the accountant in business as a result of technological advances.	A7 (b)
List ways in which the business can affect or be affected by its physical environment.	A8 (a)
Describe ways in which businesses can operate more efficiently and effectively to limit damage to the environment.	A8 (b)
Identify the benefits of economic sustainability to stakeholders.	A8 (c)
Identify a business's strengths, weaknesses, opportunities and threats (SWOT) in a market and the main sources of competitive advantage.	A9 (a)
Identify the main elements within Porter's value chain and explain the meaning of a value network.	A9 (b)
Explain the factors or forces that influence the level of competitiveness in an industry or sector using Porter's five forces model.	A9 (c)

	Syllabus reference no.
Describe the activities of an organisation that affect its competitiveness: (a) Purchasing (b) Production (c) Marketing (d) Service	A9 (d)

Exam context

Organisations need to understand and appreciate the environment in which they operate in order to maximise their potential competitive advantage. The models in this chapter form the foundation of knowledge that you will need in ACCA exams.

Chapter overview

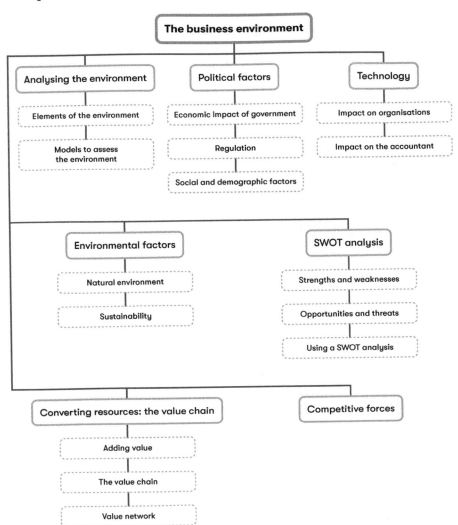

1 Analysing the environment

1.1 Elements of the environment

The environment can be described as **everything which is beyond the organisational boundary.**

Management cannot control the environment; however it influences all aspects of organisational activity and so must be viewed strategically. It comprises a number of different elements:

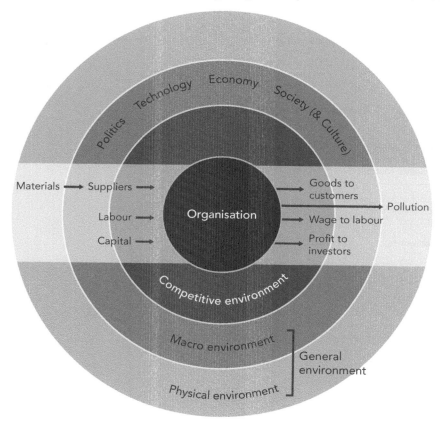

The general environment covers all the **political/legal, economic, social/cultural** and **technological** influences in the countries in which an organisation operates.

 ## Activity 1: Relevance of the environment

Consider a company specialising in building houses.

Generate as many ideas as you can as to factors in their environment that affect their business.

Solution

1.2 Models to assess the environment

Structures or frameworks have been developed which help organisations to analyse the environment. In this chapter we look at three key models which can be used to assess a company's environment:

(a) **PESTEL analysis** (Section 2 below) is used as a framework for identifying the factors that influence the macro environment:

P   Political

E   Economic

S   Social/Cultural/Fashion

T   Technology

E   Environmental

L   Legal

(b) The Value Chain is used to analyse the activities that a business performs to identify how they add value to the customer.

(c) Porter's Five Forces model analyses the competitive nature of a particular industry.

2 Political factors

Government policy influences the economic environment, the framework of laws, industry structure and certain operational issues. Political instability is a cause of risk as it means that businesses' longer-term plans cannot be achieved. Different approaches to the political environment apply in different countries. International trade is subject to a further layer of international law and regulation,

2.1 Economic impact of government

Porter notes several ways whereby the **government** can directly affect the **economic structure** of an industry. They are explained below:

Capacity expansion	Government policy can encourage firms to increase or cut their capacity. (a) The UK tax system offers 'capital allowances' to encourage investment in equipment. (b) A variety of incentives, funded by the EU and national governments, exist for locating capacity in a particular area. (c) **Incentives** are used to encourage investment by overseas firms.
Demand	• The government is a major customer. • Government can also influence demand by legislation, tax reliefs or subsidies.
Emerging industries	Can be promoted by the government or damaged by it.
Entry barriers	Government policy can discourage firms from entering an industry, by restricting investment or competition or by making it harder, by use of quotas and tariffs, for overseas firms to compete in the domestic market.
Competition	(a) The government's **purchasing decisions** will have a strong influence on the strength of one firm relative to another in the market (eg armaments). (b) **Regulations and controls** in an industry will affect the growth and profits of the industry – eg minimum product quality standards.

| | (c) As a supplier of **infrastructure** (eg roads), the government is also in a position to influence competition in an industry. |
| | (d) Governments and supra-national institutions such as the EU might impose policies which keep an industry **fragmented**, and prevent the concentration of too much market share in the hands of one or two producers. |

2.2 Regulations

In some industries, governments regulate the adoption of **new products**. This is well illustrated by the pharmaceuticals industry, where new drugs or medicines must in many countries undergo stringent testing and obtain government approval before they can be marketed.

National and supra national (e.g. WTO) bodies also affect the operating activities of some organisations, for example:

- Anti-discrimination legislation
- Health and safety legislation
- Product safety and standardisation
- Workers' rights (eg unfair dismissal, maternity leave)
- Training and education policies (which can determine the 'standard' of recruits)

Activity 2: Political factors

State in what ways government policy might affect a pharmaceutical company.

Essential reading

See Chapter 2 Section 1 of the Essential reading for more detail on the ways in which the political factors may impact on businesses.

The Essential reading is available as an Appendix of the digital edition of the Workbook.

3 Socialanddemographic factors

Changes in social attitudes impact the demand for goods and services, and so opportunities open up or close down. For example, there have been significant changes in attitudes to:

(a) Health

(b) The environment

(c) Diversity

Changes in the population can influence businesses over the longer term, for example the large spike in the birth rate after the second world war in many countries has meant that these countries now have a larger number of senior citizens (often referred to as the 'baby boomers') and many countries are experiencing a fall in birth rates.

Organisations are impacted by social and demographic factors in two ways:

(a) The population affects an organisation's supply of labour and hence its policies towards recruiting and managing human resources.

(b) Social and demographic factors influence the buying behaviour of individuals and households.

3.1 Impact on labour force

Organisations must take account of a range of factors when managing its labour force:

(a) What **skills do we need?** – recruitment, retention, motivation

(b) What **skills are available:**

    (i) Internally?

    (ii) Externally?

(c) How does the education system contribute to our **labour supply**?

3.2 Impact on buying behaviour

The impact of social and demographic trends on businesses include:

(a) Growing markets (eg for sports-related goods or holidays for senior citizens)

(b) Employee health (and its impact on employers' productivity)

(c) Declining markets for unhealthy products (eg tobacco)

(d) Consumers switching to products that conform to their beliefs (eg switching to electric cars to reduce carbon emissions)

(e) More flexible working patterns

Essential reading

See sections 2 and 3 of Chapter 2 of the Essential reading for more detail on the ways in which social, demographic and cultural changes may impact on businesses.

The Essential reading is available as an Appendix of the digital edition of the Workbook.

3.3 Government response to demographic change

Demographic changes vary from region to region. In Europe, North America, and much of Asia and Latin America, populations are ageing, as improvements in healthcare increase life expectancy, while in many countries birth rates are falling. This can lead to the following challenges:

(a) A smaller proportion of the population will be working while a larger portion of the population will rely on support in the form of pensions and healthcare.

(b) There may be a shortage of labour as the number of people of working age falls.

Governments need to plan for these long-term changes. Measures that governments might take include the following:

(a) Encouraging people to work beyond the statutory retirement age. Incentives such as more flexible pension arrangements, whereby people do not lose their pensions if they continue to work.

(b) Provision of training to update the skills of older workers.

(c) Increasing the statutory retirement age to reflect longer life expectancy.

In some countries, particularly on the African continent, a huge increase in the birth rate is forecast, which will lead to growing and much younger populations. This will mean that a higher portion of the population will be of working age. However, governments will still have challenges, and will need to:

(a) Ensure provision of sufficient housing for the larger populations.

(b) Pursue policies that will lead to a growth in jobs (eg encouraging direct foreign investment).

(c) Providing relevant education and training to give the workforce the skills they require.

4 Technology

4.1 Impact on organisations

Information systems and information technology have played a significant role in the development of the modern business environment.

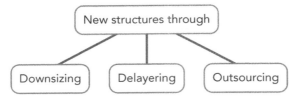

> **Delayering:** The removal of layers of middle management. Managers or staff lower down the hierarchy are empowered to make decisions previously made by middle managers.
>
> **Downsizing:** Reducing the headcount in an organisation by making redundancies. This has been driven by developments such as automation, where routine tasks that were once performed by labourers are now performed by robots.
>
> **Outsourcing:** The contacting out of specified operations or services to an external vendor.

Modern communications technology makes decentralised organisations possible, allowing decision-making to be passed down to 'empowered' workers or outsourced to external companies. This has been assisted by improved management information systems.

Delayering has gone hand in hand with a trend towards **downsizing** whereby large numbers of managers and staff have been made redundant.

There has been a trend in recent years for businesses to outsource peripheral activities to specialist organisations, enabling the business to focus on its own core activities. Activities that are commonly outsourced include (but are not limited to) IT services.

When finalising arrangements for **outsourcing IT** the following factors need to be considered:

(a) Is the system of **strategic importance**? Yes, tend towards keeping it 'in house'

(b) Can the system be relatively **isolated**? Yes, tend towards outsourcing

(c) Do we **understand the systems** enough to manage the service agreement?

4.2 Impact on accountants

The following technological advances are also having an impact on the **role of the accountant**:

(a) Routine processing

(b) Digital information and record keeping

(c) New skills required and new ways of working

(d) Reliance on IT

(e) New methods of communication and of providing customer service

(f) The view of information as a valuable resource

(g) The view of information as a commodity

Activity 3: Technology and the accountant

Discuss how you think technology will change the role of the accountant.

5 Environmental factors

5.1 Natural environment

There is increasing concern about businesses' relationship with the natural environment. Businesses may suffer **significant costs** and a **loss of reputation** if problems arise.

Much business activity takes place at some cost to the environment. Examples of impacts on the environment include:

(a) Depletion of natural resources

(b) Noise and aesthetic impacts

(c) Residual air and water emissions

(d) Long-term waste disposal (caused by excessive product packaging)

(e) Uncompensated health effects

(f) Change in the local quality of life (through for example the impact of tourism)

Failing to take sufficient account of environmental impact can have a significant impact on the business as well as the outside world.

Activity 4: Limiting damage to the environment

Suggest actions that a manufacturing company could take that would reduce the damage it causes to the environment.

Solution

5.2 Sustainability

KEY
TERM

> **Sustainability:** Meeting the needs of the present without compromising the ability of future generations to meet their needs.
>
> **Environmental sustainability:** The ability of organisations to operate without harming the environment irreversibly
>
> **Social sustainability:** The ability of organisations to have a positive impact on society, for example by creating employment and treating employees and other stakeholders fairly.
>
> **Economic sustainability:** The ability of the organisation to provide a return to shareholders over the longer term.

Businesses are recognising that in order to be economically sustainable, they need to consider not only short-term financial performance, but the wider impact they have on society and on the environment. The three types of sustainability are therefore interlinked.

Many organisations publish sustainability reports which aim to show their impact on society rather than just financial returns to shareholders. Typically, reports include the following:

- The impact the organisation has on the environment (eg the volume of carbon emissions generated)

BPP
LEARNING
MEDIA

- The use of scarce resources, such as raw materials and energy
- The use of and development of intangible resources such as human capital
- Relationships with employees and other key stakeholders

In the short term, operating in a sustainable and environmentally friendly fashion may increase the costs of a business. However, over the longer term, there can be numerous benefits.

Real life example

Oil giant BP states in its sustainability report "Our ambition is to become a net zero company by 2050 or sooner, and help the world get to net zero." *(BP 2019)*

Activity 5: Sustainability and stakeholders

What are the benefits to each of the following stakeholders of a business aiming to achieve economic sustainability?

- Shareholders
- Employees
- Customers
- Suppliers
- The local community

6 SWOT analysis

The sections above discussed the external environment and the factors that might affect organisations. As part of the strategic planning process, organisations may analyse the internal and external environments, and then summarise these using SWOT analysis.

SWOT analysis is a method of environmental analysis which looks at an organisation's internal strengths and weaknesses as well as external opportunities and threats:

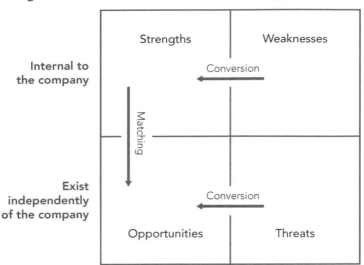

6.1 Strengths and weaknesses

An internal appraisal will identify:

(a) The areas of the organisation that have **strengths** that should be exploited by suitable strategies

(b) The areas of the organisation that have **weaknesses.** Businesses can either avoid strategies that might be affected by their weaknesses, or find ways to overcome them - for example developing new capabilities. This is what is meant by converting weaknesses into strengths.

The strengths and weaknesses analysis is intended to shape the organisation's approach to the external world. For instance, the identification of shortcomings in products could lead to a programme of product development.

6.2 Opportunities and threats

The external appraisal identifies **opportunities** that can be exploited by the organisation's strengths and anticipates environmental **threats** against which the company must protect itself.

Opportunities

(a) What opportunities exist in the business environment?

(b) What is their inherent profit-making potential?

(c) Can the organisation exploit the worthwhile opportunities?

(d) What is the comparative capability profile of competitors?

(e) What is the company's comparative performance potential in this field of opportunity?

Threats

(a) What threats might arise to the company or its business environment?

(b) How will competitors be affected?

(c) How will the company be affected

It may be possible to turn a threat into an opportunity by developing new strategies to overcome the threat that may lead to greater opportunities.?

6.3 Using a SWOT analysis

The SWOT analysis can be used in one of two ways.

(a) The organisation can develop **resource-based strategies** which enable the organisation to extend the use of its strengths. For example, a supermarket chain extends its range of own branded goods from food to other areas.

(b) The business can develop **positioning-based strategies**. In other words, identifying what opportunities are available and what the firm has to do to exploit them.

7 Converting resources: the value chain

Michael Porter (1985) says that competitive advantage is achieved by the way a firm **organises and performs activities to add value.**

7.1 Creating value

Organisations create value when they do something that customers are willing to pay for. Take a restaurant for example:

A restaurant's activities can be divided into buying food, cooking it and serving it. There is no reason why customers cannot do all these things themselves at home. However, customers are happy to pay the restaurant more than the cost of the resources. The ultimate value a firm creates is measured by the amount customers are willing to pay for its products or services above the cost of carrying out value activities. A restaurant's activities can be divided into buying food, cooking it, and serving it. There is no reason why customers cannot do all these things themselves at home. However, customers are happy to pay the restaurant more than the cost of the resources. The ultimate value a firm creates is measured by the amount customers are willing to pay for its products or services above the cost of carrying out value activities. A firm is profitable if the realised value to customers exceeds the collective cost of performing the activities.

7.2 The Value Chain

Porter's Value Chain (1985) groups an organisation's various activities into a **value chain:**

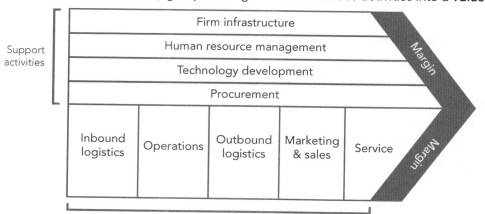

The **margin** is the excess the customer is prepared to **pay** over the **cost** to the firm of obtaining resource inputs and providing value activities. It represents the **value created** by the **value activities** themselves and by the **management of the linkages** between them.

Primary activities are directly related to production, sales, marketing, delivery and service.

Actions	Comment
Inbound logistics	Receiving, handling and storing inputs to the production system: warehousing, transport, inventory control, and so on
Operations	Convert resource inputs into a final product. Resource inputs are not only materials. People are a resource, especially in service industries
Outbound logistics	Storing the product and its distribution to customers: packaging, testing, delivery, and so on
Marketing and sales	Informing customers about the product, persuading them to buy it, and enabling them to do so: advertising, promotion, and so on
Service	Installing products and\or the act of performing the service for the client or customer. Includes all aspects of post-sales service delivery

Support activities provide purchased inputs, human resources, technology and infrastructural functions to support the primary activities.

Activity	Comment
Procurement (purchasing)	Acquire the resource inputs to the primary activities (eg purchase of materials, subcomponents equipment)
Technology development	Product design, improving processes and/or resource utilisation
Human resource management	Recruiting, training, developing and rewarding people
Firm infrastructure	Planning, finance, quality control: Porter believes they are crucially important to an organisation's strategic capability in all primary activities

Linkages connect the activities of the value chain.

(a) **Activities in the value chain affect one another**. For example, more costly product design or better quality production might reduce the need for after-sales service.

(b) **Linkages require co-ordination**. For example, Just In Time requires smooth functioning of operations, outbound logistics and service activities such as installation.

7.3 Value networks

Activities and linkages that add value do not stop at the organisation's **boundaries**. For example, when a restaurant serves a meal, the quality of the ingredients – although they are chosen by the cook – is determined by the grower. The grower has added value, and the grower's success in growing produce of good quality is as important to the customer's ultimate satisfaction as the skills of the chef.

According to *Johnson et al, (2019)*, an organisation's value chain is connected to the value chains of suppliers, distributors and customers in what may be referred to as a **value network**.

A value network extends the idea of a value chain beyond the boundaries of a business. It recognises that there is a network of businesses that together generates value for the ultimate customer. These businesses exchange both tangible (for example goods) and services with each other. Examples of services include knowledge such as collaborative design.

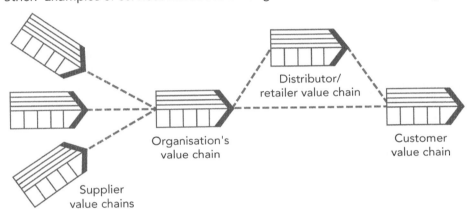

Activity 6: Value Chain

Draw two Value Chain diagrams and in each section make notes on what you would expect to see within the value chain for:

(1) A fast food restaurant

(2) A celebrity chef's restaurant

8 Competitive forces

Michael Porter (1980) argues that the pressures of **five competitive forces**, specific to the industry or organisation, will determine long-term shareholder returns.

The model may be used in two ways:

(a) To understand the **inherent attractiveness** of an industry

(b) By **understanding the impact** of each individual force on an organisation, actions may be taken to mitigate that force.

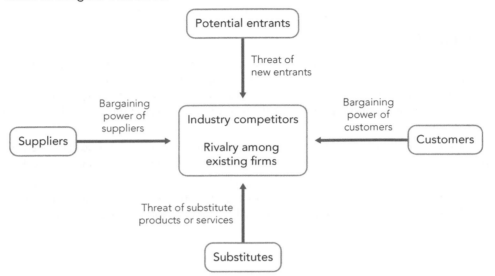

(a) **Substitutes.** The threat that alternative products or services will equally satisfy customer needs, eg substitutes for travelling to France: ferry, plane, train or even swimming!

(b) **Potential entrants.** The threat posed by an outside organisation that may try to penetrate the marketplace. Examples of barriers include economies of scale, product differentiation, capital costs, distribution channels.

(c) **Buyer power.** The power customers have to reduce prices and increase quality or to simply shop around. This depends on switching costs to change provider, the customer's relative size, and the number of buyers.

(d) **Supplier power.** The power suppliers have to increase prices and reduce quality. This depends on, for example, monopoly power and switching costs and relative size of supplier.

(e) **Competition and rivalry.** The inherent level of rivalry and competition in the industry between existing firms.

PER alert

PER performance objective PO3 requires you to demonstrate practical experience of strategy and innovation. This would mean that you need to be familiar with your employer's business, the sector in which it operates and the wider business environment, as covered in this chapter.

Essential reading

See Chapter 2 Section 4 of the Essential reading for more detail on Porter's five forces model.

The Essential reading is available as an Appendix of the digital edition of the Workbook.

Chapter summary

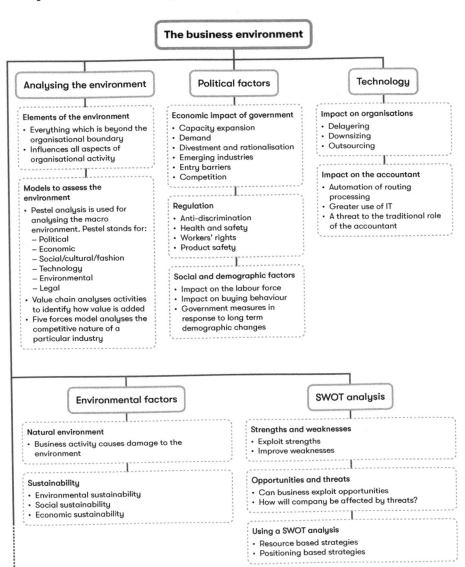

The business environment

Analysing the environment

Elements of the environment
- Everything which is beyond the organisational boundary
- Influences all aspects of organisational activity

Models to assess the environment
- Pestel analysis is used for analysing the macro environment. Pestel stands for:
  - Political
  - Economic
  - Social/cultural/fashion
  - Technology
  - Environmental
  - Legal
- Value chain analyses activities to identify how value is added
- Five forces model analyses the competitive nature of a particular industry

Political factors

Economic impact of government
- Capacity expansion
- Demand
- Divestment and rationalisation
- Emerging industries
- Entry barriers
- Competition

Regulation
- Anti-discrimination
- Health and safety
- Workers' rights
- Product safety

Social and demographic factors
- Impact on the labour force
- Impact on buying behaviour
- Government measures in response to long term demographic changes

Technology

Impact on organisations
- Delayering
- Downsizing
- Outsourcing

Impact on the accountant
- Automation of routing processing
- Greater use of IT
- A threat to the traditional role of the accountant

Environmental factors

Natural environment
- Business activity causes damage to the environment

Sustainability
- Environmental sustainability
- Social sustainability
- Economic sustainability

SWOT analysis

Strengths and weaknesses
- Exploit strengths
- Improve weaknesses

Opportunities and threats
- Can business exploit opportunities
- How will company be affected by threats?

Using a SWOT analysis
- Resource based strategies
- Positioning based strategies

Converting resources: the value chain

Adding value
- Value: customers pay more than cost

The value chain
- Primary activities
  - Inbound logistics
  - Operations
  - Outbound logistics
  - Marketing and sales
  - Service
- Support activities
  - Firm infrastructure
  - Human resource management
  - Technology development
  - Procurement

Value network
- Supplier value chains
- Organisation's value chain
- Distributor value chain

Competitive forces
- Substitutes
- Potential entrants
- Buyer power
- Supplier power
- Competition and rivalry

Knowledge diagnostic

1. Relevance of the environment

The environment influences all aspects of organisational activity so must be viewed strategically.

2. The PESTEL model

The PESTEL model is used to analyse the macro environment. Pestel stands for Political, Economic, Social, Technological, Environmental and Legal.

3. Political factors

Political factors include the economic impact of the government and the legal and regulatory framework.

4. Social factors

Social factors examine how changes in society such as demographic changes and changes in culture impact businesses, in particular the supply of labour, and changing demand for products and services.

5. Technological

Developments in IT pervade organisations and have led to delayering and downsizing, resulting in flatter organisations.

6. Environmental

Sustainability refers to operating in a way that does not compromise the needs of future generations, and can be discussed under three categories: environmental, social and economic.

7. SWOT analysis

SWOT analysis is a useful tool for summarising the results of the internal capabilities of an organisation (strengths and weaknesses) and the external environment (opportunities and threats).

8. Value chain

Porter's value chain model helps to analyse the different activities that organisations perform to help identify which of these are the drivers of value.

9. Five forces model

Porter's five forces model highlights the competitive forces that determine how attractive a particular industry is.

Further study guidance

Question practice

Now try the following from the Further question practice bank [available in the digital edition of the Workbook]:

Number	Level	Marks	Approximate time
Q5	Exam Section A	2	2 mins
Q6	Exam Section A	2	2 mins
Q7	Exam Section A	2	2 mins

Own research

Select a country of your choice and imagine that you are thinking of starting a new manufacturing business there. Using the internet, do a PESTEL analysis of the country. On the basis of your analysis, conclude whether it would be a good place to start your business.

Activity answers

Activity 1: Relevance of the environment

Environment factors affecting business:

- Demographics – (demand for retirement homes/four bed houses/high rise flats).
- Government policy on provision on new homes in the country or changes in governments.
- Changes to building regulations concerning the building of new homes eg solar panels being fitted to flats of a certain size.
- New technology to increase efficiency of property, or to increase efficiency of building property.
- Conditions in supporting industries, for example the banks and how willing they are to lend, influences demand for new homes.
- Economic factors such as changes to transaction tax/stamp duty threshold and taxes levied on house builders

Activity 2: Political factors

Ways government policy might affect a pharmaceutical company:

- The government must authorise most new drugs (eg for safety before they can be sold).
- The government, through the health service, is a major purchaser of drugs, so has significant buying power.
- Health education policies affect consumer demand.
- Funding of universities affects the science base for recruitment.
- Employment practices in all industries are influenced by the political attitudes of the government.

Note. The above is not an exhaustive list, and you may have listed other factors.

Activity 3: Technology and the accountant

The role of the accountant is already changing in the following ways:

- Many of the routine aspects of bookkeeping are performed automatically or by non-accountants (eg sales in retail businesses are recorded by the electronic point of sales systems at checkout, bank transactions feed into accounting systems from the bank).
- Much of the internal management information was traditionally provided by the management accountant. With the increase in analytical tools and databases, managers may produce their own reports directly from the system.
- Accountants are likely to have a more strategic role, helping plan the information needs of the organisation and interpreting information.

Activity 4: Limiting damage to the environment

The following are some actions that a manufacturing company could take to reduce the damage it causes to the environment:

(1) Improve energy efficiency to reduce consumption of fuels, which produce carbon emissions. Energy efficiency can be improved by using more energy efficient machinery.

(2) Switching to renewable sources of energy such as solar or wind energy.

(3) Recycling waste rather than sending it all to landfill sites.

(4) Using filters and other equipment to reduce the toxicity of emissions.

(5) Reduce packaging in final products, or introduce reusable packaging.

BPP
LEARNING
MEDIA

(6) Educate staff to be conscious of energy usage (eg turning off lights when they leave the office).

Activity 5: Sustainability and stakeholders

The benefits to stakeholders of a business aiming to achieve economic sustainability include the following:

- Shareholders: If the business is sustainable, shareholders will enjoy a return on their investment over the longer term.

- Employees: Employees will have greater job security and career progression. They may also enjoy personal development if the company invests in training.

- Customers: Customers will have a reliable supply of the goods they buy.

- Suppliers: If the business is sustainable then suppliers will also prosper as demand for inputs will continue.

- The local community will benefit because a successful business has a positive impact on the local economy, allowing supporting businesses to develop.

Activity 6: Value Chain

Support activities	Fast food	Celebrity restaurant
Firm Infrastructure	Quality control	Quality assurance
Technology development	High degree of innovation, to drive down cost	High degree of innovation, to create something 'special'
HR Management	Hire an unskilled workforce and train them in the corporate way; Low quality uniforms; Motivate by reward	Hire chef's with vast experience, less training required; High quality uniforms; Motivate by recognition
Procurement	Buying in bulk from regular suppliers; Less focus on healthy happy animals	Buying from local farms; Focus on ethically sourced meat, eggs etc

Primary activities		
Inbound Logistics	Delivered en masse, once a week	Delivered more frequently to ensure quality
Operations	Cooked in batches; Quality in producing the same burger every time	Cooked to order; Quality in creating a meal specific to the consumer
Outbound logistics	Customer takes the product to the table and collects condiments and napkins themselves	Staff wait on their customers
Sales and marketing	Branding cups, containers and bags	Word of mouth
After sales care	Limited	'Is everything alright with your meal' mentality

3

The legal framework

Learning outcomes

On completion of this chapter you should be able to:

	Syllabus reference no.
Explain how the political system and government policy affect the organisation.	A3 (a)
Describe the sources of legal authority, including supra-national bodies, national and regional governments.	A3 (b)
Explain how the law protects the employee and the implications of employment legislation for the manager and the organisation.	A3 (c)
Identify the principles of data protection and security.	A3 (d)
Explain how the law promotes and protects health and safety in the workplace.	A3 (e)
Recognise the responsibility of the individual and organisation for compliance with laws on data protection, security and health and safety.	A3 (f)
Outline principles of consumer protection, such as sale of goods and simple contracts.	A3 (g)

Exam context

It is important for business managers, including accountants, to be aware of the key laws that apply to the organisations that they manage. This chapter includes information about the laws relating to four key areas that will be relevant to most business organisations. In the Specimen Exam there were two questions in Section A relating to material covered in this chapter.

Chapter overview

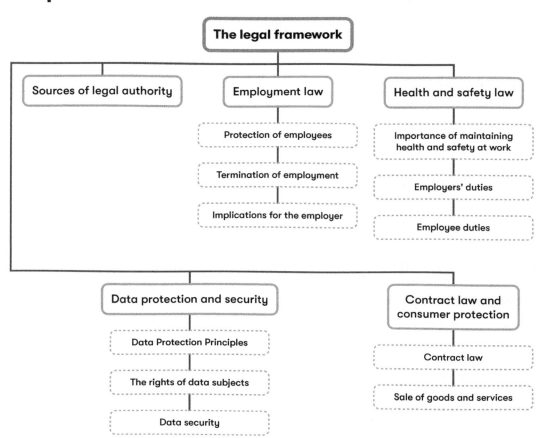

1 Sources of legal authority

The **legal framework** in which organisations operate derives from:

(a)   Parliamentary legislation

(b)   Government regulations

(c)   Treaty obligations

(d)   Official regulations

(e)   International bodies

Key legislation for business organisations includes:

- Employment law (see 2 below)
- Health and Safety (see 3 below)
- Data Protection (see 4 below)
- Sale of Goods (Consumer Rights) (see 5 below)

2 Employment law

2.1 Protection of employees

Employment law aims to protect the interests of employees. Generally, employment laws tend to cover the following areas:

- **Recruitment** in particular to ensure employers do not discriminate against particular groups
- **Minimum pay** legislation to ensure employees do not get exploited
- **Parental rights** (e.g. maternity and paternity leave) to ensure that employees are able to provide care for their children
- **Working conditions**, including health and safety (below), maximum hours of work, holidays
- **Discrimination** including equal pay for women to ensure employees are not discriminated against on the basis of factors such as gender, age or ethnicity among others
- **Bullying and harassment** at work to ensure that managers treat employees with respect
- **Discipline and grievance** procedures to ensure that employees are only dismissed if the employer has a valid reason for dismissing them or in case of redundancy
- **Redundancy provisions** requiring employees to be compensated in the case of redundancy.

2.2 Termination of employment

When terminating an individual's employment, businesses need to ensure that they do this in accordance with the law. Failure to comply with relevant laws could lead to the business being found guilty of:

- Wrongful dismissal
- Unfair dismissal

KEY TERM

Wrongful dismissal: Where an employee is dismissed and the employer has breached the terms set out in the employee's contract. An example would be failure to give the employee their contractual period of notice.

Unfair dismissal : Where the employee has been dismissed for an arbitrary reason, the onus is on the employer to prove that it was a fair dismissal

Essential reading

See Chapter 3 Section 1 of the Essential reading for more detail on termination of employment.

The Essential reading is available as an Appendix of the digital edition of the Workbook.

2.3 Implications for the employer

Some employers claim that employment laws are overly generous and add to the costs of business, while also discouraging them to take on more staff. Other employers believe that the laws are fair and that it is important that their employees are treated well.

Employers may need to employ HR experts to ensure they do not unwittingly breach employment laws.

Failure to comply with employment law could lead to the employee taking action against the employer. In the UK employees may take an employer to an employment tribunal, which is an independent body that aims to resolve disputes. An employment tribunal will listen to the employee's complaint and if they agree that the complaint is valid, they can require the employer to do one of the following:

- Pay compensation
- Improve working conditions
- Reinstate the employee if appropriate

Alternatively, employees may take employers to court, although the costs of this may be prohibitive.

Failure to comply with employment law may also give the organisation a bad reputation.

Real life example

In January 2020, TV presenter Samira Ahmed won a gender discrimination case against the BBC at an employment tribunal. She claimed that the work she performed as presenter of the BBC's 'Newswatch' programme was of 'equal value' to work performed by male presenter, Jeremy Vine who presented 'Points of View', yet Mr Vine was paid almost seven times the salary that Ms Ahmed received. Ms Ahmed claimed £700,000 in back pay.

3 Health and safety law

3.1 Importance of maintaining health and safety at work

- An employer has **legal obligations** under domestic laws.
- Accidents and illness **cost the employer money**.
- The company's **reputation** in the marketplace and society may suffer.

The **major legislation in the UK** covers a number of Acts of Parliament. EU law is important in member states. The most important piece of legislation in this area in the UK is the Health and Safety at Work Act 1974 (HMSO, 1974). Remember that UK law will not feature in the exam but you do need to be aware of health and safety best practices.

3.2 Employers' duties

A senior manager must be specified as responsible for ensuring that problems are solved and rules observed.

(a) All **work practices** must be safe.

(b) The work **environment** must be safe and healthy.

(c) All plant and equipment must be maintained to the necessary standard.

(d) Information, instruction, training and supervision should **encourage safe working practices**. Employers must provide training and information to all staff.

(e) The safety policy should be clearly **communicated** to all staff.

(f) Employers must carry out **risk assessments**, generally in writing, of all work hazards. Assessment should be continuous. They must **assess the risks to anyone else affected by their work activities**.

(g) They must **share hazard and risk information** with other employers, including those on adjoining premises, other site occupiers and all subcontractors coming onto the premises.

(h) They must **introduce controls** to reduce risks.

(i) They should **revise safety policies** in the light of the above, or initiate safety policies if none were in place previously.

(j) They must **identify employees** who are especially at risk.

(k) They must employ competent safety and health **advisers**.

The Safety Representative Regulations provide that a **safety representative** may be appointed by a recognised trade union, and for **safety committees** to be set up at the request of employee representatives. Safety representatives are entitled to paid time off work to carry out their duties.

3.3 Employee duties

(a) Take reasonable care of themselves and others

(b) Allow the employer to carry out their duties (including enforcing safety rules)

(c) Not interfere intentionally or recklessly with any machinery or equipment

(d) Inform the employer of any situation which may be a danger (this does not reduce the employer's responsibilities in any way)

(e) Use all equipment properly

Real life example

Cemex UK Operations Ltd was fined £1 million in 2019 after an accident in which a worker was killed at a site in Scotland. The conveyor on which the employee was performing repairs unexpectedly activated, and the employee was partly crushed by the conveyor's centring machine. The UK's Health and Safety Executive (HSE) concluded that Cemex should have made sure the centring machine was isolated before any repair was carried out. A lack of adequate health and safety compliance had led to a tragedy that could have been easily prevented.

Activity 1: Health and safety

1   What are costs of accidents to an organisation?

2   Which areas of health and safety would fall under the responsibility of the employer?

4 Data protection and security

Information about individuals (data subjects) stored on computer files and processed by computer could be **misused**. The internet, social media and big data technologies mean that increasingly large amounts of personal data are available and could potentially harm an individual. In 2018, the EU issued the General Data Protection Regulation (GDPR) which applies to all EU member states. The UK issued an updated Data Protection Act to bring its own laws into compliance with the GDPR. You are not required to know any particular law in detail, but just to understand the principles of data protection and security.

KEY TERM

> **Data subject:** A data subject is a person who can be identified, directly or indirectly, from data held.

Real life example

In 2018 the Royal Dutch Lawn Tennis Association sold personal data about its members, without their consent, to two of its sponsors. The data included names, gender and addresses. The sponsors contacted some of the members by post or telephone to make them some tennis related offers. The association was fined €525,000 by the Dutch Data Protection Authority for breach of the GDPR.

Activity 2: Data risks

Outline some of the potential dangers that data subjects face when organisations keep personal information about them.

Solution

4.1 Data Protection Principles

The **UK Data Protection Act** includes seven **Data Protection Principles** with which data users must comply:

Principle	Description
Lawfulness, fairness and transparency	Data can only be held if there are valid grounds to do so. Data can only be used fairly and with clarity, openness and honesty in how the data is used from the start.
Purpose limitation	Data subjects must be made aware of the purpose for recording the data from the time it is first collected. This purpose must be specified, explicit and legitimate. Should data need to be used for a different purpose in future then consent from the data subject must be obtained unless there are legal grounds to do so otherwise.
Data minimisation	Data held must be adequate (sufficient to fulfil the purpose), relevant (connected to the purpose for holding it) and not excessive (the minimum needed to fulfil the purpose).
Accuracy	Data held must be accurate and not misleading. Reasonable steps should be taken to ensure there are no inaccuracies. Any data that is found to be inaccurate or misleading must be corrected.
Storage limitation	Data must not be held for longer than is needed for the purpose it was collected and processed. There should be a justifiable data retention policy that can be justified. Data that is not needed must be deleted or anonymised.
Integrity and confidentiality (security)	Appropriate security measures regarding the risks that might arise in connection with the data must be taken.
Accountability	Organisations should take responsibility for how they use personal data and comply with the other principles. They must have appropriate measures and records in place to be able to demonstrate compliance.

4.2 The rights of data subjects

The Act establishes the following rights for data subjects:

Right	Description
To be informed	Data subjects must be informed about how their personal data is collected and used. Information that must be shared includes (for example) the purposes that their data is used for, what the retention period is and who the information is shared with. Individuals must be given this information at the time that their personal data is collected or within a month if the data was collected from another source.
Access	Individuals have the right to request information held about them either verbally or in writing. The requested information must be supplied within one month, and (in most circumstances) there should be no charge for it.
Rectification	Data subjects can request inaccurate or misleading information held about them to be rectified. Incomplete information must be made complete. The request can be made verbally or in writing and it must be completed within one month. Only in limited circumstances can the request be refused.
Erasure	This is known as the right 'to be forgotten'. Data subjects may request information held about them be destroyed. This request can be made verbally or in writing. This right only applies in certain circumstances and a reply must be sent to the data subject within one month.
Restrict processing	Data subjects can have restrictions placed on the processing of their data or have it suppressed altogether. The data can still be held, but it must not be processed. They can request the restriction verbally or in writing. The right only applies in certain circumstances and the individual must be given a response within one month.
Data portability	Data subjects can request to be sent the data held about them so they can reuse it in a different service. For example, data held by an online banking app can be requested and transferred to another app that can make use of it (such as a money manager type app).
To object	Data subjects can object to the processing of their data. Where the data is used in connection with direct marketing there is an absolute right to object. Where the data is used for other purposes, this right can be refused if there is a compelling reason to do so. The objection can be made verbally or in writing and a reply must be sent to the data subject within one month.
Automated decision making and profiling	Other data protection rights are granted to data subjects where data held about them is used to make automated decisions about them, or where data evaluation about them is automated. For example where decisions are made by bank computer systems as to whether or not to lend money to an individual. The uses of data in this way is limited and the individual must be given information about the processing. They also have the right to request human intervention or to challenge decisions made following such processing.

4.3 Data security

The **key risks** affecting data are:

(a) Human error - means that incorrect information is stored about individuals due to human error.

(b) Technical malfunction

(c) Deliberate/malicious action

(d) Hacking - hacking means unauthorised access to data, either from within the organisation, or from outside, via the internet.

Using the **Internet** brings numerous security dangers:

(a) **Viruses** - malicious programmes that are designed to disrupt the systems. They are often spread via email.

(b) Deliberate damage caused by disaffected **employees**

(c) Damage caused by **hackers**

(d) Downloading of inaccurate information and/or virus ridden software

(e) Internal information may be intercepted, but this can be avoided by encryption

(f) Communications link could break down

Data **stored electronically** is at risk of a security breach. At particular risk is:

(a) Information regarding the business's standing and competitive advantage

(b) Personal and private information

(c) Information regarding the business's security

(d) Information integral to the outcome of deadlines (eg tenders)

When data **is transmitted** over a network or telecommunications link (especially the internet) there are numerous security dangers:

(a) Corruptions such as **viruses** on a single computer can spread through the network to all of the organisation's computers.

(b) Disaffected employees have much greater potential to do **deliberate damage** to valuable corporate data or systems because the network could give them access to parts of the system that they are not really authorised to use.

Controls relating to data security are described in the chapter on control and audit.

Activity 3: Data Protection

Your managing director has asked you to recommend measures that your company, which is based in the UK, could take to ensure compliance with data protection legislation.

Required

Suggest what measures should be taken.

Solution

5 Contract law and consumer protection

Two areas of law that are relevant to the consumer are contract law and laws relating to the sale of goods. You are required to be aware of the principles of such laws.

What is written below is based on English law, but most countries adopt similar principles:

5.1 Contract law

When consumers buy goods from a retail store, or online, they are entering into a contract with the seller of the goods.

A contract must have three elements for it to be legally enforceable:

(a) **Consideration** – normally money offered, as in a contract of employment but equally as in the case of bartering, it could be a cow, a bag of rice or even the promise of a service.

(b) **Offer and acceptance** – there must be an offer and an acceptance by the two parties. Under UK law, the offer is made by the consumer and is accepted by the retailer.

(c) **Intention** to enter into a legally binding contract – this could be written or verbal. In the sale of goods it is normally assumed by the action of taking the goods to the till and paying for them.

Activity 4: Elements of a contract

A woman was walking down the High Street when she saw a bedside table in the window of a furniture shop, with a price of £30 displayed. The woman went into the shop and told the owner she wanted to buy it. She paid for the table at the cash register, and the bedside table was delivered to her home the following day.

Required

Identify each of the three elements of the contract above?

5.2 Sale of goods and services

An important area of contract law is the law concerning the **sale of goods**. UK legislation also covers contracts where the **supply of services** is the major part of the contract. For example, contracts of repair, where the supply of goods may be incidental to the provision of a service.

Imagine that you are about to enter into a contract for the purchase of some goods. What might you be concerned about?

- You may want the goods delivered for a particular occasion or **date**.
- Are the goods stolen, ie does the seller have a **right to sell the goods**?
- You would expect the goods to be the same type and quality as the description or any sample.
- The goods should be of **reasonable quality** and **suitable for their purpose**.

The UK's Consumer Rights Act 2015 (TSO, 2015) legislation covers these matters and a number of other important issues. When a consumer enters into a contract for the sale of goods, the following terms are implied, which means the consumer can assume the seller has complied with them:

- Seller's right to sell the goods – must have legal title to sell goods
- Description of the goods – goods correspond to description
- Satisfactory quality – for the purpose intended of such a good, free from minor defects and safe.

Chapter summary

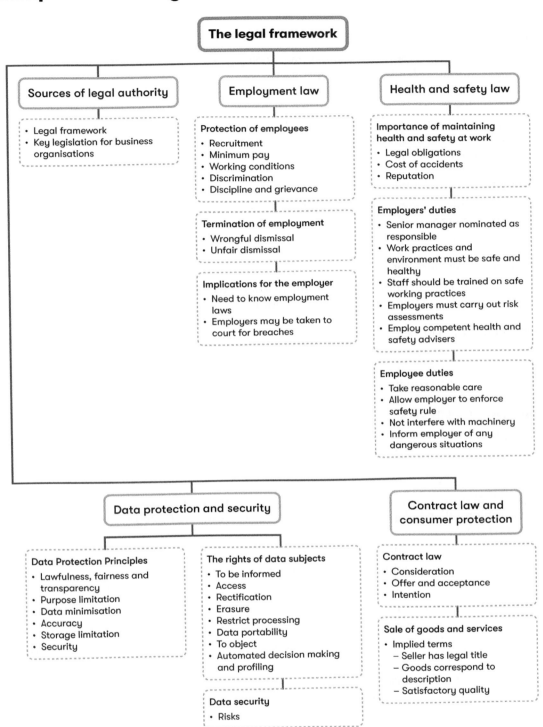

The legal framework

Sources of legal authority
- Legal framework
- Key legislation for business organisations

Employment law

Protection of employees
- Recruitment
- Minimum pay
- Working conditions
- Discrimination
- Discipline and grievance

Termination of employment
- Wrongful dismissal
- Unfair dismissal

Implications for the employer
- Need to know employment laws
- Employers may be taken to court for breaches

Health and safety law

Importance of maintaining health and safety at work
- Legal obligations
- Cost of accidents
- Reputation

Employers' duties
- Senior manager nominated as responsible
- Work practices and environment must be safe and healthy
- Staff should be trained on safe working practices
- Employers must carry out risk assessments
- Employ competent health and safety advisers

Employee duties
- Take reasonable care
- Allow employer to enforce safety rule
- Not interfere with machinery
- Inform employer of any dangerous situations

Data protection and security

Data Protection Principles
- Lawfulness, fairness and transparency
- Purpose limitation
- Data minimisation
- Accuracy
- Storage limitation
- Security

The rights of data subjects
- To be informed
- Access
- Rectification
- Erasure
- Restrict processing
- Data portability
- To object
- Automated decision making and profiling

Data security
- Risks

Contract law and consumer protection

Contract law
- Consideration
- Offer and acceptance
- Intention

Sale of goods and services
- Implied terms
  - Seller has legal title
  - Goods correspond to description
  - Satisfactory quality

Knowledge diagnostic

1. Legal framework

Laws and regulations that organisations must comply with come from various sources including parliament, treaty obligations and regulations.

2. Employment law

Employment law aims to protect the interests of employees and includes regulations relating to fair recruitment, minimum pay, acceptable working conditions, anti-discrimination measures, and discipline and grievance procedures.

3. Termination of employment

When terminating employment, employers should avoid wrongful dismissal, which means breaching the employee's employment contract, and unfair dismissal which involves dismissal for arbitrary reasons.

4. Employment law and employees

Failure of employers to adhere to employment laws could lead to fines or compensation to employees, and may harm the employer's reputation.

5. Health and safety laws

Health and safety laws are important to employers because there can be fines or punishment for breaches, costs of accidents can be high and a business's reputation might be harmed if they do not take health and safety seriously.

6. Employee's responsibility

Employees also have responsibility for health and safety issues, such as taking reasonable care themselves, and allowing employers to perform their work relating to health and safety.

7. Data Protection Act

Data protection aims to protect living individuals from the harm that they can suffer from personal information being held about them by organisations. The seven principles of the UK data protection act are:

- Lawfulness, fairness and transparency;
- Purpose limitation - data will only be held for specified purposes;
- Data minimisation - the amount of data held about an individual will not be excessive;
- Accuracy - the data held should be accurate;
- Storage limitation - the data should not be held for longer than necessary; and
- Integrity and confidentiality (security) - actions should be taken to ensure that the data is held securely.
- Accountability - organisations should be held accountable for how they use personal data and for compliance with the law

Further study guidance

Question practice

Now try the following from the Further question practice bank [available in the digital edition of the workbook]:

Number	Level	Marks	Approximate time
Q8	Exam Section A	2	2 mins
Q9	Exam Section A	2	2 mins
Q10	Exam Section A	2	2 mins
Q11	Exam Section A	2	2 mins
Q12	Exam Section B	4	5 mins

Activity answers

Activity 1: Health and safety

1 Cost of:
- Stopping production; repairs to machinery
- Poor morale
- Being sued, compensation, increased insurance
- Recruitment/training
- Bad PR

2 Employer's responsibility:
- Health and safety assessments/risk assessment
- Regular checks
- Health and safety training

Activity 2: Data risks

Potential dangers of data being held include:
- **Identity theft:** where criminals use the data subjects' identity to fraudulently make transactions in the subject's name (eg taking out bank loans in the name of the data subject)
- **Theft of assets:** for example, if bank account details and passwords are stolen, criminals can transfer money from the victims' bank accounts
- **Privacy:** people have a right to privacy. This right can be breached if data held about them is passed on to other companies or individuals without their consent
- **Reputation:** private or confidential information could be publicised, leading to a loss of reputation or even blackmail.
- **Loss of employment** or failing to obtain new employment because of confidential information becoming available to employers (eg spent criminal records).
- Being **targeted** by advertisers online or by telephone
- **Inaccurate** information being held about an individual leading to adverse consequences

Activity 3: Data Protection

Measures could include the following.
- Obtain consent from individuals to hold any sensitive personal data you need.
- Supply individuals with a copy of any personal data you hold about them if so requested.
- Consider if you may need to obtain consent to process personal data.
- Ensure you do not pass on personal data to unauthorised parties.
- Have a policy about when personal data will be destroyed.
- Ensure adequate security is in place to prevent breaches of data

Activity 4: Elements of a contract

Consideration – the store's bedside table and the customer's money

Offer and acceptance – telling the owner she wanted to buy the table was an offer, and the owner agreeing, and taking it to the cash register was acceptance by the owner.

Intention – consent to entering into a legal contract is assumed when goods are paid for

Note. Some of you may have thought the bedside table merely being displayed in the shop window for £30 is an offer, however, under UK law, this is known as an Invitation to Treat.

Skills checkpoint 1

Approaching objective test (OT) questions

Chapter overview

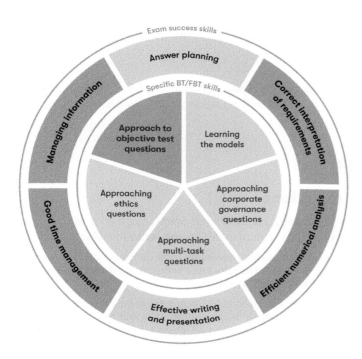

Introduction

The exam contains two sections. Section A consists of 16 objective test (OT) questions worth one mark each and 30 objective test (OT) questions worth two marks each. Section B contains six multi-task questions worth four marks each. The multi-task questions are made up of OT questions and therefore being able to answer OT questions effectively is extremely important.

OT questions

OT questions in Section A are single, short questions that are auto-marked and worth one or two marks each. You must answer the whole question correctly to earn the marks. There are no partial marks.

The OT questions in Section A aim for a broad coverage of the syllabus, and so all areas of the syllabus need to be carefully studied. You need to work through as many practice OT questions as possible, reviewing them carefully to see how correct answers are derived.

The following types of OT questions commonly appear in Section A of the BT/FBT exam:

Question type	
Multiple choice (MCQ)	Choose one correct answer from two or three options in the case of 1 mark questions, or one correct answer from four options in the case of 2 mark questions. Eg Q1 of the specimen exam
Multiple response (MR)	These are a type of multiple choice question where you need to select more than one answer from a number of given options. The question will specify how many answers need to be selected. It is important to read the requirement carefully. Eg Q8 of the specimen exam
Multiple response matching (MRM)	This question type requires you identify which of two or more categories each item in a list belongs to. For example, a question might provide a list of controls, and ask you to identify for each control whether it is a general control or an application control.

Section B questions will include six multi-task questions. These will also use OT questions, but a wider range of question types will be used in the Section B questions. The approach to these will be discussed in Skills Checkpoint 4.

Approach to OT questions

BT/FBT Skill: Approach to OT questions

A step-by-step technique for approaching OT questions is outlined below. Each step will be explained in more detail in the following sections as a 'mini exam' is answered in stages.

STEP 1 **Answer the easy questions first.** Some questions are just simple knowledge type questions and take no more than half a minute, while others might include a scenario and require more thought. By doing the easier questions first, you leave yourself longer to deal with the harder questions.

STEP 2 **Answer all questions.** There is no penalty for an incorrect answer in ACCA exams; there is nothing to be gained by leaving an OT question unanswered. If you are stuck on a question, as a last resort, it is worth selecting the option you consider most likely to be correct and moving on. Make a note of the question, so if you have time after you have answered the rest of the questions, you can revisit it.

STEP 3 **Read the requirement first!** The requirement will be stated in bold text in the exam. Identify what you are being asked to do, any technical knowledge required and what type of OT question you are dealing with. Look for key words in the requirement such as, 'which **TWO** of the following' or 'which of the following is **NOT**', etc.

STEP 4 **Apply your technical knowledge to the data presented in the question.** Take your time working through questions and make sure you read through each answer option with care. OT questions are designed so that each answer option is plausible. Work through each response option and eliminate those you know are incorrect.

Exam success skills

The following **exam success skills** are particularly relevant for the BT/FBT exam:

- **Managing information.** It is easy for the amount of information contained in a particular question to feel a little overwhelming. Active reading is a useful technique to avoid this. This involves focusing on the requirements first on the basis that, until you have done this, the detail in the scenario will have little meaning and will seem more intimidating.

- **Correct interpretation of requirements.** Identify from the requirement the type of OT question. This is especially important with multiple response options (MRO) to ensure you select the correct number of response options.

- **Good time management.** Complete all questions in the time available. One-mark OTs should take 1.2 minutes and two-mark OTs should be allocated 2.4 minutes. However, some questions may take longer than others so just make sure that you complete all of the Section A questions within 91.2 minutes (75 marks x 1.2 minutes). This will leave you with 28.8 minutes to complete Section B where you should allocate 4.8 minutes (4 marks x 1.2 minutes) to each of the six questions.

These skills will now be demonstrated using a 'mini exam'.

Skill activity

(a) **According to Mendelow's matrix, stakeholders with high interest and low power should be:** (1 mark)

○ Kept informed

○ Satisfied

○ Ignored

Note. This is an MCQ requiring one correct answer to be selected. The question does not require reading any scenario and so can be answered relatively quickly, leaving extra time for more complex questions.

(b) BCD Co is a large trading company. Steve is the administration manager and is also responsible for legal and compliance functions. Sheila is responsible for after-sales service and has responsibility for ensuring that customers who have purchased goods from BCD Co are fully satisfied. Sunny deals with suppliers and negotiates on the price and quality of inventory. He is also responsible for identifying the most appropriate suppliers of plant and machinery for the factory. Sam is the information technology manager and is responsible for all information systems within the company.

According to Porter's value chain, which of the managers is involved in a primary activity as opposed to a support activity? (2 marks)

○ Steve

○ Sunny

○ Sheila

○ Sam

Note. This is also an MCQ. However, it has four potential options and requires you to read a scenario before answering. It is therefore likely to be more time consuming than the previous question.

(c) **Indicate whether the following will cause a shift in the demand curve for a normal good, or a move along the existing demand curve:** (2 marks)

	Shift in demand	Move along the demand curve
An increase in household incomes		
A change in tastes towards another product		
A rise in the price of the good		
A rise in the price of substitute goods		

Note. This is an MRM question. You need to indicate which of two possible consequences each event will lead to. In Section A questions you need to get all parts correct to get the two marks available. This means that if you get one of the four wrong, you will lose the marks.

(d) **Which TWO of the following are the professional qualities expected of an accountant?** (2 marks)

○ Moderation

○ Authority

○ Independence

○ Scepticism

Note. This is an MRO asking for two answers to be selected. You must get them both right to obtain the 2 marks.

(e) .... comprise all those individuals or groups who have a legitimate interest in an organisation's activities.

Which word or phrase correctly completes this sentence? (1 mark)

○ Key players

○ Stakeholders

○ Shareholders

Note. This is a multiple choice question where you have to identify which word fits a gap in a sentence.

STEP 1   Answer the questions you know first.

If you are having difficulty answering a question, move on and come back to tackle it once you have answered all the questions you know.

Questions 1 and 5 should be relatively quick to do as they are just pure tests of knowledge – you either know the answer or you don't. It would make sense to answer these two questions first as it is likely that you will be able to complete them comfortably within the time allocated to each one. Any time saved could then be spent on the more complex questions that require more thought.

STEP 2   There is no penalty for an incorrect answer in FIA/ACCA exams so there is nothing to be gained by leaving an OT question unanswered. If you are stuck on a question, as a last resort, it is worth selecting the option you consider most likely to be correct, and moving on. Make a note of the question, so if you have time after you have answered the rest of the questions, you can revisit it.

For the MCQs, you have a 33% or 25% chance of getting the answer correct (depending on the number of options) so do not leave any unanswered. MRs and MRMs can also be guessed.

STEP 3   Read the requirement first!

The requirement will be stated in bold text in the exam. Identify what you are being asked to do, any technical knowledge required and what type of OT question you are dealing with. Look for key words in the requirement such as 'Which TWO of the following...', 'Which of the following is NOT...'

Question 4 requires you to choose two options not just one.

STEP 4   Apply your technical knowledge to the data presented in the question.

Take your time working through scenarios, and be sure to read through each answer option with care. OT questions are designed so that each answer option is plausible.

Let's have a look at a few of the questions in detail.

Question (1)

This is the sort of question where even if you can't remember the theory, you can have an educated guess. If people have high interest, you are not likely to completely ignore them, as they may cause trouble for the organisation, so you can eliminate that. Since the people have low power, it would not be necessary to keep them satisfied. The correct answer is therefore keep informed. A lot of questions in BT can be answered by trying to apply some logic.

Question (2)

This question essentially tests whether you know what the primary activities are in Porter's value chain. The first thing to do is read the requirement, which asks which of the managers is involved in the primary activities of Porter's value chain. The next thing to do, before reading the scenario, is to think about what the primary activities are (they are inbound logistics, operations, outbound logistics, after sales service and sales and marketing). Having done this, when you read the scenario, you will know exactly what you are looking for. This is active reading. This is much more time efficient than starting the question by reading the scenario before reading the requirement. The correct answer is Sheila.

Question (3)

The risk with this question is that if you get one of the four items wrong you will lose all the marks. This is the type of question you should leave until the end, unless you are very confident about this area.

Question (4)

This question is essentially a test of knowledge, so you either know it or you don't. The correct answer is:

- Independence
- Scepticism

Moderation – whilst admirable in many contexts – is not a professional quality specifically identified as expected of an accountant.

Authority can be an admirable quality but is not specified as a professional quality expected of an accountant.

Question (5)

The answer is stakeholders. This is a definition of stakeholders. This is the type of question where you either know the answer or you don't.

Exam success skills diagnostic

Every time you complete a few questions, use the diagnostic below to assess how effectively you demonstrated the exam success skills in answering the questions. The table has been completed below for the 'mini exam' activity to give you an idea of how to complete the diagnostic.

Exam success skills	Your reflections/observations
Managing information	Did you read each of the five requirements first? Did you actively read the scenario for each question making a note of relevant points? Eg, in question (2), ensuring you read the requirement before reading the scenario.
Correct interpretation of requirements	Did you identify the correct technical knowledge needed to answer each requirement? Again question 2 is a good example, as thinking about what the primary activities are is useful before reading the scenario. Did you identify what type of OT question you were dealing with? For example, knowing that only one correct answer is required for a multiple-choice question.
Good time management	Did you manage to answer all five questions within 9.6 mins? (8 marks in total × 1.2 minutes. Did you manage your time well by answering Questions (2) and (3) after answering the easier questions (1), (5) and (4)?
Most important action points to apply to your next question	

Summary

Being able to answer OTs is very important for the BT/FBT exam. Key skills to focus on throughout your studies will therefore include:

- Always reading the requirements first to identify what you are being asked to do and what type of OT question you are dealing with.
- Actively reading the scenario, making a note of key data needed to answer each requirement.
- Answering OT questions in a sensible order, dealing with any easier discursive style questions first.
- Applying some logic to questions where you do not know the theory.

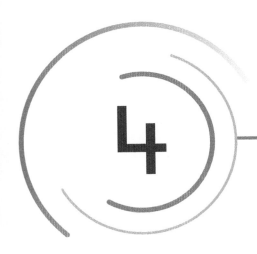

4

The macro economic environment

Learning outcomes

On completion of this chapter, you should be able to:

	Syllabus reference no.
Define macroeconomic policy and explain its objectives.	A4 (a)
Explain the main determinants of the level of business activity in the economy and how variations in the level of business activity affect individuals, households and businesses.	A4 (b)
Explain the impact of economic issues on the individual, the household and the business: (a) Inflation (b) Unemployment (c) Stagnation (d) International payments disequilibrium	A4 (c)
Describe the main types of economic policy that may be implemented by government and supra-national bodies to maximise economic welfare.	A4 (d)
Recognise the impact of fiscal and monetary policy measures on the individual, the household and businesses.	A4 (e)

Exam context

These topics are the areas that professional accountants are expected to be familiar with, and as such, should be expected to come up in the exam.

Chapter overview

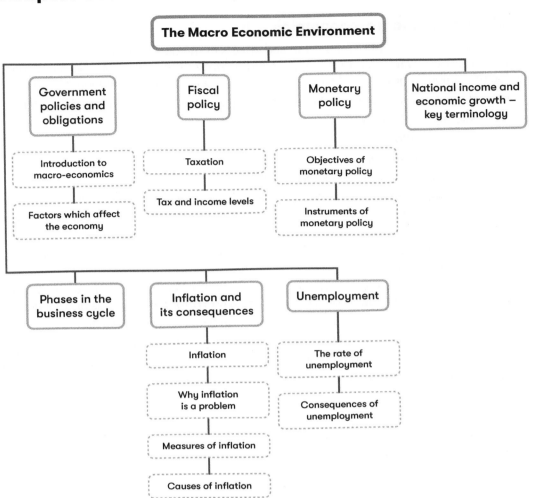

The Macro Economic Environment

Government policies and obligations
- Introduction to macro-economics
- Factors which affect the economy

Fiscal policy
- Taxation
- Tax and income levels

Monetary policy
- Objectives of monetary policy
- Instruments of monetary policy

National income and economic growth – key terminology

Phases in the business cycle

Inflation and its consequences
- Inflation
- Why inflation is a problem
- Measures of inflation
- Causes of inflation

Unemployment
- The rate of unemployment
- Consequences of unemployment

1 Government policies and obligations

1.1 Introduction to macro-economics

Macro-economics is the study of the combined effects of the decisions of individual economic units and looks at a complete national economy as a whole. The policies of macro-economics describe the actions a government takes to control economic issues, ie inflation, economic growth.

Governments seek to manage the national economy, and this may include the following aims:

(a) To achieve economic **growth**

(b) To control price **inflation**

(c) To achieve full **employment**

(d) To achieve a balance between **exports and imports**

Governments **spend money** raised by **taxation** and **borrowing** on a variety of items. Decisions by governments on spending and taxing affect the economy. If the government builds a hospital:

(a) Suppliers to government – building company wins the contract, they then employ more staff.

(b) Knock-on effect of government spending throughout the economy – the builders they employ will spend their income in shops so the shops' revenues will also grow.

(c) Taxation affects consumers' purchasing power – the builders pay income tax on earnings and VAT on what they buy. Lower rates means people can afford more goods and services.

(d) Taxes on profits affect investment returns – the building company pays tax

(e) Public sector investment benefits some companies – eg a hospital equipment company

(f) Public sector investment: longer time scale, less quantifiable benefits – healthy work force

(g) Government influences are outlined in the diagram which follows.

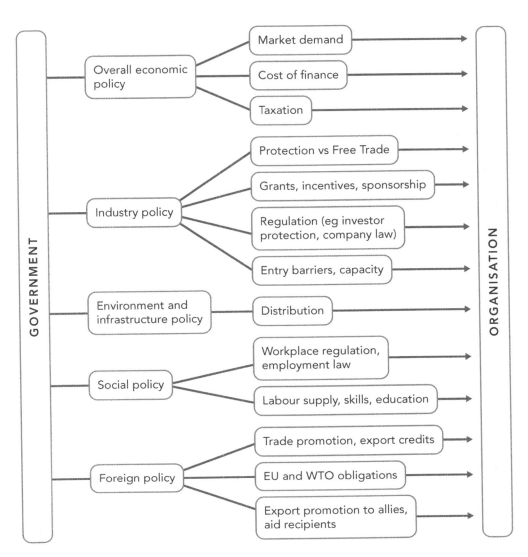

The diagram shows the relationship between GOVERNMENT (left) and ORGANISATION (right):

- Overall economic policy
  - Market demand
  - Cost of finance
  - Taxation
- Industry policy
  - Protection vs Free Trade
  - Grants, incentives, sponsorship
  - Regulation (eg investor protection, company law)
  - Entry barriers, capacity
- Environment and infrastructure policy
  - Distribution
- Social policy
  - Workplace regulation, employment law
  - Labour supply, skills, education
- Foreign policy
  - Trade promotion, export credits
  - EU and WTO obligations
  - Export promotion to allies, aid recipients

1.2 Factors which affect the economy

The economy is rarely in a stable state because of the various changing factors which influence it. These include investment levels, the multiplier effect, inflation, savings, confidence, interest rates and exchange rates.

1.2.1 The multiplier in the national economy

The concept of the **multiplier** is that an injection of a certain size into the economy leads to a much larger increase in national income. For example, the government may decide to inject $1 billion into the economy by borrowing money and spending it on an infrastructure project. The $1 billion injection will lead to an increase in national income that is much larger than $1 billion. It will increase the wages of the workers on the infrastructure project, so they will spend that money, which will increase the income of the businesses where they spend it. These businesses will then have higher income which they will spend, and so on.

1.2.2 Aggregate supply and demand

Aggregate demand: The total demand in the economy for goods and services is called the aggregate demand and it is made up of several components of the circular flow. These components include consumption, investment, government spending and exports minus imports. Put simply, the aggregate demand curve represents the sum of all the demand curves for individuals and businesses in a country.

Aggregate supply: The aggregate supply refers to the ability of the economy to produce goods and services.

Aggregate demand can be calculated using the following formula:

AD = C + I + G + (X – M)

AD = aggregate demand

C = consumption

I = investment

G = government spending

X = total exports

M = total imports

Essential reading

See Chapter 4 Section 1 of the Essential reading for more detail on the flows of income throughout the economy.

The Essential reading is available as an Appendix of the digital edition of the Workbook.

2 Fiscal policy

Fiscal policy: The use of government spending and tax policies to influence the level of demand in an economy.

The formal planning of fiscal policy (ie tax and spend policies) is set out annually (eg in the UK in the 'Budget') which has three components:

(a)   **Expenditure planning**

(b)   **Revenue raising**

(c)   **Borrowing**

If expenditure exceeds revenues the government will need to borrow. In the UK this is known as the 'Public Sector Net Cash Requirement' (**PSNCR**).

Cost push inflation occurs where the costs of factors of production rise regardless of whether or not they are in short supply. This appears to be particularly the case with wages.

If you spend more than you earn you will be overdrawn. This is the same for a government. For example, if a government spends more on building roads than it earns via taxation, it **will be running a 'budget deficit'**. When the government's income exceeds its expenditure it can repaying earlier borrowings, this is **known as having a** 'budget surplus'.

Governments can use fiscal policy to **change the level of demand** in the economy.

If a government decides to use fiscal policy to influence demand in the economy, it can choose either expenditure changes or tax changes as its policy instrument.

Increase demand by government:

(a)   **Reducing taxation,** but does not change its spending, then demand is stimulated

(b)   **Spending more,** but not altering taxation

Reduce demand by government:

(c)   **Increasing taxation** or **reducing spending**

Real life example

During the COVID-19 pandemic, many governments increased spending to increase demand in the economy after the level of economic activity fell due to the pandemic. In the UK, the government even introduced a scheme where the government paid half the price of a meal at participating restaurants and pubs in an attempt to support the hospitality industry.

2.1 Taxation

Taxation:

(a) Is a key **source of revenue** for the government

(b) Serves to **discourage certain activities** that the government want to highlight as being unhealthy or undesirable (eg tax on tobacco)

(c) **Redistributes income and wealth** (eg income support)

A good tax system should be:

* Flexible

* Efficient

* Able to attain its purpose

Taxes can be either direct or indirect.

> **Direct taxation:** Paid directly to the Revenue authority eg income, capital gains and inheritance tax.
>
> **Indirect taxation:** This is collected by the Revenue authority via a third party (a 'supplier') who passes the tax on to consumers (eg sales taxes, VAT).

Indirect taxes can be:

(a) Specific taxes charged as a fiscal sum per unit sold (eg a petrol tax per litre)

(b) 'Ad valorem taxes' charged as a fixed percentage of the price of the item (eg VAT and other sales taxes)

A government must decide how it intends to raise tax revenues, from **direct or indirect taxes**, and in what proportions tax revenues will be raised from each source.

2.2 Tax and income levels

Note the following distinctions.

(a) A **regressive tax** takes a higher **proportion** of a poor person's salary than of a rich person's. Television licences and road tax are examples of regressive taxes since they are the same for all people.

(b) A **proportional tax** takes the **same proportion** of income in tax from all levels of income.

(c) A **progressive tax** takes a **higher proportion** of income in tax as income rises. Income tax as a whole is progressive, since the first part of an individual's income is tax free due to personal allowances and the rate of tax increases in steps in the UK from 20p in £1 to 45p in £1 as taxable income rises.

Direct taxes tend to be **progressive** or **proportional**. Income tax is usually progressive, with high rates of tax charged on higher bands of taxable income. **Indirect taxes** can be **regressive**, when the taxes are placed on essential commodities or commodities consumed by poorer people in greater quantities.

Activity 1: Taxes

The government of a certain country decides to introduce a poll tax, which will involve a flat rate levy of $200 on every adult member of the population.

Required

This new tax could be described as

O Regressive

O Proportional

O Progressive

O Ad valorem

3 Monetary policy

> **KEY TERM**
>
> **Monetary policy:** The use of money supply, **interest rates**, **exchange rates** and **credit control** to influence aggregate demand.

3.1 Objectives of monetary policy

Monetary policy can be used as a means towards achieving ultimate economic objectives for inflation, the balance of trade, full employment and real economic growth. To achieve these **ultimate objectives**, the authorities will set **intermediate objectives** for monetary policy.

In the UK, the ultimate objective of monetary policy in recent years has been principally to reduce the rate of inflation to a sustainable low level. The intermediate objectives of monetary policy have related to the level of interest rates, growth in the money supply, the exchange rate for sterling, the expansion of credit and the growth of national income.

3.1.1 Money supply targets

To monetarist economists, the **money supply** is an obvious intermediate target of economic policy. This is because they claim that an increase in the money supply will raise prices and incomes and this in turn will raise the demand for money to spend. The current trend is to call this **quantitative easing**, a policy whereby a government prints more money in order to stimulate the economy.

3.2 Instruments of monetary policy

- Changing **interest rates** – higher rates lead to us saving more and so spending less and vice versa. This can be done through open market operations (issuing or buying bonds)
- Changing **reserve requirements** (the minimum balances held by banks) – increased reserves held by banks means less can be lent to customers as credit and so we have less to spend.
- Intervention to influence the **exchange rate** (buying or selling currency) – overseas goods become relatively more expensive for us if the £ is weaker and so we buy less of them.

Monetary control aims to control inflation which helps:

- Provide greater economic **certainty** through low inflation – so can plan better
- Ensure **business confidence** and so stimulate investment – through stable prices
- Stimulate economic growth and international competitiveness that should **provide higher incomes**

Activity 2: Effects of policy

How are businesses affected by fiscal and monetary policy?

4 National income and economic growth - key terminology

> **KEY TERM**
>
> **Aggregate demand:** The total planned or desired consumption demand in the economy for consumer goods and services and also for capital goods, no matter whether the buyers are households, firms or government.

4.1 Full-employment national income

If one aim of a country's economic policy is full employment, then the ideal equilibrium level of national income will be where AD and AS are in balance at the full employment level of national income, without any inflationary gap – in other words, where aggregate demand at current price levels is exactly sufficient to encourage firms to produce at an output capacity where the country's resources are fully employed.

4.2 Equilibrium national income

Demand for goods and services is in balance with available supply

4.3 Deflationary gap

Where there is **unemployment of resources** prices and wages should go down (then we could afford to buy more and so increase demand and so employment would improve). But people do not want their wages to go down even temporarily. This then creates the deflationary gap where prices stay fairly constant and output and demand change.

4.4 Stagflation

Occurs where there is a combination of **high unemployment and high inflation** caused by a price shock (eg crude oil price rises in the early 1970s) and inflexibility in supply.

5 Phases in the business cycle

The business cycle is the continual sequence of rapid growth in national income followed by a slowdown. An economy will **naturally rise and fall** without government intervention.

The four main phases of the business **cycle** are:

(a) **Recession** (point A on the graph below)

(b) **Depression** (point B on the graph below)

(c) **Recovery** (point C on the graph below)

(d) **Boom** (point D on the graph below)

(e) Recession, etc.

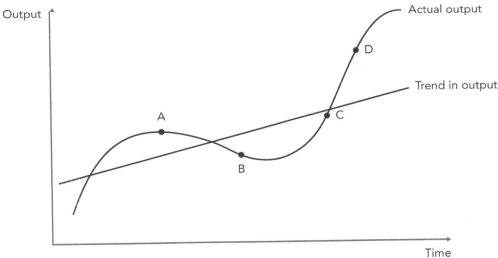

In the **'recession'** phase:

- Consumer demand/confidence falls.
- Investment projects begin to look unprofitable.
- Orders are cut, inventory levels reduced.
- Some companies unable to sell their inventories become insolvent.

If during the recession phase there is a lack of stimulus to aggregate demand a period of **'depression'** will set in.

'Recovery' is usually slow to begin due to a general lack of confidence in the economy:

- Governments look to boost demand (using fiscal/monetary policy)
- Together with confidence, output, income and employment rise.

BPP
LEARNING
MEDIA

- Investment flows into the economy.

Once the actual output has risen above the trend line the **'boom'** phase of the cycle is entered:
- Capacity and labour become fully utilised
- Further rises in demand lead to price rises
- Business is profitable and high inward investment occurs.

6 Inflation and its consequences

High rates of **inflation** are harmful to an economy. Inflation redistributes income and wealth. Uncertainty about the value of money makes business planning more difficult. Constantly changing prices impose extra costs.

6.1 Inflation

Inflation is the name given to an increase in price levels generally. It is also manifest in the decline in the purchasing power of money.

Historically, there have been very few periods when inflation has not been present. We discuss below why high rates of inflation are considered to be harmful. However, it is important to remember that **deflation** (falling prices) is normally associated with low rates of growth and even recession. It would seem that a healthy economy may require some inflation. Certainly, if an economy is to grow, the money supply must expand, and the presence of a low level of inflation will ensure that growth is not hampered by a shortage of liquid funds. (Liquidity is the ease with which assets can be converted into cash.)

6.2 Why is inflation a problem?

An economic policy objective which now has a central place in the policy approaches of the governments of many developed countries is that of stable prices. Why is a **high** rate of price inflation harmful and undesirable?

Redistribution of income and wealth

Inflation leads to a redistribution of income and wealth in ways which may be undesirable. Redistribution of wealth might take place from accounts payable to accounts receivable. This is because debts lose 'real' value with inflation. For example, if you owed $1,000, and prices then doubled, you would still owe $1,000, but the **real value** of your debt would have been halved. In general, in times of inflation those with economic power tend to gain at the expense of the weak, particularly those on fixed incomes.

Balance of payments effects

If a country has a higher rate of inflation than its major trading partners, its exports will become relatively expensive and imports relatively cheap. As a result, the balance of trade will suffer, affecting employment in exporting industries and in industries producing import-substitutes. Eventually, the exchange rate will be affected.

Uncertainty of the value of money and prices

If the rate of inflation is imperfectly anticipated, no one has certain knowledge of the true rate of inflation. As a result, no one has certain knowledge of the value of money or of the real meaning of prices. If the rate of inflation becomes excessive, and there is 'hyperinflation', this problem becomes so exaggerated that money becomes worthless, so that people are unwilling to use it and are forced to resort to barter. In less extreme circumstances, the results are less dramatic, but the same problem exists. As prices convey less information, the process of resource allocation is less efficient and rational decision-making is almost impossible.

Resource costs of changing prices

A fourth reason to aim for stable prices is the resource cost of frequently changing prices. In times of high inflation, substantial labour time is spent on planning and implementing price changes. Customers may also have to spend more time making price comparisons if they seek to buy from the lowest cost source.

Economic growth and investment

It is sometimes claimed that inflation is harmful to a country's economic growth and level of investment. Although some studies have indicated that the adverse influence of inflation on economic growth and investment appears to be small in the short term, it could affect a country's standard of living fairly significantly over the long term.

6.3 Measures of inflation

The rate of inflation is measured by price indices.

A **'basket'** of items which represent average purchases around the country is priced regularly and this forms the basis of a price index.

In the UK there are now two key price indices:

(a) **Retail Prices Index (RPI)**

 This index includes prices for all goods and services (including housing costs) purchased by UK consumers.

(b) **Consumer Prices Index (CPI)**

 This index, which excludes housing costs (council tax, rent), is calculated on the **same basis as the rest of Europe**.

 Additionally, you do need to be aware of the following indices which are sometimes useful:

(c) **RPIX**

 This is the underlying rate of inflation excluding mortgage interest payments.

(d) **RPIY**

 This is RPIX as adjusted for the effects of any VAT changes.

6.4 Causes of inflation

The following can cause inflation:

* Demand pull factor
* Cost push factors
* Import cost factors
* Expectations
* Excessive growth in the money supply

Of these causes, the most significant are the first two, demand pull and cost push inflation.

KEY TERM

Demand pull inflation: Inflation resulting from a persistent excess of aggregate demand over aggregate supply. Supply reaches a limit on capacity at the full employment level.

Cost push inflation: Inflation resulting from an increase in the costs of production of goods and services, eg through escalating prices of imported raw materials or from wage increases.

6.4.1 Demand pull inflation

Demand pull inflation occurs when the economy is buoyant and there is a high aggregate demand, in excess of the economy's ability to supply.

(a) Because aggregate demand exceeds supply, prices rise.

(b) Supply needs to be raised to meet the higher demand.

 There will be an increase in demand for factors of production, and so factor rewards (wages, interest rates, and so on) will also rise.

(c) Since aggregate demand exceeds the output capability of the economy, it should follow that demand-pull inflation can only exist when unemployment is low.

 A feature of inflation in the UK in the 1970s and early 1980s, however, was high inflation coupled with high unemployment.

6.5 Cost push inflation

Real life example

A significant concern for investors and analysts around the world right now is the *absence* of inflation, despite several years of quantitative easing which has significantly increased the level of money supply. Some analysts believe that deflationary forces – such as the increase in the global workforce caused by the rapid industrialisation in many areas of the world – have acted as a brake on inflationary pressures, but that brake may start to weaken in the near future. Recent increases in the price of gold have been taken as evidence of a general belief that inflation will increase in the future – ie inflation will increase *because* people think it will.

7 Unemployment

7.1 The rate of unemployment

The rate of unemployment in an economy can be calculated as:

$$\frac{\text{Number of unemployed}}{\text{Total workforce}} \times 100\%$$

The number of unemployed at any time is measured by government statistics.

If the flow of workers through unemployment is constant then the size of the unemployed labour force will also be constant.

7.1.1 Flows into unemployment

Flows into unemployment are:

(a) Members of the working labour force **becoming** unemployed
  (i) Redundancies
  (ii) Lay-offs
  (iii) Voluntarily quitting a job
(b) People **out** of the labour force **joining** the unemployed
  (i) School leavers without a job
  (ii) Others (for example, carers) re-joining the workforce but having no job yet.

7.1.2 Flows out of unemployment

Flows out of unemployment are:

* Unemployed people finding jobs
* Laid-off workers being re-employed
* Unemployed people stopping the search for work.

7.1.3 Unemployment statistics

In the UK, the monthly unemployment statistics published by the Office for National Statistics (ONS) count only the jobless who receive benefits.

The ONS also produces figures based on a quarterly survey of the labour force known as the International Labour Organisation measure (ILO measure) that provides seasonally adjusted monthly data. This figure is considered to be more useful because it is also an internationally comparable measure.

7.2 Consequences of unemployment

Unemployment results in the following problems.

(a) **Loss of output**. If labour is unemployed, the economy is not producing as much output as it could. Thus, total national income is less than it could be.

(b) **Loss of human capital.** If there is unemployment, the unemployed labour will gradually lose its skills, because skills can only be maintained by working.

(c) **Increasing inequalities in the distribution of income.** Unemployed people earn less than employed people, and so when unemployment is increasing, the poor get poorer.

(d) **Social costs.** Unemployment brings social problems of personal suffering and distress, and possibly also increases in crime, such as theft and vandalism.

(e) **Increased burden of welfare payments.** This can have a major impact on government fiscal policy.

7.3 Causes of unemployment

Unemployment may be classified into several categories depending on the underlying causes.

Category	
Real wage unemplymnt	This type of unemployment is caused when the supply of labour exceeds the demand for labour, but real wages do not fall for the labour market to clear. This type of unemployment is normally caused by strong trade unions which resist a fall in their wages. Another cause of this type of unemployment is the minimum wage rate, when it is set above the market clearing level.
Frictional	It is inevitable that some unemployment is caused not so much because there are not enough jobs to go round, but because of the **friction in** the labour market (difficulty in quickly matching workers with jobs), caused perhaps by a lack of knowledge about job opportunities. In general, it takes time to match prospective employees with employers, and individuals will be unemployed during the search period for a new job. Frictional unemployment is temporary, lasting for the period of transition from one job to the next.
Seasonal	This occurs in certain industries, for example building, tourism and farming, where the demand for labour fluctuates in seasonal patterns throughout the year.
Structural	This occurs where long-term changes occur in the conditions of an industry. A feature of structural unemployment is high regional unemployment in the location of the industry affected. The primary cause is a significant reduction in the level of demand.
Technological	This is a form of structural unemployment, which occurs when new technologies are introduced. (a) Old skills are no longer required. (b) There is likely to be a labour-saving aspect, with machines doing the job that people used to do. With automation, employment levels in an industry can fall sharply, even when the industry's total output is increasing.
Cyclical or demand-deficient	It has been the experience of the past that domestic and foreign trade go through cycles of boom, decline, recession, recovery, then boom again, and so on. (a) During recovery and boom years, the demand for output and jobs is high, and unemployment is low. (b) During decline and recession years, the demand for output and jobs falls, and unemployment rises to a high level. Cyclical unemployment can be long term, and a government might try to reduce it by doing what it can to minimise a recession or to encourage faster economic growth.

Seasonal employment and frictional unemployment will be short term. Structural unemployment, technological unemployment and cyclical unemployment are all longer term, and more serious.

Activity 3: Types of unemployment

Match the terms 'Structural unemployment', 'Cyclical unemployment' and 'Frictional Unemployment' with the definitions below:

	Structural/Cyclical/Frictional
Unemployment arising from a difficulty in matching unemployed workers with available jobs	
Unemployment occurring in the downswing of an economy in between two booms	
Unemployment arising from a long-term decline in a particular industry	

Essential reading

See Chapter 4 Section 2 of the Essential reading for more detail on unemployment.

The Essential reading is available as an Appendix of the digital edition of the Workbook.

8 Objective of economic growth

8.1 Economic growth

Economic growth may be measured by increases in the **real** gross domestic product (GDP) per head of the population.

It is not unusual to find economic growth measured simply as increases in total GDP, regardless of inflation and changes in population size. Over periods in which the population changes relatively little, this approach is satisfactory.

Economic growth may be **balanced**, when all sectors of the economy expand together, or **unbalanced**. Less developed countries in particular find it difficult to achieve economic growth, because many of the factors necessary for growth are absent in these countries.

Actual economic growth is the annual percentage increase in national output, which typically fluctuates in accordance with the trade cycle. **Potential economic growth** is the rate at which the economy would grow if all resources (eg people and machinery) were utilised.

8.2 Actual growth

Actual growth in the long run is determined by two factors.

- The growth in **potential output** (in other words the aggregate supply)
- The growth in **aggregate demand (AD)**

These factors should move in step with one another as we explained in Section 2.2 and Figure 3.

8.3 Potential growth

The causes of growth in **potential** output are the determinants of the capacity of the economy (the supply side) rather than actual spending (the demand side) and are as follows.

(a) There may be increases in the **amount of resources** available.

(i) **Land, raw materials**. Land is virtually in fixed supply, but new natural resources are continually being discovered.

(ii) **Labour** (the size of the working population). The output per head will be affected by the proportion of the population which is non-working.

(iii) **Capital** (eg machinery).

(b) Increases in the **productivity of resources** may result from technological progress or changed labour practices, for example.

8.4 Factors needed for sustained economic growth

Sustained economic growth depends heavily on an adequate level of new investment, which will be undertaken if there are expectations of future growth in demand. After investment has taken place on the basis of expectations, the level of income will increase, by the operation of the multiplier. But there is no reason why the actual level of income should end up increasing as much as the investing businesspeople thought it would. It follows that investment, a factor in growth, is dependent on business confidence in the future, which is reflected in expectations of growth in consumption.

8.5 Natural resources

The rate of extraction of natural resources will impose a limit on the rate of growth. Production which uses up a country's natural resources, such as oil, coal and other minerals, depletes the stock of available resources.

8.6 Technological progress

Technological progress is a very important source of faster economic growth.

- The same amounts of the factors of production can produce a higher output.
- New products will be developed, thus adding to output growth.

There can be technical progress in the labour force. If workers are better educated and better trained they will be able to produce more. For example, if there is a fault in the production process, a skilled worker will be able to deal with it quickly, whereas an unskilled worker might have to call for a superior instead.

Technological progress can be divided into three types.

(a) **Capital saving**: technical advances that use less capital and the same amount of labour per unit of output

(b) **Neutral**: technical advances that require labour and capital in the same proportions as before, using less of each per unit of output

(c) **Labour-saving**: technical advances that use less labour and the same amount of capital per unit of output.

If technological progress is of type (c) and the new technology seems to be labour-saving, then unemployment will rise unless there is either a simultaneous **expansion of demand** or a **reduction in hours** worked by each person. In the latter case there is no productivity increase associated with the technological progress.

Technological progress may therefore stimulate growth but at the same time conflict with the goal of full employment. A further consequence of this could be that those people in work would benefit from economic growth in the form of higher wages, but those people put out of work by the new technology would be left with a lower income. There is thus a danger that the rich will get richer and the poor will get poorer in spite of economic growth, and this would be regarded by many people as an undesirable development.

8.7 External trade influences on economic growth

An improvement in the **terms of trade** (the quantity of imports that can be bought in exchange for a given quantity of exports) means that more imports can be bought or alternatively a given volume of exports will earn higher profits. This will boost investment and hence growth. The rate of growth of the rest of the world is important for an economy that has a large foreign trade sector.

If trading partners have slow growth, the amount of exports a country can sell to them will grow only slowly, and this limits the country's own opportunities for investment and growth.

8.8 Advantages and disadvantages of economic growth

Economic growth should lead to a higher income per head which can in turn lead to higher levels of consumption and a better standard of living.

A country with economic growth is more easily able to provide welfare services without creating intolerable tax burdens on the community.

There are possible disadvantages to growth, however.

(a) Growth implies faster use of **natural resources**. Without growth, these resources would last longer.

(b) Much economic activity tends to create **pollution**, such as acid rain and nuclear waste. It leads to emissions which threaten to produce disruptive climatic changes through an increase in the 'greenhouse effect'. It results in more roads, new and larger towns, and less unspoilt countryside.

(c) There is a danger that some sections of the population, unable to adapt to the demands for new skills and more training, will not find jobs in the developing economy. This **structural unemployment** might create a large section of the community which gains no benefit from the increase in national income.

(d) In order to achieve growth, firms need to **invest more** and this requires financing. This finance can only come from **higher savings** which in turn require the population to consume less. In the short run, therefore, higher growth requires a cut in consumption.

9 The balance of payments

The balance of payments account is a country's bank account with the rest of the world. It relates to foreign exchange movements in a country. It consists of a current account for trading activities, a capital account and a financial account.

The **current account** is sub-divided into:

(a) Trade in goods

(b) Trade in services

(c) Income from:

    (i) Residents employed in other countries

    (ii) Returns on capital investment in other countries

(d) Transfers from

    (i) Interest payments to/from bodies in other countries

    (ii) Non-government payments to/from bodies in other countries.

The **capital account** comprises public sector flows of capital (eg government loans to other countries).

The **balance** on the **financial account** comprises flows of **capital to/from non-government sector** (eg investment in other countries).

The sum of the balance of payments accounts must **always be zero** (excluding statistical errors in collecting the data known as the 'balancing item') via the financial account.

When commentators speak of a balance of payments **surplus** or **deficit** they are only referring to the current account, which is also known as the balance of trade.

• Deficit: importing more than exporting, ie country buys more than it sells.

• Surplus: exporting more than importing, ie country sells more than buys.

A problem arises for a country's balance of payments when the country has a deficit on current account year after year, although there can be problems too for a country which enjoys a continual current account **surplus**.

The problems of a **deficit** on the current account are probably the more obvious. When a country is continually in deficit, it is importing more goods and services that it is exporting. This leads to two possible consequences.

(a) It may borrow more and more from abroad, to build up external liabilities which match the deficit on the current account, for example encouraging foreign investors to lend more by purchasing the government's gilt-edged securities.

(b) It may sell more and more of its assets. This has been happening recently in the US, for example, where a large deficit on the US current account has resulted in large purchases of shares in US companies by foreign firms.

Even so, the demand to buy the country's currency in the foreign exchange markets will be weaker than the supply of the country's currency for sale. As a consequence, there will be pressure on the exchange rate to depreciate in value.

If a country has a **surplus** on the current account year after year, it might invest the surplus abroad or add it to official reserves. The balance of payments position would be strong. There is the problem, however, that if one country which is a major trading nation (such as Japan) has a continuous surplus on its balance of payments current account, other countries must be in continual deficit. These other countries can run down their official reserves, perhaps to nothing, and borrow as much as they can to meet the payments overseas, but eventually they will run out of money entirely and be unable even to pay their debts. Political pressure might therefore build up within the importing countries to impose tariffs or import quotas.

Chapter summary

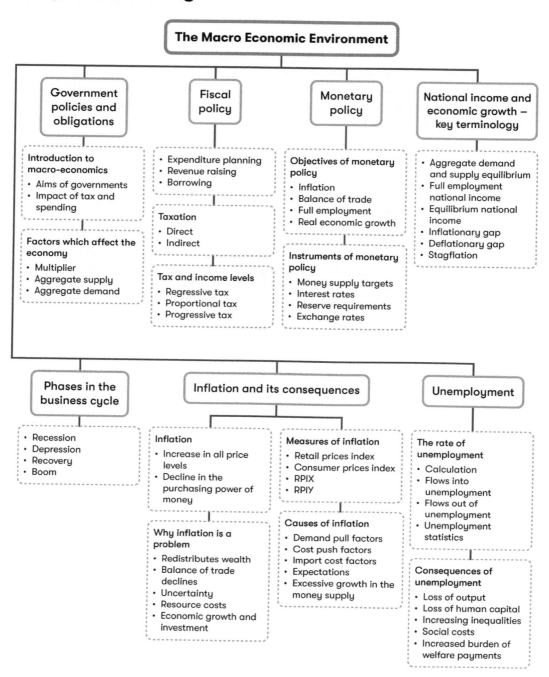

The Macro Economic Environment

Government policies and obligations

Introduction to macro-economics
- Aims of governments
- Impact of tax and spending

Factors which affect the economy
- Multiplier
- Aggregate supply
- Aggregate demand

Fiscal policy

- Expenditure planning
- Revenue raising
- Borrowing

Taxation
- Direct
- Indirect

Tax and income levels
- Regressive tax
- Proportional tax
- Progressive tax

Monetary policy

Objectives of monetary policy
- Inflation
- Balance of trade
- Full employment
- Real economic growth

Instruments of monetary policy
- Money supply targets
- Interest rates
- Reserve requirements
- Exchange rates

National income and economic growth – key terminology

- Aggregate demand and supply equilibrium
- Full employment national income
- Equilibrium national income
- Inflationary gap
- Deflationary gap
- Stagflation

Phases in the business cycle

- Recession
- Depression
- Recovery
- Boom

Inflation and its consequences

Inflation
- Increase in all price levels
- Decline in the purchasing power of money

Why inflation is a problem
- Redistributes wealth
- Balance of trade declines
- Uncertainty
- Resource costs
- Economic growth and investment

Measures of inflation
- Retail prices index
- Consumer prices index
- RPIX
- RPIY

Causes of inflation
- Demand pull factors
- Cost push factors
- Import cost factors
- Expectations
- Excessive growth in the money supply

Unemployment

The rate of unemployment
- Calculation
- Flows into unemployment
- Flows out of unemployment
- Unemployment statistics

Consequences of unemployment
- Loss of output
- Loss of human capital
- Increasing inequalities
- Social costs
- Increased burden of welfare payments

Knowledge diagnostic

1. Government policy

Governments manage the economy by using **fiscal policy, monetary policy** and **supply side policies**. These are designed to get a desired balance between the four main economic objectives – **growth, inflation, employment and balance of payments.**

2. Business cycle

The economy will pass through four phases in the business cycle and governments will seek to manage these changes in demand to achieve greater economic stability.

3. Inflation

Inflation is **rising prices** and is usually measured by an appropriate index. High inflation is damaging to an economy by creating **uncertainty** and making goods **uncompetitive** in export markets.

4. Unemployment

Unemployment has several **costs** that governments seek to mitigate; there are several **causes** of unemployment, and different **measures** are used to **monitor and reduce it.**

5. Economic growth

Economic growth is measured by increases in real gross domestic product (**GDP**) per head of population.

6. Balance of payments

The balance of payments can be considered as the UK's bank account with the rest of the world, and is affected by a number of factors, the most obvious of which are changes in foreign exchange rates.

Further study guidance

Question practice

Now try the following from the Further question practice bank [available in the digital edition of the workbook]:

Number	Level	Marks	Approximate time
Q13	Exam Section A	2	2 mins
Q14	Exam Section A	2	2 mins
Q15	Exam Section A	1	1 min
Q16	Exam Section B	4	5 mins

Activity answers

Activity 1: Taxes

The correct answer is: Regressive

A flat-rate poll tax, with no concession for the lower paid, would take a higher proportion of the income of lower-income earners than of higher-income earners. This is a regressive tax system.

Activity 2: Effects of policy

Businesses are affected by a government's tax policy (eg corporation tax rates) and monetary policy (high interest rates increase the cost of investment and depress consumer demand).

Activity 3: Types of unemployment

Structural/Cyclical/Frictional:

	Structural/Cyclical/Frictional
Unemployment arising from a difficulty in matching unemployed workers with available jobs	Frictional unemployment
Unemployment occurring in the downswing of an economy in between two booms	Cyclical unemployment
Unemployment arising from a long-term decline in a particular industry	Structural unemployment

Micro-economic factors

Learning outcomes

On completion of this chapter you should be able to:

	Syllabus reference no.
Define the concept of demand and supply for goods and services.	A5 (a)
Explain elasticity of demand and the impact of substitute and complementary goods.	A5 (b)
Explain the economic behaviour of costs in the short and long term.	A5 (c)
Define perfect competition, oligopoly, monopolistic competition and monopoly.	A5 (d)

Exam context

As you read through this chapter, make sure you understand the concepts of the market and how it impacts on individuals and businesses and how it influences the decisions they make in respect of production and consumption.

Chapter overview

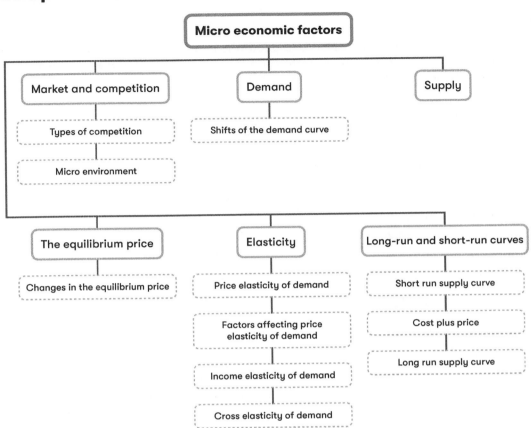

1 Market and competition

1.1 Market

A market involves **the buyers and sellers of a good who influence its price**. Markets can be worldwide, as in the case of oil, wheat, cotton and copper for example. Others are more localised, such as the housing market or the market for second-hand cars.

> **Market:** A situation in which potential buyers and potential sellers (**suppliers**) of a good or service come together for the purpose of exchange.

The way in which firms are structured and compete with one another in an industry are often described as:

- Perfect competition
- Imperfect competition
- Monopolistic competiton
- Monopoly
- Oligopoly

1.2 Types of competition

1.2.1 Perfect competition

Perfect competition is characterised by:

- **Many** small (in value) buyers and sellers which, individually, cannot influence the market price
- **No barriers** to entry or exit, so businesses are free to enter or leave the market as they wish
- **Perfect information** such that production methods and cost structures are identical
- **Homogeneous** (identical) products
- **No collusion** between buyers or sellers

The consequences of perfect competition include:

- Suppliers are '**price takers**' not 'price makers'; that is they can sell as much as they want but only at the market-determined price
- All suppliers only earn '**normal' profits**
- There is a **single selling price**

1.2.2 Imperfect competition

Is defined as **any** market structure that does not meet the conditions of perfect competition. An example of this is monopolistic competition.

1.2.3 Monopolistic competition

Monopolistic competition is characterised by:

- **Many** buyers and sellers (as in perfect competition)
- **Some differentiation** between products (not homogeneous as in perfect competition)
- **Branding** of products to achieve this differentiation
- Some (but not total) **customer loyalty**
- **Few barriers** to entry
- Significant **advertising** in many cases

Consequences of monopolistic competition include:

- Increases in prices cause loss of some customers
- Only normal profit earned in the long run (as in perfect competition)

1.2.4 Monopoly

A monopoly describes the situation where a market has only one product. It is often used, however, to describe a firm that has a very high share of the market.

The consequence of not controlling monopolies is that they can set their own prices which can lead to 'super-normal profits'.

1.2.5 Oligopoly

An oligopoly occurs when a market has a few dominant producers. These producers will all have a high level of influence and a high level of knowledge on their competitors' strategies.

Oligopolistic markets are often characterised by complex product differentiation, high barriers to entry and significant influence over prices.

If there are only two firms in an oligopoly, these are referred to as a duopoly.

1.2.6 The market mechanism

The interaction of demand and supply for a particular item.

In a free market, the **price mechanism** signals demand and supply conditions to producers and consumers. It therefore determines the activities of both producers and consumers, influencing the levels of demand for and the supply of goods.

Real life example

It is important to remember that the concepts described above are attempts to model the real world, and as such they are unlikely to be an *exact* description of any market you come across in practice. However, they are often close *enough* for us to be able to use them to get an understanding of how people and organisations are likely to behave in a given set of circumstances.

For instance, when we look at the retail market for petrol, it is usually thought of as an oligopoly - refining and distributing oil is a complex and expensive process carried out by a small number of organisations (in the UK you'd probably be thinking of BP, Shell, Texaco and maybe one or two others), requiring enormous investment, and hence has high barriers to entry.

Other industries however may prove more problematic when it comes to describing their market: if you think for a moment about buying and selling books on eBay, it is perhaps easiest to think of it as a perfect market – but is that true? Even something as standardised as a book would have variations in its design, quality, layout and so on, meaning that books cannot really be considered as homogenous. Also, there could be large retailers on eBay with the ability to dominate and influence the market – if something proves popular, they may be able to flood the market, reducing the selling price in order to gain market share, and remove competitors.

1.3 The micro environment

In the previous chapter we dealt with the issue of the *macro* environment, looking at the big picture, such as the influence of government on the economy as a whole, and how big issues like inflation, unemployment and taxation impact on the economy of the country. Now we are going to look at the picture in more detail, by considering the impact of decisions on an individual organisation, and by looking at how the immediate environment will affect its ability to trade profitably. This immediate operational environment is commonly referred to as the micro environment, and while it will be specific to each and every organisation, it is possible to identify a number of common elements such as customers, suppliers and competitors.

Essential reading

See chapter 5 Section 1 of the Essential reading for more detail on markets.

The Essential reading is available as an Appendix of the digital edition of the Workbook.

2 Demand

KEY TERM

Demand: The quantity of a good that potential purchasers would buy, or attempt to buy, if the price of the good were at a certain level.

It is perhaps best to think of demand in this way – how much people are prepared to pay to acquire a particular item – rather than to think in vague terms of somebody *wanting* something.

2.1 The demand curve

Suppose that the following *demand schedule* shows demand for biscuits by one household over a period of one month.

Price per kg	Quantity demanded at this price
£	kg
1	9.6
2	8.0
3	6.25
4	4.5
5	2.3
6	1

This is simply a table showing the quantity that people are willing to buy at a particular price. As is often the case in real life, the cheaper the item is, the more people are prepared to buy it.

We can show this schedule graphically on a demand curve (below figure), with:

(a) Price on the y axis; and

(b) Quantity demanded on the x axis.

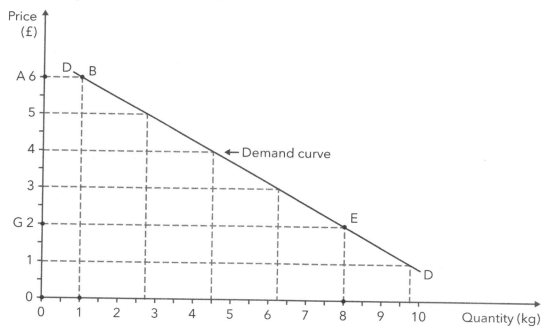

Activity 1: Demand curves

Refer to the figure above.

Let's say the price of biscuits is currently £3 per kg, and demand is approximately 6 kilograms at that price. What would be the (approximate) demand for the commodity if the price fell to £2 per kilo? And what would be the demand if the price rose to £4 per kilo?

2.2 Factors influencing demand

What factors determine demand?

- Price
- Inter-related goods: substitutes and complements
- Income levels: normal and inferior goods
- Fashion and expectations
- Income distribution

KEY TERM

Substitute goods: Goods that are alternatives to each other, so that an **increase** in the demand for one is likely to cause a **decrease** in the demand for another. Switching demand from one good to another 'rival' good is **substitution**.

Complements: Goods that tend to be bought and used together, so that an **increase** in the demand for one is likely to cause an **increase** in the demand for the other.

A change in the price of one good will not necessarily change the demand for another good. For example, we would not expect an increase in the price of televisions to affect the demand for bread. However, there are goods for which the market demand is interconnected. These interrelated goods are referred to as either **substitutes** or **complements**.

Examples of substitute goods and services
- Brands of the same commodity, like Coca-Cola and Pepsi-Cola
- Tea and coffee
- Some different forms of entertainment

Substitution takes place when the price of one good rises relative to a substitute good.

By contrast, complements are connected in the sense that demand for one is likely to lead to demand for the other.

Examples of complements
- Cups and saucers
- Bread and butter
- Motor cars and the components and raw materials that go into their manufacture

Activity 2: Substitutes and complements

What might be the effect of an increase in the ownership of domestic deep freezers on the demand for perishable food products?

2.3 Shifts of the demand curve

Here we are looking at a movement of the curve because of some change in the market which alters customers' perceptions of how attractive a particular product actually is – anything included in the list above is able to do this, and it results in different levels of demand at a particular price.

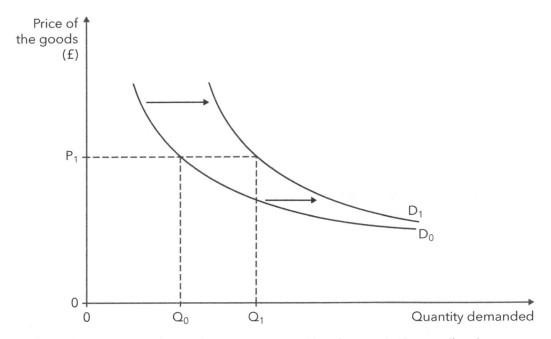

- **Movements along a demand curve** are caused by changes in the good's **price.**
- **Shifts of the demand curve** are caused by changes in any of the **other factors** which affect demand for a good, other than its price.

2.3.1 Demand, fashion and expectations

A change in fashion or tastes will also alter the demand for a product. For example, if it becomes fashionable for middle-class households in the UK to drink wine with their meals, expenditure on wine will increase.

There may be passing 'crazes', such as roller blades or skateboards. And tastes can be affected by advertisers and suppliers trying to 'create' demand for their products. However, the effect of a product becoming fashionable will be that demand for it rises without its price having to be reduced.

Activity 3: Shifts in the demand curve

Looking back at the figure above:

Required

1   What specific actions could cause the curve to move to the right?

2   What specific actions could cause the curve to move to the left?

Solution

3 Supply

KEY TERM

> **Supply:** The quantity of a good that existing suppliers or would-be suppliers would want to produce for the market at a given price.

3.1 The supply curve

The supply schedule for product Y is as follows.

Price per unit £	Quantity that suppliers would supply at this price Units
100	10,000
150	20,000
300	30,000
500	40,000

The relationship between supply quantity and price is shown as a supply curve in the following figure:

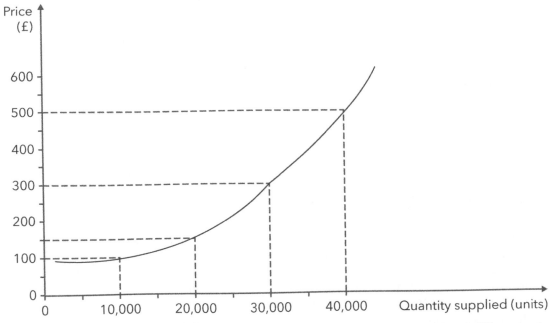

This graph shows us the amount of materials that firms are willing to supply at different prices. Notice this curve slopes upwards as it goes to the right – again, this is pretty much what you would expect; the higher the selling price is for something, the more firms are willing to make it, since they will be able to make more money from doing so.

3.2 Factors affecting supply

What factors influence supply?

- **Price** obtainable for the good
- **Prices of other goods**
- **Price of related goods** in 'joint supply'
- **Costs of making the good**
- **Changes in technology**

Essential reading

See Chapter 5 Section 2 of the Essential reading for more detail on supply.

The Essential reading is available as an Appendix of the digital edition of the Workbook.

3.3 Shifts of the supply curve

The market supply curve is the aggregate of all the supply curves of individual firms in the market. A shift of the market supply curve occurs when supply conditions (other than the price of the good itself) change.

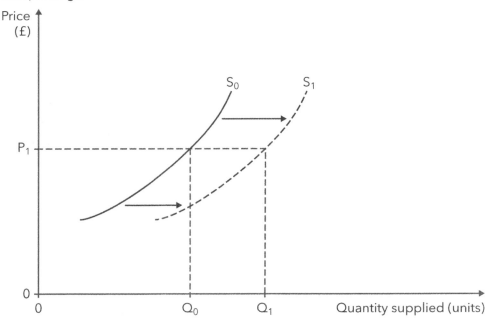

The figure above shows a shift in the supply curve from S0 to S1. A rightward (or downward) shift of the curve shows an expansion of supply and may be caused by the factors below.

(a) A fall in the cost of factors of production, for example a reduction in the cost of raw material inputs

(b) A fall in the price of other goods; the production of other goods becomes relatively less attractive as their price falls and firms are therefore likely to shift resources away from the goods whose price is falling and into the production of higher priced goods that offer increased profits. We therefore expect that (ceteris paribus) the supply of one good will rise as the prices of other goods fall (and vice versa).

(c) Technological progress, which reduces unit costs and also increases production capabilities

(d) Improvements in productivity or more efficient use of existing factors of production, which again will reduce unit cost

A shift of the supply curve is the result of changes in costs, either in absolute terms or relative to the costs of other goods. If the price of the good is P1, suppliers would be willing to increase supply from Q0 to Q1 under the new supply conditions (Figure 5.3).

Conversely, we might see a leftward (or upward) shift in the supply curve if the cost of supply increases. This would mean that at the existing price, a firm's output will decrease and less will be supplied.

An upward shift in supply could be caused by:

(a) An increase in the cost of factors of production

(b) A rise in the price of other goods which would make them relatively more attractive to the producer

(c) An increase in indirect taxes, or a reduction in a subsidy, which would make supply at existing prices less profitable.

4 The equilibrium price

> **Equilibrium price:** The price of a good at which the volume demanded by consumers and the volume businesses are willing to supply are the same.

We usually find the equilibrium price by plotting both the supply and demand curve on the graph, and noting where they cross.

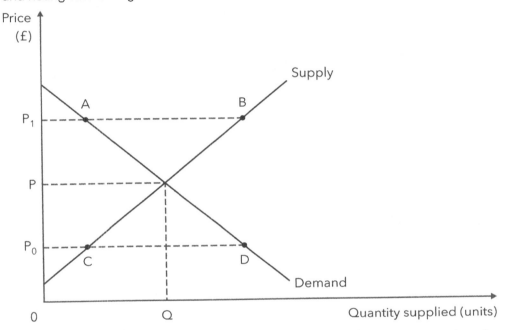

The point where the lines intersect gives us the point where the amounts produced equal the amounts that people are prepared to buy, and so there is no shortage (pushing the price up) and no excess production (pushing the price down). Of course, this equilibrium won't last forever – as we pointed out before, the curves will move as any number of factors come into play, and as the curves move to the right or left, the equilibrium price will move either up or down.

4.1 Changes in the equilibrium price

Equilibrium price, supply and demand must adjust following a shift of the demand or supply curve. There are four possibilities therefore, which are illustrated by the following diagrams:

(1) Increase in consumer incomes

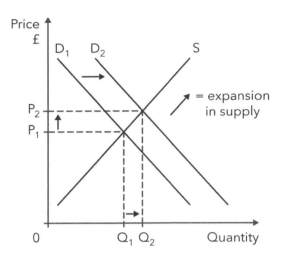

(2) Product becomes unfashionable

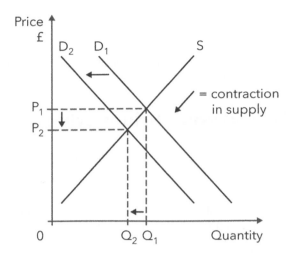

Increase in consumer incomes	Product becomes unfashionable
Prediction	**Prediction**
• Rise in market price • Rise in quantity supplied	• Fall in market price • Fall in quantity supplied

(3) Improvement in production technology

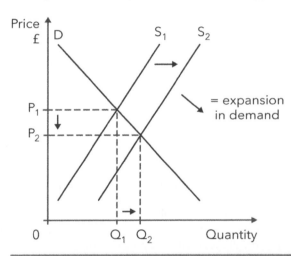

(4) Rise in factor costs

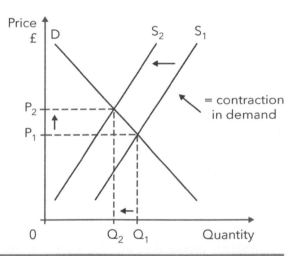

Improvement in production technology	Rise in factor costs
Prediction	**Prediction**
• Fall in market price • Rise in quantity supplied	• Rise in market price • Fall in quantity supplied

4.1.1 Price regulation

Government might introduce regulations either:

- To set a **maximum price** for a good, perhaps as part of an anti-inflationary economic policy
- To set a **minimum price** for a good below which a supplier is not allowed to fall

However, if we consider the setting of a maximum price:

- If this price is **higher than the equilibrium price**, its existence will have no effect at all on the operation of market forces; but

- If the maximum price is **lower than what the equilibrium price would be,** there will be an excess of demand over supply. The low price attracts customers but deters suppliers, so supply will fall unless there is scope for the market to exist outside government-sanctioned channels – a so-called 'black market'.

Essential reading

See Chapter 5 Section 3 of the Essential reading for more detail on the equilibrium price.

The Essential reading is available as an Appendix of the digital edition of the Workbook.

5 Elasticity

KEY TERM

Elasticity: The extent of a change in demand and/or supply given a change in price.

Elasticity, in general, refers to the relationship between two variables. Price elasticity of demand explains the relationship between **change in quantity demanded** and **changes in price**.

If prices went **up** by 10%, would the quantity demanded **fall** by the same percentage?

5.1 Price elasticity of demand (PED)

Price elasticity of demand (PED) is a measure of the extent of change in the market demand for a good in response to a change in its price.

- The demand for a good is said to be **inelastic** when **changes in price** have a relatively **small effect** on the **quantity** of the good **demanded**.
- The demand for a good is said to be **elastic** when **changes in price** have a relatively **large effect** on the **quantity** of a good **demanded**.
- 'Relatively small' and 'relatively large' here equate to 'less than 1' and 'greater than 1' respectively.

Formula to learn

$$PED = \frac{\text{Change in quantity demanded, as a percentage of original demand}}{\text{Change in price, as a percentage of original price}}$$

$$PED = \frac{\text{Proportional change in quantity}}{\text{Proportional change in price}}$$

$$= [\frac{Q2-Q1}{Q1}] \div [\frac{P2-P1}{P1}]$$

(Where P_1, Q_1 are the initial price and quantity; P_2, Q_2 are the subsequent price and quantity.)

Since demand usually increases when the price falls, and decreases when the price rises, elasticity has a negative value. **However, it is usual to ignore the minus sign**, and just describe the absolute value of the coefficient

- PED less than 1 = inelastic demand
- PED more than 1 = elastic demand
- PED = 1 = unit elasticity

BPP
LEARNING
MEDIA

Activity 4: Price elasticity of demand

The price of a good is £1.20 per unit and annual demand is 800,000 units. Market research indicates that an increase in price of 10 pence per unit will result in a fall in annual demand of 70,000 units. Assume that the demand curve is a straight line.

Required

1   Calculate the elasticity of demand when the price is initially £1.20 and the price rises to £1.30

2   Calculate the elasticity of demand when the price is initially £1.30 and the price falls to £1.20.

Solution

Activity 5: Price elasticity of demand and revenue

A shop sells 100 shirts each month at a price of £20. When the price is increased to £24, the total sales revenue rises by 14%.

Required

Within which range does the price elasticity of demand lie?

O   Under 0.15

O   Greater than 0.15 and less than 0.5

O   Greater than 0.5 and less than 1.0

O   Greater than 1.0

5.2   Special values of price elasticity of demand

There are three special values of price elasticity of demand: 0, 1 and infinity.

- **Demand is perfectly inelastic:** PED = 0

  This is the case where the demand curve is a **vertical straight line**.

- **Demand is perfectly elastic:** PED = (infinitely elastic)

  This is the case where the demand curve is a **horizontal straight line**.

- **Unit elasticity of demand:** PED = 1

  The **demand changes proportionately to a price change**.

One point to remember is that we normally assume that goods have a negative PED, and so ignore the negative sign – if something has a PED of '-2' we would just refer to it as having a PED of '2'. However, some goods do actually have a positive price elasticities of demand – if the price goes up, so does demand.

While this may seem counterintuitive, it does actually happen in real life, and such goods are referred to as:

- Giffen goods (basic items for which demand goes up when prices rise because of a lack of close substitutes)
- Veblen goods (status symbol items whose price is seen as a measure of exclusivity and quality)

Of the two, Veblen goods are more commonly found.

Real life example

Giffen goods; bread, rice and wheat are common essentials with few near-dimensional substitutes at the same price levels. An increase in price may lead to a fear of shortages in the near future, leading to stockpiling by consumers.

Veblen goods; Rolex watches are seen as exclusive – if the price were to fall by say 20%, they would be seen as less attractive by those consumers who are attracted by the idea of conspicuous consumption, but would still be seen as overly expensive by those who struggle to deal with normal day to day bills.

5.3 Factors affecting the price elasticity of demand

- Availability of substitutes
- The time horizon
- Competitors' pricing
- Luxuries and necessities
- Percentage of income spent on a good
- Habit-forming goods

5.4 Income elasticity of demand

> **Income elasticity of demand:** An indication of the responsiveness of demand to changes in household incomes.

> **Formula to learn**
>
> $$\text{Income elasticity of demand} = \frac{\% \text{ change in quantity demanded}}{\% \text{ change in household incomes}}$$

- Demand for a good is **income elastic** if income elasticity is greater than 1. These are **luxury goods.**
- Demand for a good is **income inelastic** if income elasticity is between 0 and 1. These are **normal goods** or **necessities**.
- Demand for a good is negatively income elastic where, in response to an increase in income, demand actually falls. These are **inferior goods**.

The change in quantity demanded takes the form of a **shift in the position of the demand curve**, not a movement along it, since it is **not** stimulated by a change in price.

Goods whose income elasticity of demand is positive are said to be **normal goods,** meaning that demand for them will rise when household income rises. If income elasticity is **negative**, the commodity is called an **inferior good** since demand for it falls as income rises.

Inferiority in this sense is an observable fact about the consumer's demand preferences, rather than a statement about the quality of the good itself.

Real life example

Inter-city bus travel is an example of an inferior good. Bus travel is cheaper than air or rail travel, but takes longer. When consumers have limited income, they are prepared to forgo the increased time taken to travel in return for the cheaper cost. However, as their income increases, they will choose the more rapid modes of transport over the slower, albeit cheaper, bus travel. Therefore demand for bus travel will fall as income rises.

Activity 6: Income elasticity of demand

What will be the effect on price, quantity demanded and quantity supplied of luxury sports cars, given a significant reduction in income tax?

Solution

5.5 Cross elasticity of demand

Cross elasticity of demand: Cross elasticity of demand: A measure of the responsiveness of demand for one good to changes in the price of another good.

Formula to learn

$$\text{Cross elasticity of demand} = \frac{\text{\% change in quantity of good A demanded *}}{\text{\% change in the price of good B}}$$

*(given no change in the price of A)

Cross elasticity depends upon the degree to which goods are substitutes or complements.

- If the two goods are **substitutes** cross elasticity will be positive.
- If the goods are **complements** cross elasticity will be negative.
- For **unrelated goods**, such as tea and oil, cross elasticity will be 0.

Real life example

For example, assume bread and butter are complements. If the price of bread increases, demand for bread and then, in turn, butter will decrease. So, as a fraction, we have a negative value (quantity of butter demanded) over a positive value (increase in price) meaning the cross elasticity of demand is negative.

Essential reading

See chapter 5 Section 4 of the Essential reading for more detail on Elasticity.

The Essential reading is available as an Appendix of the digital edition of the Workbook.

6 Long run and short run cost curves

KEY
TERM

Marginal cost: The increase in total cost from selling one additional unit of a product or service

Marginal revenue: The increase in total revenue from selling one additional unit of a product or service.

6.1 Short run supply curve

A firm's short run average cost curve is U shaped. Initially, as output rises, the average cost falls, due to economies of scale. However, at a certain point, represented by the bottom of the U, if production increases further, the average cost starts to rise again, dues to diseconomies of scale.

The marginal cost curve initially lies below the average cost curve, but starts to rise steeply. It passes through the average cost curve at the bottom of the U shape, then rises more steeply than average costs.

If we assume there is a single, constant selling price for all firms, then a firm's average revenue (AR) and marginal revenue (MR) will be identical. We can show this as Price = Average Revenue = Marginal Revenue.

The relationships are shown in the diagram below:

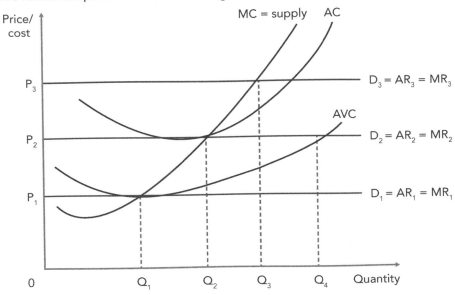

If a firm wishes to maximise profits, it will always produce the quantity such that marginal cost = marginal revenue. Why is this? Consider the case where the price is P_1:

*   If a firm is producing less than Q_1 then the marginal cost is less than the marginal revenue. Producing one more unit increases total revenue by more than it increases costs. It is worth producing more to increase profits. This will be the case up until Q_1, where marginal cost equals marginal revenue.

- Once output exceeds Q_1 then the marginal cost becomes greater than marginal revenue. The increase in total costs if one more unit is produced is more than the increase in total revenue. Profits would fall if output is increased.
- A profit maximising firm will therefore produce the quantity such that the marginal cost = the marginal revenue.

We can see in the figure above that at price P_1 the firm supplies Q_1 output, because MC = MR_1. When price rises to P_2, the output increases to Q_2 and so on, provided that the firm has the capacity to increase its sales output. In these conditions, the firm's **marginal cost curve becomes its supply curve**.

6.1.1 Cost plus pricing

The idea of the marginal cost curve representing the supply curve is the traditional theory of a firm's short run supply curve. However, more recent theories of the firm incorporate a cost-plus pricing approach.

Under a cost-plus pricing approach, a firm adds a profit margin to its average cost at any level of output in order to establish its selling price. This alternative theory produces a horizontal supply curve.

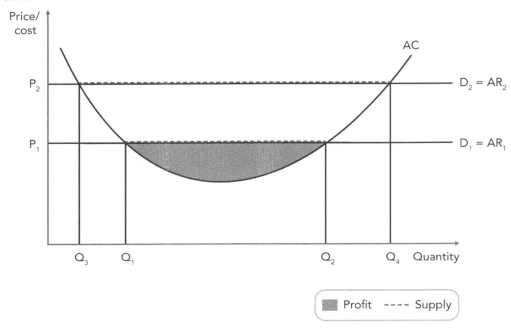

A rational (profit maximising, or loss minimising) firm will only supply where AR > AC. So the minimum and maximum levels of output occur at Q_1 and Q_2 respectively, at price P_1; that is, where AR crosses the AC curve (AC = AR). Changes in the market price will lead to changes in output. (Note, we are still assuming a single, constant selling price for all firms in the industry.) A higher price (P_2) will lead to a new supply curve, between Q_3 and Q_4.

6.2 Long run supply curve

In traditional theory, the **marginal cost curve remains the supply curve** in the long run. However, it may no longer be upward sloping. The supply curve was upward sloping in the short run because of the impact of diminishing returns on the marginal cost curve. However, this is only a short run phenomenon, because the constraint of one factor of production being fixed is only a short run condition.

In the long run, the supply curve could still be upward sloping (if the firm suffers from diseconomies of scale) but it could equally be downward sloping to the right if the firm benefits from economies of scale. The curve could even be horizontal if the firm's marginal cost remained constant at all levels of output.

Chapter summary

Micro economic factors

Market and competition

Types of competition
- Perfect competition
- Imperfect competition
- Monopolistic competition
- Oligopoly
- The market mechanism

Micro environment
- Individual organisations

Demand

- The demand curve
- Factors influencing demand

Shifts of the demand curve
- Movements along the demand curve
- Shifts of the demand curve
- Factors causing a shift
- Factors influencing demand

Supply

- The supply curve
- Factors influencing supply
- Shifts of the supply curve

The equilibrium price

Changes in the equilibrium price
- Increase in consumer incomes
- Product becomes unfashionable
- Improvement in production technology
- Rise in factor costs

Elasticity

Price elasticity of demand
- Measure of change in demand given change in price
- Elastic
- Inelastic
- Special values of price elasticity of demand
  – Perfectly inelastic
  – Perfectly elastic
  – Unit elasticity

Factors affecting price elasticity of demand
- Availability of substitutes
- The time horizon
- Competitors' pricing
- Luxuries and necessities
- Percentage or income spent on a good
- Habit-forming goods

Income elasticity of demand
- Responsiveness to change in household incomes

Cross elasticity of demand
- Responsiveness to change in price of another product
- Substitutes
- Complements
- Unrelated goods

Long-run and short-run curves

Short run supply curve
- Produce to point where marginal cost = marginal revenue
- If selling price constant
- Short run curve – marginal cost curve above AVC

Cost plus price
- Horizontal supply curve
- Min and maximum quantities where AR crosses AC curve

Long run supply curve
- Marginal cost curve remains supply curve
- Capital not constrained in long term
- Slope of curve depends on economies of scale in long term

BPP LEARNING MEDIA

Knowledge diagnostic

1. Market

A market can be defined as a situation in which potential buyers and potential suppliers of a good or service come together for the purpose of exchange.

2. Demand

Demand is concerned with the quantity of a good that potential purchasers would buy, or attempt to buy, if the price of the good were at a certain level.

3. Supply

Supply is concerned with the quantity of a good that existing suppliers or would be suppliers would want to produce for the market at a given price.

4. Equilibrium price

Equilibrium price is the price of a good at which the volume demanded by consumers and the volume businesses are willing to supply are the same.

5. Elasticity

Elasticity can be considered from a number of perspectives, the principle ones being

- Price elasticity of demand
- Income elasticity of demand
- Cross elasticity of demand

Further study guidance

Question practice

Now try the following from the Further question practice bank [available in the digital edition of the workbook]:

Number	Level	Marks	Approximate time
Q17	Exam Section A	2	2 mins
Q18	Exam Section A	2	2 mins
Q19	Exam Section A	2	2 mins
Q20	Exam Section A	2	2 mins
Q22	Exam Section A	2	2 mins

Further reading

There is an article on the ACCA website entitled 'Introduction to micro-economics' that is relevant to material in this chapter. You are strongly advised to read this article in full as part of your preparation for the FBT exam.

Activity answers

Activity 1: Demand curves

Demand rises to (approximately) 8 kg at the reduced price of £2 per kilo. If the price rises to £4 per kilo, demand falls to (approximately) 4.5 kg.

Notice that in this example we are considering what happens if we move *along* the demand curve.

Activity 2: Substitutes and complements

Effect of increase:

(1) Domestic deep freezers and perishable products are complements because people buy deep freezers to store perishable products.

(2) Perishable products are supplied either as fresh produce (for example, fresh meat and fresh vegetables) or as frozen produce, which can be kept for a short time in a refrigerator but for longer in a freezer. The demand for frozen produce will rise, while the demand for fresh produce will fall.

(3) Wider ownership of deep freezers is likely to increase bulk buying of perishable products. Suppliers can save some packaging costs, and can therefore offer lower prices for bulk purchases.

Activity 3: Shifts in the demand curve

1   Just look at the curve for a second. As it moves to the right the amount demanded at Price P has increased from Q0 to Q1. Maybe this has been caused by people having more money to spend, or maybe a famous film star has been seen with the product and more people are interested in owning it as a result – there is no single 'right' answer to this; there could be many factors causing the shift.

2   If the curve moves to the left, it means that there is *less* demand at any given price; so maybe the product is less fashionable – maybe a new alternative has been developed, rendering the product less attractive. Think of what happened to the sale of fountain pens when the ballpoint pen came out – the demand for the fountain pens fell dramatically.

Activity 4: Price elasticity of demand

1   At a price of £1.20, annual demand is 800,000 units.

For a price rise:

$$\% \text{ change in quantity } \frac{70,000}{800,000} \times 100\% = 8.75\% \text{ (fall)}$$

$$\% \text{ change in price } \frac{10p}{120p} \times 100\% = 8.33\% \text{ (rise)}$$

$$\text{Price elasticity of demand at price } = \frac{-8.75}{8.22} = -1.05$$

Ignoring the minus sign, the price elasticity at this point is 1.05. Demand is **elastic** at this point, because the elasticity is greater than one.

2   At a price of £1.30, annual demand is 730,000 units.

For a price fall from £1.30 of £0.10:

% change in demand 70,000/730,000 × 100% = 9.59% (rise)

% change in price 10p/130p × 100% = 7.69% (fall)

Price elasticity of demand = -1.25

Or, 1.25 ignoring the minus sign

Demand is even more *elastic* at this point than it was at £1.20.

Activity 5: Price elasticity of demand and revenue

The correct answer is: Greater than 0.15 and less than 0.5

Total revenue at £20 = 100 × $20 = $2,000

Total revenue at £24 = $2,000 × 1.14 = $2,280 (A price increase of 20%)

Number sold at $24 = $2,280 ÷ 24 = 95 (a fall in quantity demanded of 5%)

Therefore the PED = -.05/0.20 = -0.25 , so we would say the PED is 0.25.

Activity 6: Income elasticity of demand

The demand curve for sports cars will shift to the right. Price, quantity demanded and quantity supplied will all go up.

The effect of a cut in income tax is to leave households with more to spend. Sports cars are a luxury good, so their income elasticity of demand is likely to be quite high. The percentage increase in demand for the cars is therefore likely to be greater than the percentage increase in after-tax household income.

We can illustrate the change diagrammatically:

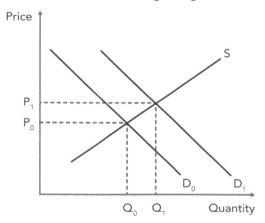

The shift in the demand curve (from D_0 to D_1) means that the equilibrium quantity demanded and supplied shifts from Q_0 to Q_1 and the equilibrium price increases from P_0 to P_1.

Business organisation structure

Learning outcomes

On completion of this chapter you should be able to:

	Syllabus reference no.
Explain the informal organisation and its relationship with the formal organisation.	B1 (a)
Describe the impact of the informal organisation on the business.	B1 (b)
Describe Mintzberg's components of the organisation and explain the different ways in which organisations may be structured: (a) Entrepreneurial (b) Functional (c) Matrix (d) Divisional: (geographical, by product, or by customer type) (e) Boundaryless: (virtual, hollow or modular)	B2 (a)
Explain basic organisational structure concepts: (a) Separation of ownership and management (b) Separation of direction and management (c) Span of control and scalar chain (d) Tall and flat organisations (e) Outsourcing and offshoring (f) Shared services approach	B2 (b)
Explain the characteristics of the strategic, tactical and operational levels in the organisation in the context of the Anthony hierarchy.	B2 (c)
Explain centralisation and decentralisation and list their advantages and disadvantages.	B2 (d)

Exam context

This chapter lays the foundation for an understanding of what organisations are and how they are controlled. It also introduces the concept of stakeholders, which is examinable in FBT but also feeds into later ACCA exams.

Chapter overview

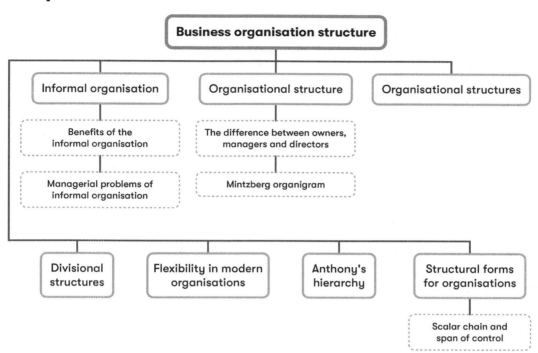

1 Informal organisation

An informal organisation always exists alongside the formal one. This consists of social relationships, informal communication networks, behavioural norms and power/influence structures, all of which may 'bypass' formal organisational arrangements. This may be detrimental or beneficial to the organisation, depending how it is managed.

When people work together, they establish social relationships and customary ways of doing things. Unlike the formal organisation, the informal organisation is loosely structured, flexible and spontaneous. It embraces such mechanisms as:

(a) Social relationships and groupings (eg cliques) within – or across – formal structures

(b) The 'grapevine', 'bush telegraph', or informal communication which bypasses the formal reporting channels and routes

(c) Behavioural norms and ways of doing things, both social and work-related, which may circumvent formal procedures and systems (for good or ill). New members must 'learn the ropes' and get used to 'the way we do things here'

(d) Power/influence structures, irrespective of organisational authority: informal leaders are those who are trusted and looked to for advice.

Real life example

Just think about the place where you work. No doubt there are individuals that you feel more at ease with than others, and equally, some people you prefer not to work with. The workplace, like any other place where people congregate is affected by the relationships that arise between individuals – and in some cases, these relationships can benefit or be detrimental to the organisation. Think about the restrictions that exist in your workplace; for instance, many organisations insist that if two members of staff develop a serious attachment, one of them is required to relocate to another department because of concerns that the judgement of either party may be compromised by the relationship.

1.1 Benefits of the informal organisation

(a) **Employee commitment.** The meeting of employees' social needs may contribute to morale and job satisfaction, with benefits in reduced absenteeism and labour turnover.

(b) **Knowledge sharing.** The availability of information through informal networks can give employees a wider perspective on their role in the task and the organisation, potentially stimulating 'big picture' problem-solving, cross-boundary co-operation and innovation.

(c) **Speed.** Informal networks and methods may sometimes be more efficient in achieving organisational goals, where the formal organisation has rigid procedures or lengthy communication channels, enabling decisions to be taken and implemented more rapidly.

(d) **Responsiveness.** The directness, information-richness and flexibility of the informal organisation may be particularly helpful in conditions of rapid environmental change, facilitating both the mechanisms and culture of anti-bureaucratic responsiveness.

(e) **Co-operation.** The formation and strengthening of interpersonal networks can facilitate team working and co-ordination across organisational boundaries. It may reduce organisational politics – or utilise this positively by mobilising effective decision-making coalitions and bypassing communication blocks.

1.2 Managerial problems of informal organisation

Each of the positive attributes of informal organisation could as easily be detrimental if the power of the informal organisation is directed towards goals unrelated to, or at odds with, those of the formal organisation.

(a) Social groupings may act collectively against organisational interests, strengthened by collective power and information networks. Even if they are aligned with organisational goals, group/network maintenance may take a lot of time and energy away from tasks.

(b) The grapevine is notoriously inaccurate and can carry morale-damaging rumours.

(c) The informal organisation can become too important in fulfilling employees' needs: individuals can suffer acutely when excluded from cliques and networks.

(d) Informal work practices may 'cut corners', violating safety or quality assurance measures.

Managers can minimise problems by:

- Meeting as many employee needs through the formal organisation as possible
- Using the informal, charismatic leaders to motivate workers
- Managers working as part of the informal organisation

2 Organisational structure

2.1 The difference between owners, managers and directors.

Before starting to look at the different organisational structures, it is worthwhile spending some time considering what we mean when talk about management in an organisation.

The first point to note is that managers are usually distinct from the owners of a business. Owners will delegate authority to managers to run the company in the best interests of the owners, but managers will need to be motivated to do this – they will need to be incentivised to operate the company in an efficient and effective way to reward the owners for risking their capital.

This topic is the main part of Section 5 of the syllabus 'Governance and social responsibility in business'.

Equally it is important to appreciate that the people at the top of the organisation – the directors of a limited company – tend to have a much longer-term outlook than more junior managers. They also tend to look at the whole company, rather than say a particular department or division.

Note that the higher up the organisation a manager climbs, the more likely he or she is to have an external, longer term, group-wide perspective.

2.2 Mintzberg organigram

Henry Mintzberg believes that all organisations can be analysed into five components, according to how they relate to the work of the organisation and how they prefer to co-ordinate.

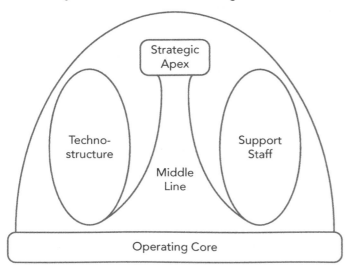

The following table summarises the details you need to know about the five components

Strategic apex	Ensures the organisation follows its mission Manages the organisation's relationship with the environment	Direct supervision (especially in small businesses)
Operating core	The operating core is the people directly involved in the production of the goods and services that the organisation produces.	Mutual adjustment; standardisation of skills
Middle line	Converts the desires of the strategic apex into the work done by the operating core.	Standardisation of outputs (results)
Technostructure	Analysers determine the best way of doing a job. Planners determine outputs (eg goods must achieve a specified level of quality). Personnel analysts standardise skills (eg training programmes).	Standardisation of work processes or outputs
Support staff	Ancillary services such as public relations, legal counsel, the cafeteria. Support staff do not plan or standardise production. They function independently of the operating core.	Mutual adjustment

Note that the strategic apex, middle line and operating core make up the basic triangle often used to depict an organisation's structure.

2.2.1 Strategic Apex

The board of directors of an organisation is nearly always its strategic apex, but remember that every organisation has somebody that makes a decision about how it will be run; a window cleaner is an example of a sole trader – and he would have to make decisions about what tools he wants to buy or if he wants to continue carrying out his rounds. He would be *both* strategic apex and operating core.

2.2.2 Operating core

The operating core is usually the people who carry out the work of the organisation, and very often come into regular contact with the customers. Often the operating core is made up of low skilled workers on low wages. In some organisations, however, the operating core may consist of highly skilled, highly paid persons. A surgeon is part the operating core of a hospital for example. A surgeon may get paid substantially more than the manager who oversees them. At BPP, the operating core would include the writer of this workbook and would also include the staff who teach in the classroom.

2.2.3 Middle line

Think in terms of any manager who exists below the strategic apex. They organise and encourage the operating core, or the managers below them. At BPP the manager of the publishing teams would be an example of the middle line.

2.2.4 Technostructure

Think in terms of the people who report on performance. At BPP it would include the finance team that prepare monthly management accounts, carry out variance analysis and so on.

2.2.5 Support staff

At BPP, these would be the people whose work does not impact directly on teaching or writing, such as the HR department or the legal team, but it also includes the people who come into the head office to clean the windows.

Activity 1: Mintzberg

State which of Mintzberg's five components correctly describes each of the following staff/departments:

Staff/ departments	Mintzberg
Manager of a retail outlet supervising 40 staff	
A salesman responsible for 20 corporate accounts	
The owner of a start-up internet company employing two staff.	
The IT department seeking to harmonise internal systems	
The HR department which provides assistance to business managers	

Essential reading

See Chapter 6 Section 1 of the Essential reading for more detail on details of Business organisation structure.

The Essential reading is available as an Appendix of the digital edition of the Workbook.

3 Organisational structures

There are four structures: entrepreneurial, functional, matrix and divisional. As the divisional is perhaps the most common, we'll look at the divisional structure in Section 4.

Exam questions in this area often focus on the advantages and disadvantages of the different structures, so make sure you are comfortable with them.

3.1 Entrepreneurial

A fluid structure with little or no formality. Suitable for small start-up companies, the activities and decisions are dominated by a key central figure (the owner/entrepreneur).

The strategic apex exerts a pull to centralise, leading to the simple structure.

The strategic apex wishes to retain control over decision-making, and so exercises a pull to centralise (Mintzberg, 1979). Mintzberg believes that this leads to a simple structure. It is often associated with small organisations, such as perhaps a firm that provides decorating services to local customers. Notice that there are no managers other than the strategic apex, simply because none are needed.

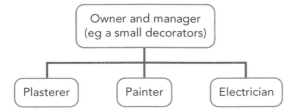

The key characteristics of the entrepreneurial structure are as follows:

(a) The simple structure is characteristic of small, young organisations. The strategic apex is a small group, or possibly one person, which exercises direct control over the people making up the operating core. There is little, if any, role for technical or support staff.

(b) In small firms, a single entrepreneur or management team will dominate (as in the power culture). If it grows, the organisation might need more managerial skills than the apex can provide. Strategies might be made on the basis of the manager's hunches.

(c) Centralisation is advantageous, as it reflects management's full knowledge of the operating core and its processes. However, senior managers might intervene too much.

(d) This structure can handle an environment that is relatively simple but fast moving, where standardisation cannot be used to co-ordinate activities.

(e) Co-ordination is achieved by direct supervision, with few formal devices. It is thus flexible.

(f) This structure has its own particular characteristics: wide span of control; no middle line and hence minimal hierarchy; and no technostructure, implying little formalisation or standardisation of behaviour.

3.2 Functional

This structure is created via separate departments or 'functions'. Employees are grouped by specialism, and departmental targets will be set. Formal communication systems will be set up to ensure information is shared. At its most simple, the organisation will look like this:

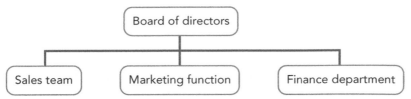

Functional organisation involves grouping together people who do similar tasks. Primary functions in a manufacturing company might be production, sales, finance and general administration. Sub-departments of marketing might be market research, advertising, PR, and so on.

Advantages include:

- **Expertise is pooled** thanks to the division of work into specialist areas.
- It **avoids duplication** (eg one management accounts department rather than several) and enables economies of scale.
- It **facilitates** the recruitment, management and development of functional specialists.
- It suits **centralised** businesses.

Disadvantages include:

- It **focuses** on internal **processes** and **inputs, rather than the customer and outputs**, which are what ultimately drive a business. Inward-looking businesses are less able to adapt to changing demands.
- **Communication problems** may arise between different functions, which each have their own jargon.
- **Poor co-ordination**, especially if rooted in a tall organisation structure. Decisions by one function/department involving another might have to be referred upwards, and dealt with at a higher level, thereby increasing the burdens on senior management.
- Functional structures create **vertical barriers to information and work flow.**

3.3 Matrix

A matrix organisation crosses a functional with a product/customer/project structure.

- The finance manager for their work in accounting and finance for their functional department; and

- The project manager C for their work on the project team: budgeting, management reporting and payroll relevant to the project, say.

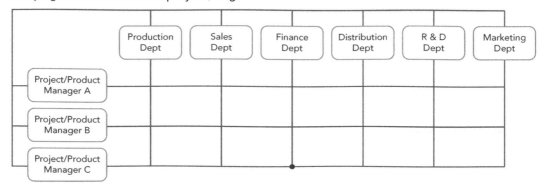

Advantages of matrix organisation include:

(a) Greater flexibility of:

    (i) People. Employees develop an attitude geared to accepting change, and departmental monopolies are broken down.

    (ii) Workflow and decision-making. Direct contact between staff encourages problem solving and big-picture thinking.

    (iii) Tasks and structure. The matrix structure may be readily amended, once projects are completed.

(b) Inter-disciplinary co-operation and a mixing of skills and expertise, along with improved communication and co-ordination.

(c) Motivation and employee development: providing employees with greater participation in planning and control decisions.

(d) Market awareness: the organisation tends to become more customer/quality focused

(e) Horizontal workflow: bureaucratic obstacles are removed, and department specialisms become less powerful.

There are disadvantages, however.

(a) Dual authority threatens a conflict between functional managers and product/project/area managers.

(b) An individual with two or more bosses may suffer stress from conflicting demands or ambiguous roles.

(c) Cost: product management posts are added, meetings have to be held, and so on.

(d) Slower decision-making due to the added complexity.

Real life example

The matrix structure is most commonly associated with large organisations – it was originally developed for the Boeing company in the 1970s. Boeing found it useful because they worked in a project based environment – an order would come in for a large number of planes for a particular customer, and they would accommodate the specific needs of those high fee paying customers. (It's not like a car manufacturer that makes cars on a production line and holds any unsold cars in stock until required.) Boeing is *huge*. As a large organisation, it has the resources to support an extensive sophisticated co-ordinating mechanism (ie the technostructure) which allows it to overcome some of the problems associated with the matrix structure. Smaller firms lack this, and so would find that the matrix structure would not work.

4 Divisional structures

When an organisation reaches a certain size, it may be appropriate to structure it into divisions or 'semi-autonomous' blocks. These divisions may focus on a particular geographic area or a particular product or even customer type.

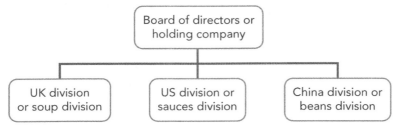

In a divisional structure some activities are decentralised to business units or regions (we shall discuss centralisation and decentralisation in more detail later on in this chapter).

4.1 Divisionalisation

> **Divisionalisation:** Divisionalisation is the division of a business into autonomous regions or product businesses, each with its own revenues, expenditures and capital asset purchase programmes, and therefore each with its own profit and loss responsibility.

Each division of the organisation might be:

- A subsidiary company under the holding company
- A profit centre or investment centre within a single company
- A strategic business unit (SBU) within the larger company, with its own objectives.

4.2 Requirements of successful divisionalisation

Successful divisionalisation requires certain key conditions.

(a) Each division must have properly delegated authority, and must be held properly accountable to head office (eg for profits earned).

(b) Each unit must be large enough to support the quantity and quality of management it needs.

(c) The unit must not rely on head office for excessive management support.

(d) Each unit must have a potential for growth in its own area of operations.

(e) There should be scope and challenge in the job for the management of each unit.

(f) If units deal with each other, it should be as an 'arm's length' transaction.

The advantages and disadvantages of divisionalisation may be summarised as follows.

Advantages	
Focuses the attention of management below 'top level' on business performance	In some businesses, it is impossible to identify completely independent products or markets for which separate divisions can be set up.
Reduces the likelihood of unprofitable products and activities being continued	Divisionalisation is only possible at a fairly senior management level, because there is a limit to how much discretion can be used in the division of work. For example, every product needs a manufacturing function and a selling function.
Encourages a greater attention to efficiency, lower costs and higher profits	There may be more resource problems. Many divisions get their resources from head office in competition with other divisions.

Advantages	
Gives more authority to junior managers, and so grooms them for more senior positions in the future (planned managerial succession)	
Reduces the number of levels of management, meaning that the top executives in each division should be able to report directly to the chief executive of the holding company	

Activity 2: Different structures

Which type of structure would be appropriate for each of the organisations listed below?

Organisation	Appropriate structure
A family run restaurant with 10 staff	
A small manufacturing company with 250 staff	
Johnson and Johnson who have 197 strategic business units	
BPP Professional Education	

4.3 Centralisation and decentralisation – the role of head office in divisions

Divisions will normally report to head office on a range of performance-related matters. The level of autonomy given to divisional heads is dependent on the level of centralisation required.

Centralised organisations retain much of the power and decision making at head office.

Decentralised organisations delegate more business decisions to divisional heads.

A **centralised** organisation is one in which authority is concentrated in one place.

We can look at centralisation in two ways.

(a) Geography. Some functions may be centralised rather than 'scattered' in different offices, departments or locations.

So, for example, secretarial support, IT support and information storage (filing) may be centralised in specialist departments (whose services are shared by other functions) rather than carried out by staff/equipment duplicated in each departmental office.

(b) Authority. Centralisation also refers to the extent to which people have to refer decisions upwards to their superiors. Decentralisation therefore implies increased delegation, empowerment and autonomy at lower levels of the organisation.

4.3.1 Advantages and disadvantages of centralisation

Centralisation offers greater control and co-ordination; **decentralisation** offers greater flexibility.

The table below summarises some of the arguments in favour of centralisation and decentralisation.

Pro centralisation	Pro decentralisation/delegation
Decisions are made at one point and so are easier to co-ordinate.	Avoids overburdening top managers, in terms of workload and stress
Senior managers can take a wider view of problems and consequences.	Improves motivation of more junior managers who are given responsibility
Senior management can balance the interests of different functions – eg by deciding on the resources to allocate to each.	Greater awareness of local problems by decision makers (geographically dispersed organisations are often decentralised on a regional/area basis for this reason)
Quality of decisions is (theoretically) higher due to senior managers' skills and experience.	Greater speed of decision-making, and response to changing events, since no need to refer decisions upwards. This is particularly important in rapidly changing markets.
It is possibly cheaper, by reducing number of managers needed and so lower costs of overheads.	Helps develop the skills of junior managers: supports managerial succession
Crisis decisions are taken more quickly at the centre, without need to refer back.	Separate spheres of responsibility can be identified: controls, performance measurement and accountability are better.
Policies, procedures and documentation can be standardised organisation-wide.	Communication technology allows decisions to be made locally, with information and input from head office if required.

Activity 3: Centralisation and decentralisation

Suggest two benefits and two drawbacks of both centralisation and decentralisation.

5 Flexibility in modern organisations

Modern management writers such as **Charles Handy** and **Tom Peters** rate flexibility as a key critical success factor for competitive organisations today.

Some recent trends have emerged from the focus on flexibility:

(a) **Flat structures**. The flattening of hierarchies does away with levels of organisation which lengthened lines of communication and decision-making. Flat structures are more responsive because there is a more direct relationship between the organisation's strategic centre and the operational units serving the customer. We look at the details of flat and tall structures in Section 7 of this chapter.

(b) In **modular organisations** different elements or components of the product or service the organisation produces are outsourced to different suppliers. The retained people within the organisation assemble or combine these elements to produce the final product or service. This structure enables the organisation to be more flexible and to respond to market needs more quickly, but also depends on reliable suppliers. For example, a motor vehicle dealership may recognise that its sales, repair and customer service modules are performing well, but that its finance and accounting services are inefficient. The dealership may, as a result, outsource that module.

(c) **Boundaryless organisations** remove both the internal barriers that separate the hierarchy levels, different functions and different departments, and also remove the barriers between the organisation and its suppliers, customers and competitors. To help eliminate boundaries, managers may use virtual, hollow or modular structures. This helps to eliminate bureaucracy and helps to reduce costs.

(d) **Virtual organisations**. The organisation may consist of individuals, teams, companies or stakeholders. Members are geographically dispersed and the organisation usually only exists electronically on the internet, without any physical premises. This creates cost savings from not having the costs associated with physical locations, such as rent. For example, Amazon operates as a virtual retailer without incurring the cost of retail premises. These organisations are entirely reliant on their technology and any problems could affect the operation of the organisation.

(e) In a **hollow organisation** people and activities are split between core and non-core competencies. All non-core processes and activities are outsourced.

Real life example

The sports shoe and clothing manufacturer Nike outsources production to sub-contractors – but the activity seen as core and key, product design, is retained in-house. Such organisations can then focus on their core activities, but this structure depends on being able to find reliable subcontractors.

6 Anthony's hierarchy

Robert Anthony classified management activities into three categories.

Managerial activity can be described in the following hierarchy (Anthony, 1965).

(a) **Strategic management** (carried out by senior management) is concerned with direction setting, policy making and crisis handling. The time frame of decisions made at strategic management level would typically have implications for three to five years.

(b) **Tactical management** (carried out by middle management) is concerned with establishing means to the corporate ends, mobilising resources and innovating (finding new ways to achieve business goals). Decisions made at this level would have medium-term implications.

(c) **Operational management** (carried out by supervisors and operatives) is concerned with routine activities to carry out tactical plans. Decisions at this level would deal with short-term matters.

Real life example

Consider the position of a manufacturing company that is trying to grow. It may decide to grow by entering new geographic markets, so it has to decide which markets it wants to enter or remain in – it may for instance decide to enter the retail market in Peru. This would be a strategic level decision. How it competes in the Peruvian market (by perhaps making its products cheaper than its competitors) is an example of a tactical management decision. How it actually makes the products and runs its factories is an example of an operational management decision.

7 Structural forms for organisations

7.1 Scalar chain and span of control

As organisations grow in size and scope, different organisational structures may be suitable.

The scalar chain and span of control determine the basic shape. The scalar chain relates to levels in the organisation, and the span of control the number of employees managed.

Tall organisations have a:

(a) Long scalar chain (via layers of management)

(b) Hierarchy

(c) Narrow span of control

Flat organisations have a:

(a) Short scalar chain (less layers)

(b) Wide span of control

> **Span of control:** Span of control or **'span of management'** refers to the number of subordinates responsible to a superior.

In other words, if a manager has five subordinates, the span of control is five.

A number of factors influence the span of control.

(a) A manager's capabilities limit the span of control: there are physical and mental limitations to any single manager's ability to control people and activities.

(b) The nature of the manager's workload

The more non-supervisory work in a manager's workload:

*   The narrower the span of control
*   The greater the delegation of authority to subordinates
*   The geographical dispersion of subordinates: dispersed teams require more effort to supervise.

7.2 Tall and flat organisations

Recent trends have been towards delayering organisations of levels of management. In other words, tall organisations (with many management levels, and narrow spans of control) are turning into flat organisations (with fewer management levels, and wider spans of control) as a result of technological changes and the granting of more decision-making power to frontline employees.

The span of control concept has implications for the length of the scalar chain.

> **Scalar chain:** The chain of command from the most senior to the most junior.
>
> **Tall organisation:** An organisation which, in relation to its size, has a large number of levels of management hierarchy. This implies a **narrow** span of control.
>
> **Flat organisation:** An organisation which, in relation to its size, has a small number of hierarchical levels. This implies a **wide** span of control.

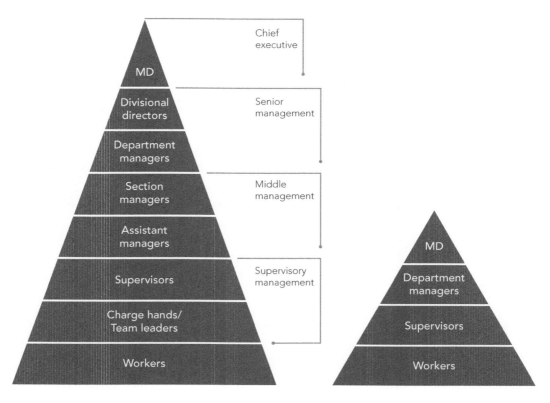

			Chief executive
MD			
Divisional directors			Senior management
Department managers			
Section managers			Middle management
Assistant managers			
Supervisors			Supervisory management
Charge hands/ Team leaders			
Workers			

Tall

MD	
Department managers	
Supervisors	
Workers	

Flat

The advantages and disadvantages of these organisational forms can be summarised as follows.

Tall organisation

For	
Narrow control spans	Inhibits delegation
Small groups enable team members to participate in decisions	Rigid supervision can be imposed, blocking initiative
A large number of steps on the promotional ladders – assists management training and career planning	The same work passes through too many hands Increases administration and overhead costs Slow decision making and responses, as the strategic apex is further away.

Flat organisation

For	Against
More opportunity for delegation	Requires that jobs **can** be delegated. Managers may only get a superficial idea of what goes on. If they are overworked they are more likely to be involved in crisis management
Relatively cheap	Sacrifices control
In theory, speeds up communication between strategic apex and operating core	Middle managers are often necessary to convert the grand vision of the strategic apex into operational terms

Activity 4: Span of control

The span of control refers to the chain of command from the most senior to the most junior.

True or false?

Essential reading

See Chapter 6 Section 2 of the Essential reading for more detail on details on flexibility in modern organisations.

The Essential reading is available as an Appendix of the digital edition of the Workbook.

Chapter summary

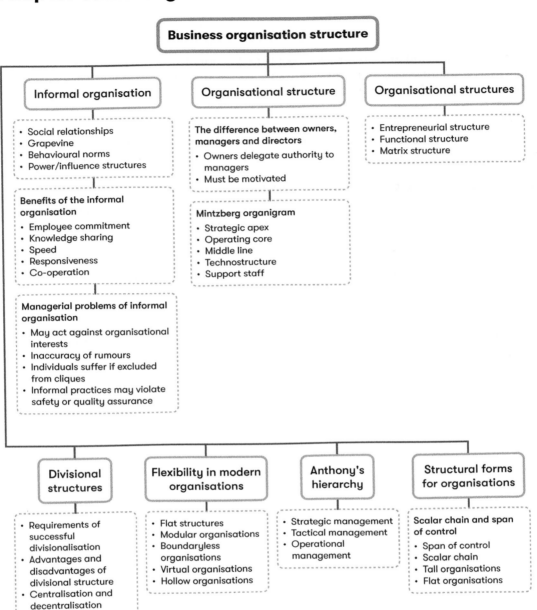

Business organisation structure

Informal organisation
- Social relationships
- Grapevine
- Behavioural norms
- Power/influence structures

Benefits of the informal organisation
- Employee commitment
- Knowledge sharing
- Speed
- Responsiveness
- Co-operation

Managerial problems of informal organisation
- May act against organisational interests
- Inaccuracy of rumours
- Individuals suffer if excluded from cliques
- Informal practices may violate safety or quality assurance

Organisational structure

The difference between owners, managers and directors
- Owners delegate authority to managers
- Must be motivated

Mintzberg organigram
- Strategic apex
- Operating core
- Middle line
- Technostructure
- Support staff

Organisational structures
- Entrepreneurial structure
- Functional structure
- Matrix structure

Divisional structures
- Requirements of successful divisionalisation
- Advantages and disadvantages of divisional structure
- Centralisation and decentralisation

Flexibility in modern organisations
- Flat structures
- Modular organisations
- Boundaryless organisations
- Virtual organisations
- Hollow organisations

Anthony's hierarchy
- Strategic management
- Tactical management
- Operational management

Structural forms for organisations

Scalar chain and span of control
- Span of control
- Scalar chain
- Tall organisations
- Flat organisations

Knowledge diagnostic

1. Informal organisation

An **informal organisation** always exists alongside the formal one. This consists of social relationships, informal communication networks, behavioural norms and power/influence structures, all of which may 'bypass' formal organisational arrangements.

2. Mintzberg

Henry Mintzberg described organisational forms that show the elements of the organisation including strategic apex, middle line, operating core, technostructure and support staff.

3. Organisational structures and divisional structures

Henry Mintzberg described organisational forms that show the elements of the organisation including strategic apex, middle line, operating core, technostructure and support staff

4. Flexibility in modern organisations

Recent trends have emerged from the focus on flexibility in modern organisations. This has given rise to a number of new organisational structures.

5. Anthony's levels

Robert Anthony defined the organisation into three levels which are strategy, tactics and operations.

Further study guidance

Question practice

Now try the following from the Further question practice bank [available in the digital edition of the Workbook]:

Number			
Q23	Exam Section A		2 mins
Q24	Exam Section A	2	2 mins
Q25	Exam Section A	2	2 mins
Q26	Exam Section A	2	2 mins
A27	Exam Section B	4	

Further reading

There is an article on the ACCA website entitled 'Mintzberg's theory on organisations' which is relevant to material in this chapter. You are strongly advised to read this article in full as part of your preparation for the FBT exam.

Activity answers

Activity 1: Mintzberg

Mintzberg's five components:

Staff/departments	Mintzberg
Manager of a retail outlet supervising 40 staff	The middle line
A salesman responsible for 20 corporate accounts	The operating core
The owner of a start-up internet company employing two staff.	The strategic apex
The IT department seeking to harmonise internal systems	The technostructure
The HR department which provides assistance to business managers	Support staff

- Since the manager is not part of the board of directors, he would be part of the middle line
- The salesman is dealing with the customers daily , so would be part of the operating core.
- The owner of the internet company, being the person who makes the decisions about the overall direction of the business, would be considered the strategic apex
- The IT department seeking to harmonise internal systems would be part of the technostructure.
- The HR department does not get involved directly in what the organisation does, so would be thought of as part of the support staff.

Activity 2: Different structures

For BPP, the matrix would be by syllabus, and for each syllabus area there are marketing, production and subject managers etc.

Organisation	Appropriate structure
A family run restaurant with 10 staff	Entrepreneurial
A small manufacturing company with 250 staff	Functional
Johnson and Johnson who have 197 strategic business units	Divisional
BPP Professional Education	Matrix

Activity 3: Centralisation and decentralisation

Advantages/Disadvantages:

Centralisation		
Advantages	Quick decisions Strategic view	Motivational Local focus
Disadvantages	Loss of local focus Loss of autonomy	Costly Lack of direction

Activity 4: Span of control

False. This refers to the scalar chain. The span of control refers to the number of subordinates responsible to a superior.

7

Organisational culture and committees

Learning outcomes

On completion of this chapter you should be able to:

	Syllabus reference no.
Describe the activities of an organisation that affect its competitiveness: (a) Purchasing (b) Production (c) Marketing (d) Service	A9 (d)
Describe the roles and functions of the main departments in a business organisation: (a) Research and development (b) Purchasing (c) Production (d) Direct service provision (e) Marketing (f) Administration (g) Finance	B2 (e)
Explain the role of marketing in an organisation: (a) The definition of marketing (b) The marketing mix (c) The relationship of the marketing plan to the strategic plan	B2 (f)
Define organisational culture.	B3 (a)
Describe the factors that shape the culture of the organisation.	B3 (b)
Explain the contribution made by writers on culture: (a) Schein – determinants of organisational culture (b) Handy – four cultural stereotypes (c) Hofstede – international perspectives on culture	B3 (c)
Explain the purposes of committees.	B4 (a)
Describe the types of committee used by business organisations.	B4 (b)

	Syllabus reference no.
List the advantages and disadvantages of committees.	B4 (c)
Explain the roles of the Chair and Secretary of a committee.	B4 (d)
Explain the relationship between accounting and other key functions within the business, such as procurement, production and marketing.	C1 (a)
Explain financial considerations in production and production planning.	C1 (b)
Identify the financial issues associated with marketing.	C1 (c)
Identify the financial costs and benefits of effective production planning.	C1 (d)
Explain the contribution of the accounting function to the formulation, implementation and control of the organisation's policies, procedures and performance.	C2 (a)
Identify and describe the main financial accounting functions in business: (a) Recording financial information (b) Codifying and processing financial information (c) Preparing financial statements	C2 (b)
Identify and describe the main management accounting and performance management functions in business: (a) Recording and analysing costs and revenues (b) Providing management accounting information for decision-making (c) Planning and preparing budgets and exercising budgetary control	C2 (c)
Identify and describe the main finance and treasury functions: (a) Calculating and mitigating business tax liabilities (b) Evaluating and obtaining finance (c) Managing working capital (d) Treasury and risk management	C2 (d)

Exam context

The role of the various departments in an organisation is something that could be easily examined in a Section A question. Cultural influences provide a good source of potential exam questions for both Sections. The specimen exam contained a number of questions on topics covered in this chapter.

Chapter overview

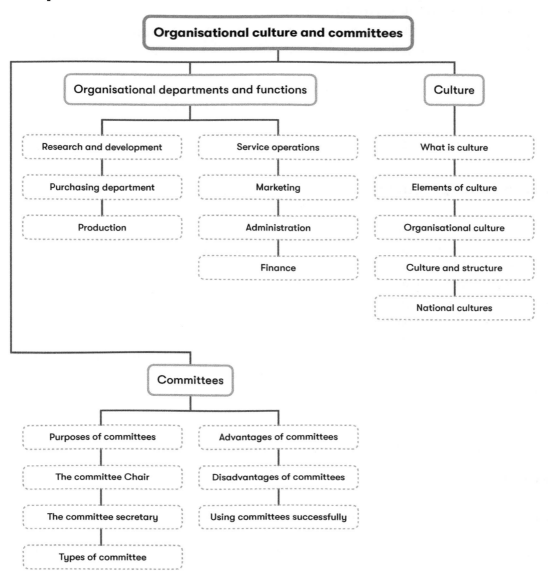

1 Organisational departments and functions

1.1 Research and development

Organisations undertake research and development in order to **improve their products and processes**; thus enabling them to remain competitive in the marketplace.

Research types:

- **Pure** – No immediate commercial advantage (eg looking for a cure for the common cold)
- **Applied** – Specific application (eg have a cure but need to make it safe!)

An 'R&D' department will be involved in the development of brand new products as well as enhancements to existing ones. It will also be involved with improving the manufacturing processes.

1.2 Purchasing (procurement)

The purchasing department is responsible for the **acquisition of material resources and business services** used by the organisation.

Purchasing managers have to obtain the **best purchasing mix** from suppliers bearing in mind four factors in order to obtain the best value for money:

- Price - should consider best value over time
- Quality - the level of quality will depend on the needs of user departments
- Quantity - obtaining a balance between avoiding delays in production by running out of inventory, and the costs of holding too much inventory
- Delivery - the lead time between placing and delivery of an order should be considered when selecting suppliers

Effective purchasing achieves the following:

- Obtains best value for money
- Quality targets
- Optimal inventory levels

1.3 Production

The production function plans, organises, directs and controls the necessary activities to provide products and services, creating outputs which have added value over the value of inputs.

Activity	
Obtain **inputs** to the production 'system', such as plant facilities, materials and labour	Inputs: timber, screws, nails, adhesives, varnish, stain, templates, cutting tools, carpenters
Adding of value. The activities below occupy most of the production manager's attention. • Scheduling jobs on machines • Assigning labour to jobs • Controlling the quality of production and/or service delivery • Improving methods of work • Managing materials and equipment, to avoid waste	Operations: sawing, sanding, assembly, finishing
Create **outputs**, ie finished products and services	Outputs: tables, chairs, cabinets, and so on

1.3.1 Production management decisions

Longer term decisions

These are related to setting up the production organisation:

- Selection of equipment and processes
- Job design and methods
- Factory location and layout
- Ensuring the right number and skills of employees

Short-term decisions

These are concerned with the running and control of the organisation.

- Production and control
- Labour control and supervision
- Quality management
- Inventory control
- Maintenance

1.3.2 Relationship with other functions

Longer-term decisions, particularly relating to design and the innovation of improved products, cannot be taken by the production department alone; its activities must be **integrated with other functions** in the firm.

- **Product design** is co-ordinated with **R&D**. Production should advise R&D as to the consequences of particular designs for the manufacturing process.
- **Job design** will involve consultation with **human resources** specialists.
- The quantities needed to be produced will be notified by the **sales department**.
- The **human resources department** will be involved in managing the workforce.
- The **finance department** might indicate the resources available for new equipment.

1.4 Service operations

Many products have a service element (eg after sales warranty and service), whilst some businesses are purely service orientated (eg healthcare, education).

Service issues that make them different from providing goods to customers:

Simultaneous – production and consumption of the service takes place at the same time (eg a hairstyle)

Heterogenous – the quality of service varies each time it is performed. It can depend on who delivers it and when.

Intangible – unlike goods, there are no substantial material or physical aspects to a service. A service cannot be packaged in a bag and carried home, such as a live musical performance.

Perishable – services cannot be stored, which means they have to be performed when needed.

1.5 Marketing

> **Marketing:** 'The management process which identifies, anticipates, and satisfies **customer needs** profitably' (Chartered Institute of Marketing).

1.5.1 Marketing activities

A popular misconception is that marketing means advertising or selling. As the definition above shows, marketing is far broader, as it is about identifying what customers want and making sure that the products or services that the business provide meet those needs. The main activities in marketing include:

(a) **Sales support**. The emphasis in this role is essentially reactive: marketing supports the direct sales force. It may include such activities as telesales or telemarketing, responding to inquiries, co-ordinating diaries, customer database management, organising exhibitions or other sales promotions, and administering agents. These activities usually come under a sales and marketing director or manager.

(b) **Marketing communications**. The emphasis in this role is more proactive: marketing promotes the organisation and its product or service at a tactical level. It typically includes activities such as providing brochures and catalogues to support the sales force.

(c) **Operational marketing**. The emphasis in this role is for marketing to support the organisation with a co-ordinated range of marketing activities including marketing research; brand management; product development and management; corporate and marketing communications; and customer relationship management. Given this breadth of activities, planning is also a function usually performed in this role but at an operational or functional level.

(d) **Strategic marketing**. The emphasis in this role is for marketing to contribute to the creation of competitive strategy. As such, it is practised in customer-focused and larger organisations. In a large or diversified organisation, it may also be responsible for the co-ordination of marketing departments or activities in separate business units.

1.5.2 The marketing mix

KEY TERM

> **Marketing mix:** The set of controllable variables and their levels that the organisation uses to influence the target market. These variables are product, price, place and promotion (*McCathy 1964*).

The **marketing 'mix'** comprises four 'Ps':

(a) **Product**

The actual physical products or services that are being sold. The marketing function endeavours to ensure that the products are what the customers require and/or communicates the benefits of the products to the consumers.

(b) **Place**

Marketing helps to decide where the consumer can obtain the product (eg website or store) and how the product is distributed (eg delivered or collect).

(c) **Promotion**

This includes all marketing communications which inform potential customers about the products on offer. Promotion should create:

(i) Awareness of the product

(ii) Interest in the product

(iii) Desire to purchase the product

(iv) Action in purchasing the product

(d) **Price**

The price of a product has to deliver a profit to the organisation, but at the same time must be set at the right level for the consumer.

Sometimes prices are pitched at a low level to persuade purchasers to buy. This is known as '**penetrating pricing**' and often occurs in the early stages of the product life cycle (eg household products).

'**Price skimming**' is where prices are set very high to maximise profits, even though this will restrict demand (eg new high technology products).

Price is often used as a competitive weapon.

Activity 1: The marketing mix

Consider how you would market Product Princess, a new cosmetic, to the teenage market.

Required

How would you use the 4Ps of the marketing mix to go after that market and successfully sell this new product?

1.5.3 Marketing strategy and corporate strategy

So, what is the relationship between marketing and strategic management? The two are closely linked since there can be no corporate plan which does not involve products/services and customers.

Corporate strategic plans aim to guide the overall development of an organisation. Marketing planning is subordinate to corporate planning but makes a significant contribution to it and is concerned with many of the same issues. The marketing department is probably the most important source of information for the development of corporate strategy. The corporate audit of product/market strengths and weaknesses, and much of its external environmental analysis is directly informed by the **marketing audit**.

Specific marketing strategies will be determined within the overall corporate strategy. To be effective, these plans will be interdependent with those for other functions of the organisation.

(a) The **strategic** component of marketing planning focuses on the direction which an organisation will take in relation to a specific market, or set of markets, in order to achieve a specified set of objectives.

(b) Marketing planning also requires an **operational** component that defines tasks and activities to be undertaken in order to achieve the desired strategy. The **marketing plan** is concerned uniquely with **products** and **markets**.

Marketing management aims to ensure the company is pursuing effective policies to promote its products, markets and distribution channels. This involves exercising strategic control of marketing, and the means to apply strategic control is known as the **marketing audit**. Not only is the marketing audit an important aspect of **marketing control,** but it can also be used to provide much information and analysis for the **corporate planning process.**

Essential reading

See Chapter 7 Section 1 of the Essential reading for more detail on the marketing function.

The Essential reading is available as an Appendix of the digital edition of the Workbook.

1.6 Administration

In many organisations administrative functions are carried out at head office as much as possible. When this is the case, the administration function is said to be **centralised**. A **centralised** administration department involves as many administrative tasks as possible being carried out at a single central location.

1.6.1 Advantages of a centralised administrative office

(a) It provides **consistency,** for example the same account codes are likely to be used no matter which part of the organisation submits an invoice. Everyone uses the same data and information.

(b) It gives better **security/control** over operations and it is easier to enforce standards.

(c) **Head office** is in a better position to know what is going on.

(d) There may be **economies of scale** available, for example in purchasing computer equipment and supplies.

(e) Administration staff are in a **single location** and more expert staff are likely to be employed. Career paths may be more clearly defined.

1.6.2 Disadvantages of a centralised administration office

(a) Local offices might **have to wait** for tasks to be carried out.

(b) There is a **reliance on head office** as local offices are less self-sufficient.

(c) A system fault or hold-up at head office will **impact across the organisation**.

1.7 Finance

The finance function has four primary roles:

- **Raising money**
- **Recording** and controlling what happens to the money
- Providing **information** to managers
- **Reporting** to shareholders and others

Money is raised from a variety of **equity and debt** sources as required by the organisation's strategic plan.

The finance function produces **financial accounts** for its shareholders and ensures that all transactions are properly recorded in accordance with the law.

A key feature of the finance function is **treasury management.** Treasury management **plans and controls** the **sources and uses of funds** by the organisation. This is achieved by a range of techniques.

(a) **Cash budgeting**, daily, weekly, monthly, quarterly and annually

(b) Arranging **a bank overdraft facility**; borrowing funds in the money markets and capital markets

(c) **Repaying** sums borrowed when the loans mature

(d) Comparing actual **cash flows** against budget

(e) Possibly, the **cashier's duties** of making payments to suppliers, paying wages and banking receipts

Managing **foreign currency dealings**, to limit the firm's exposure to the risk of losses arising from changes in exchange rates

The finance function produces **management accounts**, which are used by the organisation to control its activities and to help make general management decisions.

(a) Planning

   (i) The finance function draws up budgets which direct and allocate resources.

   (ii) The finance function also produces forecasts of anticipated future results.

(b) Decision-making. The finance function is often involved in assessing and modelling the expenditure and cash flow implications of proposed decisions.

(c) Control

   (i) Budgets are also used to monitor performance. The finance function regularly provides information comparing budgeted revenues and costs for a period, with actual results and comparisons from previous months.

   (ii) Management accountants are involved in assessing the contribution which products, services, processes and other operations make to overall profitability.

   (iii) Costing based on predetermined standards provides the information which enables managers to identify weaknesses and look for remedies all in a timely manner.

The success of management accountants in meeting their job objectives will depend on:

- The quality of the information they provide
- Whether the information they provide to other managers is used properly

Essential reading

Section 2 of Chapter 9 of the essential reading discusses the role of the finance function in more detail.

The Essential reading is available as an Appendix of the digital edition of the Workbook.

2 Culture

2.1 What is culture?

Culture can be described as 'the way we do things around here'.

Schein (1985) defines organisational culture as 'the set of shared, taken for granted implied assumptions that a group holds and that determines how it perceives, thinks about and reacts to its environment'.

2.2 Elements of culture

According to Schein there are three elements of culture which build on each other:

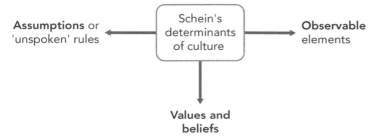

(a) **The first level.** The **observable**, expressed or 'explicit' elements of culture.

   (i) **Behaviour**: norms of personal and interpersonal behaviour; customs and rules about behaviour that is acceptable or unacceptable.

   (ii) **Artefacts**: concrete expressions such as architecture and interior design (eg of office premises), dress codes and symbols.

   (iii) **Attitudes**: patterns of collective behaviour such as greeting styles, business formalities, social courtesies and ceremonies.

(b) **The second level.** Beneath these observable phenomena lie **values and beliefs** and the professed culture, which give the behaviour and attitudes their special meaning and significance. For example, the design of office space may imply status and honour, or reflect the importance of privacy within a culture: it 'means' more than the observable features. Values and beliefs may be overtly expressed in slogans or the mission statement.

(c) **The third level.** Beneath these observable phenomena lie values and beliefs and the professed culture, which give the behaviour and attitudes their special meaning and significance. For example, the design of office space may imply status and honour, or reflect the importance of privacy within a culture: it 'means' more than the observable features. Values and beliefs may be overtly expressed in slogans or the mission statement.

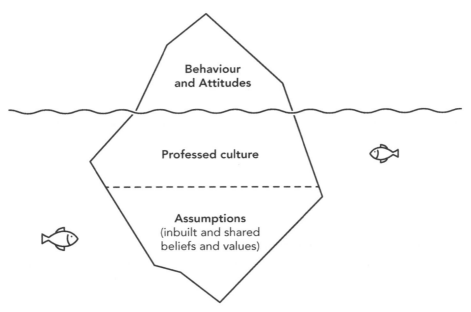

Behaviour and attitudes are observable to outsiders, but professed culture and assumptions are not, despite often being the more important aspect of culture. This is similar to an iceberg, in that what can be seen above the significant part of the structure.

2.3 Organisational culture

Organisations have differing cultures. These are sets of values, norms (standards of behaviour) and beliefs, which are reflected in different organisation structures and systems.

There are five observable aspects of culture that can be identified (and memorised as **CRABS**).

Customs

Rituals

Artefacts

Beliefs and values

Symbols

Examples of these aspects include the following:

Item	
Beliefs and values, which are often unquestioned	'The customer is always right'.
Customs	In the City of London, standard business dress is still generally taken for granted and even 'dress down Fridays' have their rules.
Artefacts	Microsoft encourages communication between employees by setting aside spaces for the purpose.
Rituals	In some firms, salespeople compete with each other, and there is a reward, given at a ceremony, for the salesperson who does best in any period.
Symbols	Corporate logos are an example of symbols, but they are directed outwards. Within the organisation, symbols can represent power: dress, make and model of car, office size and equipment and access to facilities can all be important symbols.

Activity 2: Organisational culture

Give an example of each of the observable aspects, of culture using your organisation.

2.4 Culture and structure

Different types of organisational structure are associated with different types of culture. Charles Handy (2007) named four types of organisational culture after the names of Greek Gods:

Zeus **Power culture**	Apollo **Role culture**
The organisation is controlled by a key central figure, owner or founder. Power is direct, personal, informal. Suits small organisations where people get on well.	Classical, rational organisation: bureaucracy. Stable, slow-changing, formalised, impersonal. Authority based on position and function.
Athena **Task culture**	Dionysus **Person culture**
Management is directed at outputs: problems solved, projects completed. Team based, horizontally structured, flexible, valuing expertise – to get the job done.	The purpose of the organisation is to serve the interests of the individuals who make it up: management is directed at facilitating, administering.

2.4.1 Power culture (ZEUS) - Key features

(a) Central power source, eg owner manager

(b) Control through trust

(c) Flexible and reactive

2.4.2 Role culture (Apollo)

Features based around functional 'pillars':

(a) The pillars are co-ordinated at the top by a narrow band of senior management.

(b) Likely to be regulated and hierarchical.

2.4.3 Task culture (Athena)

(a) Job or project orientated

(b) Team based

(c) Very adaptable

(d) Horizontally structured

2.4.4 Person culture (Dionysus)

(a) A culture based on self-interest

(b) Management through facilitation and administration

It is possible for **different cultures to occur in different parts of the same organisation,** especially large ones with many departments and sites. This is an example of the '**contingency approach**' where 'it all depends'.

2.5 National culture

National Cultural dimensions influence the way in which people work and the way in which they expect to be managed.

Global organisations in particular need to be sensitive to these particular issues.

Hofstede (2011) carried out cross-cultural research at 66 national offices of IBM and formulated one of the most influential models of work-related cultural differences.

The Hofstede model describes four main dimensions of difference between national cultures, which impact on all aspects of management and organisational behaviour: motivation, team working, leadership style, conflict management and HR policies.

(a) **Power** distance: the extent to which unequal distribution of power is accepted

    (i)   **High** PD cultures (as in Latin, near Eastern and less developed Asian countries) accept greater centralisation, a top-down chain of command and closer supervision. Subordinates have little expectation of influencing decisions.

    (ii)   **Low** PD cultures (as in Germanic, Anglo and Nordic countries) expect less centralisation and flatter organisational structures. Subordinates expect involvement and participation in decision-making. (Japan is a medium PD culture.)

(b) **Uncertainty avoidance**: the extent to which security, order and control are preferred to ambiguity, uncertainty and change

    (i)   **Low** UA cultures (as in Anglo and Nordic countries) respect flexibility and creativity. They have less task structure and written rules, more generalists and greater variability. There is more tolerance of risk, dissent, conflict and deviation from norms.

    (ii)   **High** UA cultures (as in Latin, near Eastern and Germanic countries and Japan) respect control, certainty and ritual. They value task structure, written rules and regulations, specialists and experts, and standardisation. There is a strong need for consensus: deviance and dissent are not tolerated. The work ethic is strong.

(c) **Individualism**: the extent to which people prefer to live and work in individualist (focusing on the 'I' identity) or collectivist (focusing on the 'we' identity) ways

    (i)   **High** individualism cultures (as in Anglo, more developed Latin and Nordic countries) emphasise autonomy and individual choice and responsibility. They prize individual initiative. The organisation is impersonal and tends to defend business interests: task achievement is more important than relationships. Management is seen in an individual context.

    (ii)   **Low** individualism (or collectivist) cultures (as in less developed Latin, near Eastern and less developed Asian countries) emphasise interdependence, reciprocal obligation and social acceptability. The organisation is seen as a 'family' and tends to defend employees' interests: relationships are more important than task achievement. Management is seen in a team context. (Japan and Germany are 'medium' cultures on this dimension.)

(d) **Masculinity**: the extent to which social gender roles are distinct (Note that this is different from the usual sense in which the terms 'masculine' and 'feminine' are used.)

    (i)   **High** masculinity cultures (as in Japan and Germanic and Anglo countries) clearly differentiate gender roles. Masculine values of assertiveness, competition, decisiveness and material success are dominant. Feminine values of modesty, tenderness, consensus, focus on relationships and quality of working life are less highly regarded, and confined to women.

    (ii)   **Low** masculinity (or Feminine) cultures (as in Nordic countries) minimise gender roles. Feminine values are dominant – and both men and women are allowed to behave accordingly.

Activity 3: National culture and management style

Here are three cases:

(1)   The newly appointed Spanish (more developed Latin) R&D manager of a UK (Anglo) firm asks to see the Rules and Procedures Manual for the department.

(2)   A US-trained (Anglo) manager attempts to implement a system of Management by Objectives (MbO) in Thailand (less developed Asian).

(3)   A Dutch (Nordic) HR manager of a US (Anglo) subsidiary in the Netherlands is instructed to implement downsizing measures.

Required

According to the Hofstede model, what issues might arise in each of the cases above?

3 Committees

3.1 Purposes of committees

Committees exist within organisations for many purposes. At the board level there may be committees such as the risk committee which monitor the risks that the organisation faces. There may other less formal committees such as social committees. The purposes of such committees typically include:

(a) **Creating new ideas.** Group creativity may be achieved by a brainstorming committee or think tank.

(b) **Communication.** They can be an excellent means of **communication**. For example, they can be used to exchange ideas and get feedback before a decision is taken or to inform managers about policies, plans, actual results, and so on.

(c) **Democratic.** They are democratic, because they allow for greater **participation** in the decision-making process. **Problem solving** can be facilitated by consultations between interested parties.

(d) **Combining abilities.** Committees enable the differing skills of its various members to be brought together to deal with a problem. In theory, the quality of committee decisions should be of a high standard.

(e) **Co-ordination.** Committees should enable the maximum co-ordination of all parties involved in a decision to be achieved, for example in co-ordinating the budgets of each department and compiling a master budget.

(f) **Representation.** Committees enable all relevant interests to be involved in the decision-making process and they bring together the specialised knowledge of working people into a working combination.

(g) **Recommendations.** Making **recommendations** for others to follow is a key output from committee processes.

3.2 The committee chair

There are a number of recognised qualities of a good chair (though common sense may dictate many others, varying with circumstances).

(a) The chair will have to give **immediate rulings** on points of dispute or doubt, so they should have:

    (i) A sound knowledge of the relevant issues

    (ii) An ability to make up his/her mind

    (iii) Skill in communicating clearly, but tactfully and in a courteous manner

(b) The chair should be and be seen to be **impartial**. There will be times when criticism is expressed which they personally may find unfair, or when there is a strong clash of opinion between other committee members. In either situation, whatever their personal views, the Chair should treat opponents with equal fairness.

(c) The chair should have the **discretion** to know when to insist on **strict observance** of correct procedure, and when a certain amount of **relaxation** will ease the tension.

(d) The chair should be **punctual** and regular in attendance at meetings. If they cannot give the duties the appropriate amount of time and attention, they should consider resigning.

3.3 The committee secretary

(a) Duties **before** committee meeting:

    (i) Fixing the date and time of the meeting

    (ii) Choosing and preparing the location of the meeting

    (iii) Preparing and issuing various documents

(b) Duties **at** the meeting: assisting the chair, making notes

(c) Duties **after** the meeting: preparing minutes, acting on and communicating decisions

3.4 Types of committee

Committees can be classified according to the **power** they exercise.

(a) **Executive committees** have the power to govern or administer. The board of directors of a limited company is itself a 'committee' appointed by the shareholders, to the extent that it governs or administers.

(b) **Standing committees** are formed for a particular purpose on a **permanent basis**. Their role is to deal with routine business delegated to them at weekly or monthly meetings.

(c) **Ad hoc committees** are formed to complete a particular task (eg fact-finding and reporting on a particular problem before being wound up).

(d) **Sub-committees** may be appointed by committees to relieve the parent committee of some of its routine work.

(e) **Joint committees** may be formed to co-ordinate the activities of two or more committees; for example, representatives from employers and employees may meet in a joint consultative committee. This kind of committee can either be permanent or appointed for a special purpose.

(f) **Management committees** in many businesses contain executives at a number of levels; not all the decisions in a firm need to be taken by the board.

3.5 Advantages of committees

(a) **Consolidation of power and authority**. The pooled authority of a committee may enable a decision to be made for which an individual's authority would not be sufficient. Examples of a **plural executive** include a board of directors or the cabinet of the government.

(b) **Delegation**. A committee can further delegate responsibility, for example to a subcommittee.

(c) **Blurring responsibility**. When a committee makes a decision, no individual will be held responsible for the consequences of the decision.

(d) **Delay**. A committee is used to gain time (eg a manager may set up a committee to investigate a problem when they want to delay their decision, or a company may refer a labour relations problem to a committee to defer a crisis with a trade union).

3.6 Disadvantages of committees

(a) They are **apt to be too large for constructive action**, since the time taken by a committee to resolve a problem tends to be in direct proportion to its size.

(b) Committees are **time consuming and expensive**. In addition to the cost of highly paid executives' time, secretarial costs will be incurred.

(c) **Delays may occur if matters of a routine nature are entrusted to committees**; committees must not be given responsibilities which they would carry out inefficiently.

(d) **Operations may be jeopardised by the frequent attendance of executives at meetings**, and by distracting them from their real duties.

(e) **Incorrect or ineffective decisions** may be made, if members are unfamiliar with the issues. Occasionally, there may be a **total failure to reach any decision at all**.

(f) The fact that there is no individual responsibility for decisions might invite **compromise** instead of clear-cut decisions. Moreover, members may avoid responsibility for poor results arising from decisions taken by the committee. Weak management can hide behind committee decisions.

3.7 Using committees successfully

(a) Well-defined areas of authority, timescales of operations and purpose should be specified in writing.

(b) The **chair** should have the qualities of leadership to co-ordinate and motivate the other committee members.

(c) The committee should not be so large as to be unmanageable.

(d) The members of the committee should have the necessary skills and experience to do the committee's work; where the committee is expected to liaise with functional departments, the members must also have sufficient status and influence with those departments.

(e) Minutes of the meetings should be taken and circulated by the **secretary**, with any action points arising out of the meetings notified to the members responsible for doing the work.

(f) In order to conduct business and make decisions there is usually a minimum number of members required to be in attendance at the meeting. This minimum number of members is known as a quorum and it is usually over 50% of members.

(g) Above all, an efficient committee must provide benefits that justify its cost.

(h) Finally, if at all possible, the committee should be allowed plenty of time to reach decisions, enabling members to form subgroups.

PER alert

PER performance objective PO3 requires you to demonstrate contribution to strategy and innovation. Knowledge of organisational culture and working effectively with internal committees on business issues and challenges, may help in this context.

Chapter summary

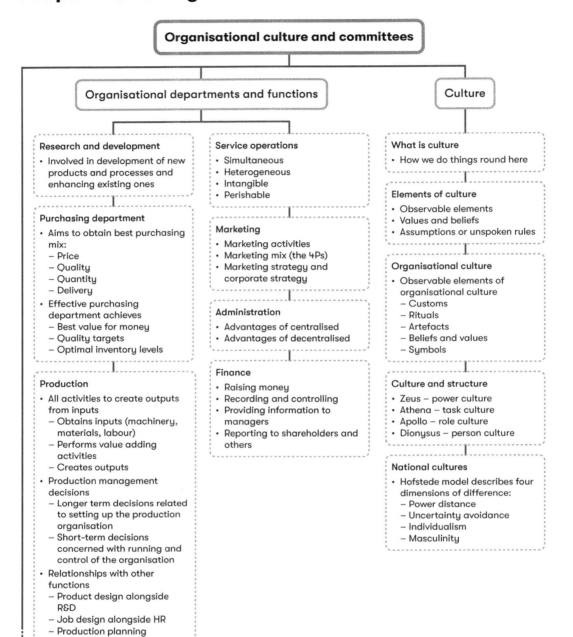

Organisational culture and committees

Organisational departments and functions

Research and development
- Involved in development of new products and processes and enhancing existing ones

Purchasing department
- Aims to obtain best purchasing mix:
  – Price
  – Quality
  – Quantity
  – Delivery
- Effective purchasing department achieves
  – Best value for money
  – Quality targets
  – Optimal inventory levels

Production
- All activities to create outputs from inputs
  – Obtains inputs (machinery, materials, labour)
  – Performs value adding activities
  – Creates outputs
- Production management decisions
  – Longer term decisions related to setting up the production organisation
  – Short-term decisions concerned with running and control of the organisation
- Relationships with other functions
  – Product design alongside R&D
  – Job design alongside HR
  – Production planning alongside sales department
  – Investment decisions with finance department

Service operations
- Simultaneous
- Heterogeneous
- Intangible
- Perishable

Marketing
- Marketing activities
- Marketing mix (the 4Ps)
- Marketing strategy and corporate strategy

Administration
- Advantages of centralised
- Advantages of decentralised

Finance
- Raising money
- Recording and controlling
- Providing information to managers
- Reporting to shareholders and others

Culture

What is culture
- How we do things round here

Elements of culture
- Observable elements
- Values and beliefs
- Assumptions or unspoken rules

Organisational culture
- Observable elements of organisational culture
  – Customs
  – Rituals
  – Artefacts
  – Beliefs and values
  – Symbols

Culture and structure
- Zeus – power culture
- Athena – task culture
- Apollo – role culture
- Dionysus – person culture

National cultures
- Hofstede model describes four dimensions of difference:
  – Power distance
  – Uncertainty avoidance
  – Individualism
  – Masculinity

Committees

Purposes of committees
- Creating new ideas
- Communication
- Democratic
- Combining abilities
- Coordination
- Representation
- Recommendations

The committee Chair
- Has to make immediate rulings
- Should be impartial
- Should have discretion over procedures

The committee secretary
- Preparing for committee meetings
- Making notes
- Preparing minutes, acting on decisions

Types of committee
- Executive committees
- Standing committees
- Management committees

Advantages of committees
- Sharing authority
- Delegation
- Blurring of responsibility

Disadvantages of committees
- Slow to make decisions
- Time consuming and expensive
- May remove executives from other tasks

Using committees successfully
- Chair with good leadership qualities
- Committee should not be too large
- Members of the committee should have the relevant skills
- Should allow plenty of time to reach decisions

Knowledge diagnostic

1. Organisational departments and functions

May include a research and development function, purchasing function, production, marketing, admin, and finance

2. Purchase function

The purchase function is responsible for the right purchase mix – Price, Quality, Quantity, and Delivery. It aims to achieve value for money and source the right quality of inputs. It also aims to optimise inventory levels.

3. Marketing

Marketing aims to anticipate and satisfy customer needs, profitably. Marketing activities include supporting sales, promoting the organisations, market research and strategic marketing. The company may use the marketing mix – the four Ps of Product, Place, Promotion and Price.

4. Finance function

The finance function's primary roles are raising money, recording and controlling the company's resources, providing information to management, and reporting to shareholders and other external stakeholders. The finance function may also include a treasury department.

5. Culture

The culture of an organisation includes observable elements such as customs, rituals, artefacts, overt beliefs and values and symbols. Unobservable elements include assumptions and unstated values and beliefs. Culture may also be associated with structure, and Handy proposed four types of culture: Power (Zeus), Role culture (Apollo), Task culture (Athena) and Person culture (Dionysus). National culture is influenced by four dimensions: Power distance, Uncertainty avoidance, Individualism and Masculinity.

6. Committees

Committees may be set up at various levels within an organisation, such as sharing ideas, enabling more democratic decision making and combining differing skills. The chair of a committee must be able to ensure the committee is effective.

Further study guidance

Question practice

Now try the following from the Further question practice bank [available in the digital edition of the Workbook]:

Number			
Q28	Exam Section A	2	2 mins
Q29	Exam Section A	1	1 min
Q30	Exam Section b	4	6 mins

Further reading

There is an article on the ACCA website entitled 'The role of marketing' that is relevant to material in this chapter. You are strongly advised to read this article in full as part of your preparation for the FBT exam.

Activity answers

Activity 1: The marketing mix

The following is one possible approach to using the 4Ps. It is not the only approach, so if your answer is different from this, it does not mean that your answer is 'wrong'.

Product:

- Natural ingredients
- Colourful packaging
- Brand clearly displayed (teenagers tend to be brand sensitive)

Price:

- Dependent on brand although premium brand may not mean premium price as teenagers cannot afford
- Would not be cheap product as again teenagers tend not to want cheap products

Place:

- High Street stores to attract the teenagers to buy
- Supermarkets for parents to have access to purchase for the kids
- Internet would depend on a variety of factors, one key issue is would it be environmentally and economically viable

Promotion

- Instagram groups, interactive website attached to the parent company's site
- Promoted by famous celebrities known to the teenage population
- BOGOF/vouchers for discounts

Activity 2: Organisational culture

Examples of the things you may have considered under each heading are given below, but this is not an exhaustive list:

Customs – appraisal cycles, start and finish times

Rituals – break times, cakes on birthdays, social activities

Artefacts – language, smart phones

Beliefs and values – mission statements

Symbols – logo, uniform

(Also: workings methods, communication methods, dress code, rules, working methods, hours.)

Activity 3: National culture and management style

Possible issues:

(1) A high-UA manager, expecting to find detailed and generally adhered-to rules for everything, may be horrified by the adhocracy of a low-UA organisation: if they attempt to impose a high-UA culture, there may be resistance from employees and management.

(2) A high-individuality manager may implement MbO on the basis of individual performance targets, results and rewards: this may fail to motivate collectivist workers, for whom group processes and performance is more important.

(3) A low-masculinity manager may try to shelter the workforce from the effects of downsizing, taking time for consultation, retraining, voluntary measures, and so on: this may seem unacceptably 'soft' to a high-masculinity parent firm.

Skills checkpoint 2

Learning the models

Chapter overview

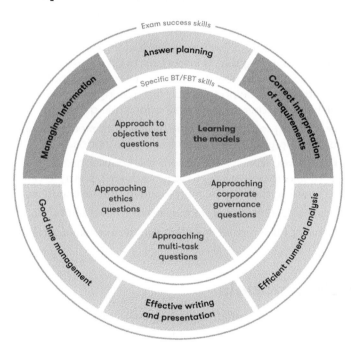

Introduction

Within the syllabus for BT/FBT are many models and theories that you need to learn. The examiner reports that exam questions on simpler theories such as Porter's five forces, Maslow, Blake and Mouton enjoy higher pass rates, while questions on more complex theories, such as Belbin and Shein have lower pass rates in Section A of the exam.

In Section B the examiner mentions Schein, Hofsted, Herzberg, McGregor Vroom, Belbin and as models that candidates have difficulties with. The examiner does acknowledge that there are many topics covered in the BT/FBT syllabus, and advises candidates to aim for breadth, rather than spending too much time focusing on some topics at the expense of others.

This section aims to help you develop techniques to learn the various models.

Approach to studying

As you work through the chapters in the Workbook, a good approach to studying the models is to do the following:

- Look at the chapter overview – this gives you the 'big picture' and puts into context how the models fit in. In Chapter 2, for example, the overview shows you that you are looking at the external factors that impact on a business. You can see that there are boxes for Political Factors, Technology and so on. So already you are becoming aware of the factors that you will study in more detail. You will notice one model, which is Porter's Five Forces.

- As you begin to study the model, read through the section dealing with the model fairly quickly initially, again to get the overall picture of what is involved in the model.

- Once you have done this, go through and read it again – reflectively. As you look at each part of the model, try to think of real life examples, or reflect on whether you can understand the logic of what you are reading. When studying Porter's five forces model for example, the first 'force' is the threat of new entrants. Think about why that is important to an industry. Think about the industry you work in – would it be easy for new competitors to set up in that business, or not? If not, what is stopping them? By doing this, you are gaining a deeper understanding of the models which will help you answer the application style questions

- Close your book, take a piece of paper, and try to summarise the model from memory. Write as much as you can remember before opening your book again to fill in any gaps.

- Make some notes. Active learning is a good way to help you absorb the knowledge, Just highlighting the main points is not a particularly active way to learn a theory, so try to put more effort in. Perhaps try some of the memory techniques mentioned in the next section.

- Having 'mastered' the model in this way, have a break before moving onto the next mode

- Once you have completed a chapter, attempt the further question practice recommended, to test your knowledge.

Techniques for memorising models

A mnemonic is a system that is used to help memorise something. Mnemonics are a good way of remembering the main parts of a model. This section provides examples of some types of mnemonics that you might find useful in learning the models and theories in the BT/FBT syllabus:

Acronyms

An acronym is a good way of learning a list. You arrange the list in such a way that the first letter of each item in the list spells a word that you can remember. An example is SPAMSOAP, which can be used to remember the different types of internal control (see Chapter 10):

Segregation of duties

Physical

Authorisation

Management

Supervision

Organisation

Arithmetic and accounting

Personnel

Stories and associations

Other types of mnemonic include stories and associations. In Belin's team roles, which is covered in Chapter 14, there are nine different roles that members can play in a team. A good way to remember each of these roles is to take a team that you know and try to match each role in Belbin's model with somebody in that team, then learn the name given by Belbin to that person – for example, John = Shaper, Janet = Chair etc. The team could be any type of team – a work team, a sports team, even a group of friends.

Test yourself

Test yourself continuously. Perhaps make a list of all the models as you come across them, on a notepad document on your phone. When you have a spare five minutes, take a model from the list, and write down on a piece of paper the key points of that model, if you can remember them. The more often you review a model, the more likely you are to remember it. As you get closer to the exam, you should hopefully find that you can remember all of the models.

Workbook features

The chapter summaries are another useful tool that may help you revise models. The chapter summaries are like a skeleton – they contain the bones of the theory. Look at the summaries and see how much you can remember to flesh out the bones. If you can't remember that much, you should go back and read through that section of the chapter. These are supplemented by the learning diagnostics at the end of the chapter.

Application of knowledge

While some of the questions in the BT/FBT exam are pure tests of knowledge, there are also questions that aim to test your understanding, by giving you a short scenario and requiring you to apply your knowledge in some way. This is particularly the case in Section B of the exam. It is therefore important when studying that you do not just learn the 'what' of each model, but also the 'why'. You need to understand the model in other words. Taking Porter's five forces, for example, it would not be enough to simply be able to list the five forces. You would need to understand how each force affects the competitive nature of the environment. This skill is acquired while studying. Always ask yourself 'what is the point of this model, how does it help?'.

Application is also helped by practising questions too. It is essential that you do plenty of question practice. In the workbook, there are plenty of questions within the chapters and the further question practice at the end. You also have the questions in the revision question bank. Aim to work through all of these questions at least twice, and note down those that you get wrong, so you can come back to them again later. Practising questions will reinforce your learning process – it is often said that you learn by your mistakes, so when you get a question wrong, think of that as an opportunity to fill in a gap in your knowledge.

Skills practice

As you work through the chapters in the workbook, try the techniques above to help you learn more effectively.

- Read through the model once quickly
- Read the model again, reflectively
- Close your book and see how much of the model you can remember
- Write some notes – try to think of interesting mnemonics – ways to help you remember the model
- Attempt the questions in the chapter and the further question practice
- Keep a list of models and continuously test yourself

8

Corporate governance and social responsibility

Learning outcomes

On completion of this chapter you should be able to:

	Syllabus reference no.
Explain the agency concept in relation to corporate governance.	B5 (a)
Define corporate governance and social responsibility and explain their importance in contemporary organisations.	B5 (b)
Explain the responsibility of organisations to maintain appropriate standards of corporate governance and corporate social responsibility.	B5 (c)
Briefly explain the main recommendations of best practice in effective corporate governance: (a) Executive and non-executive directors (b) Remuneration committees (c) Audit committees (d) Public oversight	B5 (d)
Explain how organisations take account of their social responsibility objectives through analysis of the needs of internal, connected and external stakeholders.	B5 (e)
Identify the social and environmental responsibilities of business organisations to internal, connected and external stakeholders.	B5 (f)

Exam context

Corporate governance and social responsibility is an issue for all corporate bodies, both commercial and not for profit. There were two questions in the specimen exam relating to corporate governance.

Chapter overview

1 Introduction to corporate governance

KEY TERM

> **Corporate governance:** The system by which organisations are **directed and controlled** by their **senior officers**

1.1 The agency problem

Corporate governance issues generally arise from the **separation between ownership and control** in organisations

- Small organisations where the owner and the manager are the same person do not cause corporate governance issues
- With larger organisations, the owners (shareholders) and the controllers (directors and managers) are not the same parties. Their interests may diverge, eg shareholders will want dividends and an increase in the value of their share, whereas managers may want higher remuneration and bigger status.

The **agency concept** is a situation where one party, the principal, hires another party, the agent, to act on their behalf. When applied to corporate governance, the shareholders are the **'principal'** and the directors are the **'agent'**.

The agency concept is more relevant for larger organisations where there is a greater degree of separation between ownership and management.

Management may follow their own interests rather than the owners'. This is known as the **agency problem**.

Activity 1: Agency

Give some examples of actions that directors of a large company might take, if there are no controls, that are not in the interests of its shareholders.

Solution

Essential reading

See Chapter 8 Section 1 of the Essential reading for more detail on the role of corporate governance.

The Essential reading is available as an Appendix of the digital edition of the Workbook.

1.2 Developments in corporate governance

Corporate governance has become increasingly high profile over the last thirty years due to a number of factors including:

(a) High-profile **corporate scandals** (eg BHS, Wirecard, Parmalat)

(b) Increasingly **active** and **international shareholders**

(c) Increasing **media scrutiny**

(d) Globalisation highlighting **businessculture differences around the world**

(e) Developments in **financial reporting**

1.2.1 Sarbanes-Oxley Act 2002

In the US, the Sarbanes-Oxley Act was introduced in 2002. Companies listed on US stock markets must comply with the act. The main provisions of the act are:

- The majority of the board of directors must be independent.
- The CEO and CFO must certify that the financial statements are accurate.
- Companies must form an audit committee made up entirely of independent directors.
- The auditors must review and report on the effectiveness of the internal control procedures.
- The Public Company Accounting Oversight Board (PCAOB) was set up (see Chapter 9).

1.2.2 OECD Principles

In 1999 the Organisation for Economic Co-operation and Development (OECD) published the first edition of its *Principles of corporate governance*. These are intended to provide guidance for countries that wish to improve their corporate governance regulations, and for companies that wish to adopt best practice. The most recent edition of the OECD principles was issued in 2016.

1.2.3 UK Corporate Governance Code

The UK Corporate Governance Code was developed over many years:

- In 1992 the Cadbury Committee on best practice made recommendations relating primarily to the structure of the board of directors
- The Greenbury Committee of 1995 looked at remuneration of directors.
- The Higgs report of 2003 dealt with the role of non-executive directors.
- The Smith report of 2003 looked at audit committees.

In 2003 these reports and committee recommendations were combined into the 'Combined Code on corporate governance.' Since 2018 it is now referred to as 'UK Corporate Governance Code'. The UK code is principles-based, which means it sets out principles of good governance, leaving it up to organisations to decide how to adhere to these principles. This is in contrast to the Sarbanes Oxley act in the US, which adopts a rules-based approach.

Essential reading

See Chapter 8 Section 2 of the Essential reading for more detail on corporate governance.

The Essential reading is available as an Appendix of the digital edition of the Workbook.

Activity 2: Poor corporate governance

What might the features of poor corporate governance be?

Solution

2 Best practice

2.1 The board of directors

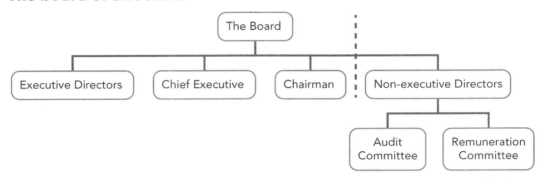

2.1.1 Role of board

A **director** is someone who works for a company and is charged with the conduct and management of its affairs. The directors collectively are referred to as the board of directors, who are elected by the shareholders.

Stewardship theory links to Corporate Governance as it views the directors as stewards of the company assets on behalf of the owners.

The role that should be taken by the board has been much debated. For example, they may include major decisions such as:

(a) Mergers and acquisitions

(b) Acquisitions and disposals of major assets

(c) Investments

(d) Capital projects

(e) Bank and other borrowings

2.1.2 Role of the chair

The chair is the leader of the board of directors. It is the chair's responsibility to ensure that the board operates efficiently and effectively, promoting regular attendance at meetings, and full involvement by all members. The chair decides the scope of each meeting and is responsible for ensuring that all matters are discussed fully.

2.1.3 Role of the chief executive officer

The chief executive officer (CEO) is the leader of the executive team and is responsible for the day-to-day management of the organisation. As well as attending board meetings, the CEO will usually chair the management committee or executive committee. While most companies have monthly board meetings, it is common for management/executive committee meetings to be held more often.

2.1.4 Role of company secretary

The company secretary is effectively the chief administrative officer and is appointed by the company's directors. They are legally responsible for acting on the company's behalf to undertake specific requirements.

Duties which fall under the remit of the company secretary typically include:

- Filing the company's financial statements and annual return with the companies supervisory authorities

- Maintaining statutory books and records, ie a register of directors and shareholders and any charges held on the company assets

- Safeguarding legal documents including share certificates, certificates of incorporation and other official documentation

- Organising board meetings of shareholders and taking formal minutes

In addition to these duties, the company secretary is required to establish and maintain a registered office for official communications.

2.2 Board members

Corporate governance codes in a number of countries have made several recommendations in relation to the board, including the following:

(a) Individual directors should have **relevant expertise for the role**, which complement each other.

(b) The board should **receive appropriate information** in a timely manner which is sufficiently clear, including non-financial information.

(c) The performance of the board and its members should be **assessed** annually (eg by shareholders).

(d) The roles of **chair and chief executive should be separated** to prevent domination of the board by one person.

2.3 Non-executive directors

Non-executive directors have **no management responsibilities**. It is intended that they act as a **balance to executive management** and advise the board on issues such as strategy, performance, risk and remuneration of the executive directors.

Non-executive directors can **broaden the experience** and perspective available to the board, and can offer reassurance to shareholders and other outside parties.

Non-executive directors **must be independent** of the company, for example, they are not expected to have business or financial connections with the company, and have time-limited appointments.

In certain countries, the concept of non-executive directors is taken further. For example, in Germany all public companies must have a **two-tier board**. The management board comprises executive directors and the supervisory board comprises non-executive directors, partly elected by shareholders and partly by employees.

Activity 3: Selecting non-executive directors

What do you think are some of the problems around the selection and recruitment and role of non-executive directors?

Solution

Real life example

Philip Green, a British retailer, acquired the BHS retail chain for £200 million in 2000. He sold it for £1 in 2016, and the company subsequently became bankrupt. At the date when Mr Green sold BHS, the company's pension fund was running a deficit of £571 million. The bankruptcy of BHS and the pension deficit were due in large part to the fact that during his period of ownership, there was little investment in the stores or the pension fund, while Mr Green's family received dividends of £400 million.

A report by the UK Parliamentary Committee into the affair reached the following conclusions: "We saw meagre evidence of the type of constructive challenge that good board should provide. These weak governance arrangements allowed the overarching interest of the Green family to prevail and facilitate the flow of money offshore to the ultimate owner of the parent company, Lady Green".

2.4 Remuneration and audit committees

Non-executive directors can exercise oversight of executive directors by operating through committees of the main board. These may include key areas of board activity including audit, senior manager's remuneration, risk management and senior appointments. You only need to know about the role of the audit and remuneration committees for your exam.

The following table summarises the key information about these two committees:

	Remuneration committee	Audit committee
Membership	Eg 2–3 non-executive directors	Eg 2–3 non-executive directors, at least one of whom must have recent, relevant financial experience
Remit	Remuneration policy and specific packages for executive directors and senior management	Internal controls with the organisation, liaison with external auditors, oversight of internal auditors
	Key objectives: (a) Procedures for determining remuneration are formal and transparent (b) Bonuses should arise from achievement of measurable performance (c) All board remuneration and benefits are transparent in the statutory accounts (d) Remuneration packages align the interests of management and shareholders	*Key objectives:* (a) An independent channel is available to report any control issues (b) Resolving any auditor recommendations and auditor/management disputes (c) Financial and control systems in place are adequate, including an effective internal audit function (d) Adequate risk monitoring is in place

Essential reading

See Chapter 8 Section 3 of the Essential reading for more detail on the roles of the remuneration and audit committees.

The Essential reading is available as an Appendix of the digital edition of the Workbook.

2.5 Reporting on corporate governance

Companies listed on a Stock Exchange may be required to provide information on corporate governance (eg the following are a requirement for the London Stock Exchange, and derive from the UK Corporate Governance Code):

(a) A **narrative statement** of how the principles of the corporate governance code have been applied

(b) A **statement of compliance** with the Code throughout the accounting period, or reasons for non-compliance

(c) Information about the **board of directors**

(d) **Committee reports** (eg of the Remuneration and Audit Committees)

(e) A statement of **effectiveness of internal controls**

Activity 4: Governance issues

Techpoint plc is a medium-sized public company that produces a range of components used in the manufacture of computers.

The board of directors consists of chair Max Mallory, chief executive Richard Mallory and finance director Linda Mallory, all of whom are siblings. There are five other unrelated executive directors. All directors receive bonuses based on sales. The company's sales are made by individual salesmen and women, each of whom have the authority to enter the company into contracts unlimited in value without the need to refer to a superior or consult with other departments.

It is this flexibility that has enabled the company to be very profitable in past years. However, a number of bad contracts in the current year have meant that the finance director has reclassed them as 'costs' to maintain healthy sales and to protect the directors' bonuses.

Required

What are the corporate governance issues at Techpoint plc?

3 Corporate social responsibility

KEY TERM

> **Corporate Social Responsibility:** The idea that organisations, especially (but not only) companies, have an **obligation to consider the interests** of customers, employees, shareholders, communities, and ecological considerations in all aspects of their operations.

3.1 Approaches to social responsibility

Proactive strategy – Taking full responsibility for its actions

Reactive strategy – Waiting until there is a public reaction before amending the company's ways

Defence strategy – Attempting to avoid additional obligations caused by a particular problem

Accommodation strategy – Accommodating concerns of the public and governments to prevent stricter legislation being introduced

3.2 Pros and cons of CSR

Some arguments for/against companies embracing corporate social responsibility are:

For CSR	Against CSR
Power – Large companies can be very powerful and, as they are not democratically accountable, may infringe on others' rights if they do not exercise self-restraint	**Key objective** – Companies can benefit societies most by operating efficiently and maximising wealth for shareholders
Infrastructure – Companies depend on society's infrastructure to function	**Taxation** – Companies already fund society's infrastructure via taxes
Externalities – A company's operations may have social and environmental consequences which need to be addressed, eg pollution, environmental damage	**Sovereignty** – It should be up to shareholders to donate to charities if they wish to, not for companies to undertake charitable activities

For CSR	Against CSR
Public Relations – Adopting corporate social responsibility can result in a better image and greater customer and employee loyalty	**Payback –** Companies should already be focused on anything that will enhance shareholder value without labelling it corporate social responsibility

3.3 Ethical stance

Ethical stance means the position that a person or organisation takes when faced with ethical questions.

The range of ethical stances, as described by *Johnson and Scholes (2005)* includes:

(a) **Short-term shareholder interest**

The organisation is responsible for its ethical stance in the short-term interests of shareholders, but the government has a wider longer-term remit.

(b) **Long-term shareholder interest**

The organisation takes a wider view of its ethical responsibilities by:

(i) Corporate image enhancement

(ii) Presentation of pressure for legal regulation

(c) **Multiple stakeholder obligations**

The organisation accepts the legitimacy of the expectations of stakeholders other than shareholders.

(d) **Shaper of society**

This is a more demanding role that **'multiple stakeholder obligations'** and is largely the preserve of public sector organisations.

3.4 Analysis of stakeholders

CSR can also be viewed within the context of the stakeholders of the organisation, and the extent to which it meets the needs of the different stakeholders.

Refer back to Chapter 1 for information on stakeholders.

PER alert

PER performance objective PO4 requires you to contribute to the effective governance, risk management and control of an organisation. The material covered in this chapter will help in this context.

Chapter summary

Corporate governance and social responsibility

Introduction to corporate governance

The agency problem
- Principal (owner)
- Agent (director)

Developments in corporate governance
- Sarbanes-Oxley Act
- OECD Principles
- UK Corporate Governance Code

Best practice recommendations

The board of directors
- Role of board
- Role of chair
- Role of chief executive
- Role of company secretary

Board members
- Relevant expertise
- Receive appropriate information
- Assessment
- Separation of role of Chair and Chief Executive

Non-executive directors
- No management responsibilities
- Broaden experience of board
- Must be independent

Remuneration and audit committees
- 2-3 non executive directors
- Remuneration responsible for remuneration of executive directors
  - Remuneration of executive directors
- Audit committee responsible for:
  - Internal controls
  - Liaison and oversight of external auditors

Reporting on corporate governance
- How principles have been applied
- Statement of compliance
- Information about board
- Committee reports
- Effectiveness of internal controls

Corporate social responsibility

Approaches to social responsibility
- Proactive
- Reactive strategy
- Defence strategy
- Accommodation strategy

Ethical stance
- Short term shareholder interest
- Long term shareholder interest
- Multiple stakeholder obligations
- Shapeholder of society

Analysis of stakeholders
- Refer to chapter 1

Knowledge diagnostic

1. Corporate governance

Corporate governance is the system by which organisations are **directed and controlled** by their **senior officers**.

2. Board of directors

A **director** is someone who works for a company and is charged with the conduct and management of its affairs. The directors collectively are referred to as the board of directors, who are elected by the shareholders.

3. Executive and non-executive directors

Executive directors take the decisions about how the business will be run; however, **non-executive directors** provide **specialist advice** and **independent oversight** of those decisions.

4. Committees

Committees including non-executive directors cover areas such as **remuneration** and **audit**. Companies are often required to publish information relating to corporate governance as a **requirement of stock exchange listing**.

5. Best practice

Best practice corporate governance regulations aim to ensure that:

- Appropriate people with the right skills are appointed to the board
- There are sufficient non-executive directors to provide scrutiny over the CEO and other executive directors
- Remuneration is fair and not excessive
- The company's system of internal controls is monitored to ensure it is effective

6. Corporate Social Responsibility (CSR)

Organisations often recognise obligations over and above those to the internal and connected stakeholders. They see an obligation to the wider community and environment. CSR policies can cover things such as **working conditions**, **charitable donations** and **ecological policies** such as waste and energy use.

Further study guidance

Question practice

Now try the following from the Further question practice bank [available in the digital edition of the Workbook]:

Number	Level		
Q31	Exam Section A	2	2 mins
Q32	Exam Section A	2	2 mins
Q33	Exam Section A	1	1 min
A34	Exam Section A	2	2 mins
Q35	Exam Section B	4	5 mins

Further reading

There is an article on the ACCA website entitled 'Corporate governance: the board of directors and standing committees' that is relevant to material in this chapter. You are strongly advised to read this article in full as part of your preparation for the FBT exam.

Activity answers

Activity 1: Agency

The following are some obvious examples, but the list is not exhaustive:

(1) Managers may award themselves large pay rises or benefits in kind (eg expensive company cars).

(2) Managers may make acquisitions to increase their own status (empire building). If they pay too much for these acquisitions, shareholders will not benefit.

(3) Managers may not work to their full potential, taking their salary for the minimum effort.

(4) Managers may award contracts to their friends in other companies rather than obtaining the best value for money from other suppliers.

Activity 2: Poor corporate governance

Features of poor corporate governance:

- Dominance of the Board and company by one individual or a small group
- Excessive remuneration and perks
- Lack of transparency
- In extreme cases, corruption or illegality

Poor corporate governance can lead to **reputational damage** and sometimes **bankruptcy.**

Activity 3: Selecting non-executive directors

Problems in selecting and recruiting non-executive directors include the following:

- Are they genuinely independent? They are ultimately appointed by the executive directors.
- Can be hard to recruit, especially if there are strict requirements on experience, eg must have been a director of a listed company.
- They usually have significant other responsibilities so may have limited time available
- Executives may ignore their views.

Activity 4: Governance issues

The main corporate governance issues are:

(1) **Domination by a small group**

   All the key directors are related which gives them power over the other executives.

(2) **Short-term view**

   Directors' bonuses are based on short-term sales and have resulted in the manipulation of accounts to achieve them.

(3) **Lack of supervision**

   The sales force can tie the company into large loss-making contracts without any checks. There is no authorisation or communication with other departments which means the company may take on contracts that it cannot fulfil. The company has been hit hard with bad contracts in the current year.

The role of accounting

Learning outcomes

On completion of this chapter you should be able to:

	Syllabus reference no.
Explain the contribution of the accounting function to the formulation, implementation, and control of the organisation's policies, procedures, and performance.	C2 (a)
Identify and describe the main financial accounting functions in business: (a) Recording financial information (b) Codifying and processing financial information (c) Preparing financial statements	C2 (b)
Explain basic legal requirements in relation to retaining and submitting proper records and preparing and auditing financial reports.	C3 (a)
Explain the broad consequences of failing to comply with the legal requirements for maintaining and filing accounting records.	C3 (b)
Explain how the international accountancy profession regulates itself through the establishment of reporting standards and their monitoring.	C3 (c)
Explain the various business purposes for which the following financial information is required. (a) The statement of profit or loss (b) The statement of financial position (c) The statement of cash flows (d) Sustainability and integrated reports	C4 (a)
Describe the main purposes of the following types of management accounting reports. (a) Cost schedules (b) Budgets (c) Variance reports	C4 (b)
Identify an organisation's system requirements in relation to the objectives and policies of the organisation.	C5 (a)
Describe the main financial systems used within an organisation.	C5 (b)

	Syllabus reference no.
(a) Purchases and sales invoicing (b) Payroll (c) Credit control (d) Cash and working capital management	
Explain why it is important to adhere to policies and procedures for handling clients' money.	C5 (c)
Identify business uses of computers and IT software applications. (a) Spreadsheet applications (b) Database systems (c) Accounting packages	C5 (g)
Describe and compare the relative benefits and limitations of manual and automated financial systems that may be used in an organisation.	C5 (h)

Exam context

This chapter looks at the role of the accounting function and at the regulatory environment for financial accounting. The topics covered in this chapter are highly examinable - there were several questions in the Specimen paper that relate to material covered here.

Chapter overview

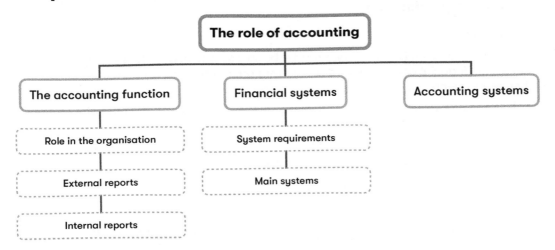

1 The accounting function

1.1 Role in the organisation

1.1.1 Main function

The accounting function is part of the broader business system, and does not operate in isolation. It handles the financial operations of the organisation, but also provides information and advice to other departments.

Typically large organisations structure their accounting functions on the lines of:

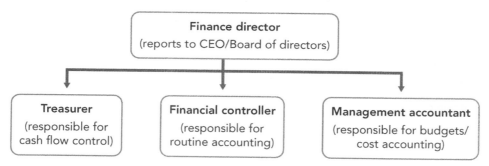

Accounts are produced to aid management in planning, control and decision-making and to comply with statutory regulations. **The accounting department must be adequate to fulfil these functions.** An organisation's accounting department is affected by the nature of its business transactions and the sort of business it is. An appropriate accounting department will depend upon:

- **Size** of the organisation
- **Type** of organisation
- **Structure** of organisation
- **Legal jurisdiction** of the organisation

The accounting department will provide the basis for financial information used internally and externally.

1.1.2 Policies and procedures

In any organisation there is a need for order, co-ordination and control to ensure efficiency. To achieve this, management often implements rules and procedures. For example, there will be authorisation policies for the purchase of non-current assets, procedures for choosing new suppliers, procedures for accepting new customers, etc.

Policies and procedures may be grouped in the form of a **policy manual**, perhaps stored on the organisation's computer network for easy reference. Although a policy manual is to be recommended as a form of control over the activities of employees, care must be taken that strict adherence to the rules does not create inflexibility.

Many organisations have an **internal audit department**, which is designed to alleviate the risks of error and fraud. Internal auditors are employees of the company, but most internal audit departments aim to retain independence from the other departments. One of the roles of an internal audit department will be to ensure that staff are complying with the company's policies and procedures.

1.1.3 Handling clients' money

In some industries, the nature of the business means that money is held on behalf of clients. Examples include:

- Banks
- Fund managers and financial services
- Lawyers
- Accountants

There must be strict policies over how client money is held. In particular, the money held by clients should be held in separate accounts from those of the rest of the business, so that they do not get confused and should the company itself go bankrupt, then the clients' money will be safe.

Regulations relating to handling clients' money are issued by industry regulators - in the UK for example, the financial services industry is regulated by the Financial Conduct Authority. Businesses must also comply with regulations relating to money laundering, and are required to ensure clients are not using the client accounts for money laundering purposes. Money laundering is described in Chapter 11.

The accounting department will be responsible for monitoring clients' money.

1.1.4 Performance

An important area of responsibility for the finance department is performance management and measurement. This involves setting targets for other departments and monitoring their performance against those targets. An example of this is the budget.

1.2 Financial accounting

Financial accounting is primarily concerned with providing information to external stakeholders, particularly shareholders. Financial accounting involves:

- Recording transactions in 'books of prime entry'.
- Analysing and categorising transactions and posting them to the ledgers.
- Finally, the transactions are summarised in the financial statements.

Essential reading

See Chapter 1 Section 1 of the Essential reading for more detail on what financial accounting involves.

The Essential reading is available as an Appendix of the digital edition of the Workbook.

1.3 The regulatory system

1.3.1 Requirements

Most countries have laws that require companies to:

- Keep proper accounting records.
- File financial statements with the government's company registration body (Companies House in the UK). These financial statements are then available for inspection by members of the public.

There may be a requirement to have the financial statements audited by an independent accountant. The role of auditors is discussed in Chapter 10. In the UK, an audit is required for all companies above a given size, according to criteria related to revenue, value of assets and number of employees.

Activity 1: Government's company registration body

Why is there a requirement for financial statements to be available for inspection by members of the public? Who might be interested in inspecting the financial statements?

1.3.2 Regulation of unincorporated entities

While most of the regulations above apply only to companies, other forms of business entity are required to comply with some regulations relating to accounting, eg:

- Businesses registered for sales tax (VAT) are required to keep records of their sales and expenses to support the numbers in their sales tax returns.

- Taxpayers are required to maintain records of their income to support their tax returns, and such returns might include profits of unincorporated businesses.
- Charities may be required to report to charity regulators.

Activity 2: Proper accounting records

What do you think is meant by proper accounting records?

1.3.3 Consequences of failing to comply with regulations

- Companies can be fined for failing to keep proper accounting records or for failing to file the financial statements with the government's company registration body on time. If companies persistently fail to file accounts on time they can be 'stuck off' by the company registration body.
- Inaccurate or late tax returns can lead to audits and investigations by tax authorities, which can lead to fines and tax penalties.
- The auditors may issue a 'qualified' audit opinion, if in their opinion there are any serious misstatements in the financial statements, or if the company has not kept proper accounting records.
- Public oversight boards (eg FRC in the UK) review financial statements on a sample basis to ensure that the accounts comply with relevant regulations. If they do not, the companies may be required to re issue the accounts.
- Where the company has issued financial statements that are designed to intentionally mislead the users, the directors are guilty of fraud, which is a criminal activity. They may therefore face jail or other sanctions.
- Directors or officers of companies may be subject to criminal procedures for failing to adhere to the accounting regulations.
- If a listed company fails to publish financial statements within the required deadline (eg four months after the financial year end in the UK) the company's listing on the stock market can be suspended. This means that it will no longer be possible to buy or sell the company's shares.

1.3.4 Regulation by the accounting profession

While company law sets out the basic accounting requirements that govern companies, detailed guidance is often provided by the accountancy profession. The accountancy profession is made up of accountancy bodies such as the ACCA which oversee the activities of their members. The profession is often independent of the government, although governments do oversee the activities of the professions to ensure that they are acting in the public interest.

The following regulatory bodies regulate the accountancy profession:

- **The International Accounting Standards Board** (IASB) is responsible for issuing International Financial Reporting Standards (IFRS). The IASB is a non-profit organisation whose members include representatives of accountancy bodies and representatives of users of the financial statements. IFRS provide detailed guidance on treatment of specific items in the financial statements - for example IFRS 15 deals with recognition of revenue. IFRS standards have been adopted in many countries around the world. Within the EU, listed companies must prepare financial statements in accordance with IFRS.
- **The International Federation of Accountants** (IFAC) is a global accountancy body. It's membership is made up of 170 accounting bodies throughout the world, including ACCA. IFAC aims to ensure that accountants throughout the world operate to a consistently high standard. IFAC issues a code of ethics (see Chapter 19) and also issues international auditing standards.
- **National accounting standards bodies** set accounting standards for use within particular countries. In the UK, for example, the Financial Reporting Council (FRC) issues accounting standards for UK companies. It should be noted that these do not apply to listed companies in the UK, as they must adopt IFRS.

- **Stock exchanges** set requirements relating to the provision of financial and other information by companies whose securities are listed on their exchanges. In the US, the **Stock Exchange Commission** (SEC) oversees the reporting requirements of all companies listed on US stock markets.
- Public oversight boards monitor and review the activities of the accounting profession. In some countries they are government bodies, while in others they are private sector. Examples include:
  - Financial Reporting Review Panel in the UK which reviews published financial statements on a sample basis, to ensure that they are compliant with relevant accounting standards and guidance.
  - Public Company Accounting oversight board (PCAOB) in the US which oversees the audit of public (listed) companies. It was set up under the Sarbanes-Oxley Act in the wake of the Enron scandal.

2 Financial information

2.1 External reports

External reports are produced primarily for shareholders, but other stakeholders might also be interested in the information provided. The main reports included in the financial statements are:

- Statement of profit and loss (income statement or profit and loss account)
- Statement of financial position (balance sheet)
- Statement of cash flows

Companies might also prepare other non-financial reports such as sustainability reports or integrated reports.

2.1.1 Statement of profit and loss

The statement of profit and loss shows the revenue and costs of the business for a particular period, and the resulting profit.

It aims to show the financial performance of the business for the period. In particular, users will be interested in how much profit has been generated.

2.1.2 Statement of financial position

The statement of financial position lists the assets and liabilities of the business at a particular point in time. It also shows the owners' equity - that is share capital plus retained profits.

The statement of financial position shows two important categories of information:

- How much the company owns - net assets means total assets minus total liabilities. This is referred to as the financial position of the company.
- Whether or not the business has sufficient cash and other liquid assets to meet its liabilities when they become due. This is referred to as the liquidity.

Users may also be interested in the return that the business generates on these assets, and may calculate ratios such as return on capital employed. Such ratios are covered in the financial accounting exam.

2.1.3 Statement of cash flows

The income and expenses in the statement of profit and loss are recognised in the period to which they relate (accruals concept) which may not be the same as the date when cash is received and paid, eg depreciation is recognised as an expense in the profit and loss account each year of the life of an asset, while the cash is usually paid at the start of the asset's life.

The statement of cash flows provides information about cash received and paid out during a period.

BPP LEARNING MEDIA

Activity 3: Shareholders

How will shareholders use the information provided in each of the three financial statements?

2.1.4 Sustainability and integrated reports

Financial statements have limitations:

- They provide only financial information, so ignore the other impacts that an organisation has on society.
- They provide only historic information. Users of the accounts are interested in the future prospects of a business.

Many businesses now provide sustainability reports, which detail how sustainable the business model is. Refer back to Chapter 2 for information about sustainability.

Integrated reporting is a new approach to corporate reporting, which aims to provide a holistic view of the performance of an organisation by looking not only at financial performance, but on the impact the business has on nature and society as a whole. An integrated report aims to be concise, as there has been much criticism recently about the amount of detail required in Financial Statements. Integrated Reporting standards are issued by the International Integrated Reporting Council. Adoption of integrated reporting is mandatory in some countries (eg South Africa) but voluntary in others.

2.1.5 Management accounting

Management accounting refers to provision of internal financial information to help managers with the following:

- Planning
- Controlling
- Decision making

Unlike external information, there are no regulations governing the management accounting information. Typically management accounts may include:

Cost schedules - showing costs incurred categorised into appropriate categories

Budgets - a budget is a financial plan for a period, showing expected revenues and costs.

Variance reports - are produced regularly, showing differences between actual and budgeted costs and revenues. These aim to identify problems which managers need to focus on solving.

The role of management accounting was discussed in Chapter 7.

3 Financial systems

KEY TERM

Financial systems: The people, procedures and computing equipment that record all of the sales and expenses of the organisation and provide relevant financial information to management and external stakeholders.

3.1 System requirements

The system requirements of a business will depend on several factors:

- Size of the business
- Volume of transactions
- Nature of the business
- Location/ dispersion of the business

Effective systems and procedures should ensure that:
- Relationships with customers are effectively managed
- Relationships with suppliers are effectively managed
- Office functions interrelate properly and are not duplicated

Activity 4: Sales systems

Contrast the sales system requirements of a large supermarket group, operating over 100 stores, with a small food retailer with only one small store.

3.2 Main systems

Businesses come in all shapes and forms. However, there will be a number of types of transaction which will be common to most businesses.
- Making sales
- Paying employees
- Making purchases
- Purchasing non-current assets
- Paying expenses

This diagram shows, in a simplified form, the flow of funds, documentation and information.

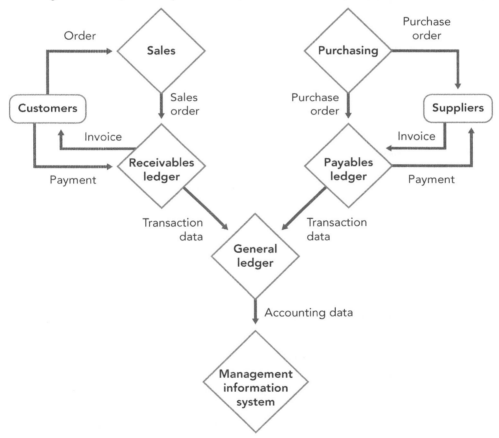

The following sections describe how these systems operate in a typical company.

3.2.1 Sales invoicing

In a retail organisation sales are made on the shop floor. The customer is given an invoice at the checkout.

In **manufacturing organisations** the system is more complex:

(a) Sales orders are taken by the sales department.

(b) Orders are authorised by credit control department.

(c) Confirmed orders are sent to stores for despatch.

(d) Copies of the order are sent to the accounts department.

(e) When the goods are despatched a despatch note is sent to the accounts department.

(f) The sales ledger team in the accounts department send the invoice to the customer based on the information in the order and despatch note.

(g) The credit control team monitor the outstanding amounts receivable from customers, and record cash payments when they are received.

3.2.2 Purchase invoicing

(a) Stores manager/user departments complete a purchase requisition.

(b) Requisitions are authorised by an appropriate manager (eg department manager).

(c) Purchase department selects a supplier and places an order for each approved requisition.

(d) Goods are received - receiving department checks that all goods accepted are matched to an order.

(e) Copies of satisfied orders are sent to accounts department.

(f) Purchase invoice is received. Purchase ledger department check invoice against appropriate purchase. order, and record the invoice for payment.

(g) Payment is made on the appropriate date.

3.2.3 Payroll

Large organisations may have a payroll department. Smaller companies may outsource payroll to an agency. The principles of operating the payroll are:

(a) Human resources department sends details of new employees to payroll department along with pay methods (monthly, weekly, fixed salary, hourly rate).

(b) For employees on variable remuneration, line managers send details of hours worked weekly or monthly to the payroll.

(c) For each employee, payroll clerk calculates total gross pay, tax and other deductions, and net pay.

(d) Payroll is authorised by a senior manager and employees are paid.

3.2.4 Credit control

When sales are made on credit, there is a risk that customers will not pay. This has to be balanced against the sales that would be lost if credit is refused. This is the job of the credit control department.

(a) **New customers** - credit checks are run and a credit limit established for a customer.

(b) When customers place orders, credit control checks that the order would not take the customer's balance above their credit limit. If it would then the credit controller will either:

(i) Increase the credit limit (after appropriate checks)

(ii) Block the order until customer has paid outstanding invoices to take the balance back below the credit limit.

(c) Credit controller monitor the outstanding receivables balances to identify overdue balances. Collection procedures are put in place to encourage the customer to pay.

(d) Ultimately if a customer refuses to pay an outstanding debt, the company may take legal action.

Essential reading

See Chapter 9 Section 3 of the Essential reading for more detail on financial systems and controls.

The Essential reading is available as an Appendix of the digital edition of the Workbook.

4 Accounting systems

4.1 Computerised accounting systems

The principles behind computerised accounting are the same as those of manual accounting. **Computerised accounting** tends to rely on accounting packages which comprise **several modules** (eg sales ledger, purchase ledger).

Manual systems are usually inferior to computerised systems.

Activity 5: Manual accounting systems

What are the disadvantages of a manual accounting system?

Solution

4.2 Integrated accounting software

Integrated accounting software has automatic links between separate accounting modules thus meaning data needs only to be processed once and all files are updated.

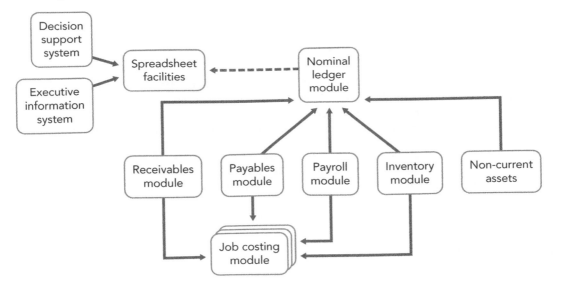

Integrated accounting systems have the following advantages and disadvantages:

Advantages	
One entry updates others	Greater computer memory needed
Users specify reports	Fewer facilities than specialist modules
Users' workload is simplified	

5 Databases and spreadsheets

5.1 Databases

A database is a **'pool' of data** that can be used by a variety of people for a variety of applications:

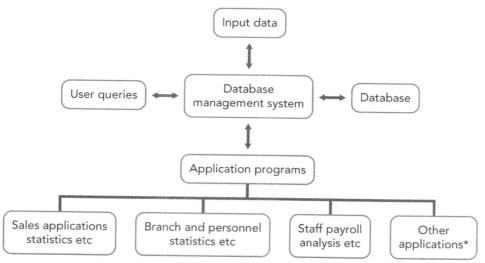

The range of applications which make use of a database will vary widely, depending on what data is held in the database files.

A database allows all of the information within an organisation to be held centrally and accessed by the different applications that use it. Controls will be in place within the database management system to ensure that people can only update or amend data that is relevant to their role, and security controls will mean that the data is only accessible to authorised persons.

Advantages	Disadvantages
No duplication of effort/data	Breakdown especially if complex
Easy to manage updates	Access issues

5.2 Spreadsheets

KEY TERM

> **Spreadsheets:** A spreadsheet is essentially an electronic piece of paper divided into rows and columns with a built-in pencil, eraser and calculator. It provides an easy way of performing numerical calculations.

The intersection of each column and row of a spreadsheet is referred to as a cell. A cell can contain text, numbers or formulae. Use of a formula means that the cell which contains the formula will display the results of a calculation based on data in other cells. If the numbers in those other cells change, the result displayed in the formula cell will also change accordingly. With this facility, a spreadsheet is used to create financial models.

Below is a spreadsheet processing budgeted sales figures for three geographical areas for the first quarter of the year.

	A	B	C	D	E
1	BUDGETED SALES FIGURES				
2		Jan	Feb	Mar	Total
3		£'000	£'000	£'000	£'000
4	North	2,431	3,001	2,189	7,621
5	South	6,532	5,826	6,124	18,482
6	West	895	432	596	1,923
7	Total	9,858	9,259	8,909	28,026

Spreadsheets have many uses, both for accounting and for other purposes. It is perfectly possible, for example, to create proforma statements of financial position and statements of comprehensive income on a spreadsheet, or set up the notes for financial accounts, like the non-current assets note.

Chapter summary

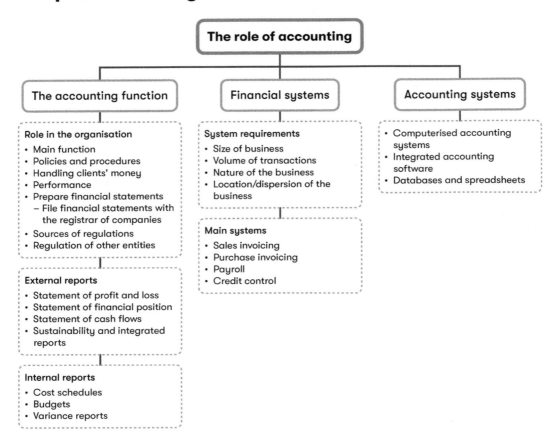

The role of accounting

The accounting function

Role in the organisation
- Main function
- Policies and procedures
- Handling clients' money
- Performance
- Prepare financial statements
  - File financial statements with the registrar of companies
- Sources of regulations
- Regulation of other entities

External reports
- Statement of profit and loss
- Statement of financial position
- Statement of cash flows
- Sustainability and integrated reports

Internal reports
- Cost schedules
- Budgets
- Variance reports

Financial systems

System requirements
- Size of business
- Volume of transactions
- Nature of the business
- Location/dispersion of the business

Main systems
- Sales invoicing
- Purchase invoicing
- Payroll
- Credit control

Accounting systems
- Computerised accounting systems
- Integrated accounting software
- Databases and spreadsheets

Knowledge diagnostic

1. Role of finance

The finance department handles the financial operations of an organisation. It also provides information and advice to other departments, ensures adherence to financial policies and procedures, monitors financial performance and prepares financial statements.

2. Regulations

Most countries have regulations that require companies to keep proper accounting records and to file financial statements with the government company registration body.

3. Sources of regulations

Accounting regulations come from several sources, including laws (eg Companies Act), accounting standards issued by professional bodies, and international financial reporting standards that may be applicable to listed companies.

4. External information

External information comprises a statement of profit and loss, a statement of financial position and a statement of cashflows. This information might be supplemented by sustainability reports or integrated reports which aim to provide information about the non-financial impact that an organisation has.

5. Internal information

Internal information is provided to help businesses plan , control and make decisions. Examples include costs schedules, budgets and variance reports.

6. Financial systems

Financial systems aim to record and classify transactions and prepare financial statements. Key financial systems include sale invoicing, purchase invoicing, payroll and credit control

Further study guidance

Question practice

Now try the following from the Further question practice bank [available in the digital edition of the Workbook]:

Number	Level	Marks	
Q36	Exam Section A	1	1 min
Q37	Exam Section A	2	2 mins
Q38	Exam Section A	2	2 mins
Q39	Exam Section A	2	3 mins
Q40	Exam Section A	2	2 mins
Q41	Exam Section A	2	2 mins
Q42	Exam Section B	4	5 mins

Activity answers

Activity 1: Government's company registration body

The requirement to file financial statements is the price that companies pay for their limited liability status. People who lend money to the company cannot hold the owners of the company liable for the company's debts, therefore they need to have information about the company's finances before doing business with it. The following members of the public may be interested in inspecting the financial statements:

- Lenders (eg banks) analyse the financial statements to ensure that the company can afford to repay their loans
- Suppliers who sell on credit want to know that the company can afford to pay their debts
- Employees want to see how well the company is performing so that they can evaluate their job security and possibly negotiate higher salaries if the company is performing well.
- Tax authorities want to ensure that the companies are declaring their profits in their tax returns
- Residents living next to the company's premises might be interested in how well the company is performing as they want to understand potential social contributions that the company could make.

Note. Shareholders are not included in the list, as shareholders should be sent copies of a company's accounts automatically, so would not have to go to the company registration body to inspect them.

Activity 2: Proper accounting records

Proper accounting records:

- All transactions should be recorded
- There should be a clear system for coding and classifying the transactions so that the financial statements and tax returns can be prepared accurately.
- It should be possible for auditors to verify the balances in the financial statements by identifying supporting documents such as invoices from suppliers.
- The records should be kept in a safe and secure manner. Many tax authorities are happy for documents to be stored digitally.
- The records should be kept for the number of years specified by tax authorities or other regulators.

Activity 3: Shareholders

Statement of financial position - shareholders will use this information to look at the value of the assets that the company holds. They will also be interested in the ability of the company to meet its liabilities as they become due (the liquidity of the company).

Statement of profit and loss - this will be used to assess the performance of the company. Shareholders will be interested in how revenues have increased over prior years, and about how well costs are being controlled. The statement may also be used to make forecasts about future profits, so that shareholders can decide whether to keep their investment.

Statement of cash flows - this will be used for similar purposes as the statement of profit and loss. The difference is it shows the cash generated, rather than the profits made, and some investors are more interested in the cash generating ability of a business rather than the accounting profits. Cash flow is also an important indicator of liquidity - profitable businesses have gone out of business because they used up more cash that they could generate.

Activity 4: Sales systems

The volume of transactions in the large supermarket group means that the supermarket would need a system that can quickly record sales at the checkouts, using electronic point of sales systems, that automatically record each sale by scanning bar codes on the items at the checkouts. In the small retailer, a manual cash register may be sufficient to record sales (although most stores these days do use EPOS systems).

In the supermarket, the system will have to deal with a huge number of transactions. It will therefore have to have the capacity to do this. It will require a network, linking all the checkouts to a central system that will summarise the daily sales.

In the retailer, no network will be required. Daily sales totals (from the cash register daily reports) could be entered into an accounting system manually.

The supermarket will need to maintain perpetual inventory records, whereby inventory is updated each time a sale is made. This will enable the supermarket to ensure inventory is replenished when needed, and provide useful information to management about trends in sales.

A small retailer will be able to perform manual inventory counts and will notice if any particular lines of inventory are running low as they will see the empty shelves.

Activity 5: Manual accounting systems

Disadvantages of a manual accounting system:

(1)   Lower productivity

(2)   Slower processing speeds

(3)   Greater risk of errors

(4)   Information less accessible

(5)   More difficult to make alterations/corrections

(6)   Not suitable for large amounts of data

(7)   Inconsistent quality of output

10

Control, security and audit

Learning outcomes

On completion of this chapter you should be able to:

	Syllabus reference no.
Identify and describe the main audit and assurance roles in business. (a) Internal audit (b) External audit	C2 (e)
Explain the main functions of the internal auditor and the external auditor and how they differ.	C2 (f)
Recommend improvements to accounting systems to prevent error and fraud and to improve overall efficiency.	C5 (e)
Explain why appropriate controls are necessary in relation to business and IT systems and procedures.	C5 (f)
Explain internal control and internal check.	C6 (a)
Explain the importance of internal financial controls in an organisation.	C6 (b)
Describe the responsibilities of management for internal financial control.	C6 (c)
Describe the features of effective internal financial control procedures in an organisation, including authorisation.	C6 (d)
Identify and describe the types of information technology and information systems used by the business organisation for internal control.	C6 (e)
Describe general and application systems controls in business.	C6 (f)
Describe cloud computing as a capability in accountancy and how it creates benefits for the organisation.	C8 (a)
Explain how automation and artificial intelligence (AI) in accounting systems can affect the role and effectiveness of accountants.	C8 (b)
Describe how the application of big data and data analytics can improve the effectiveness of accountancy and audit.	C8 (c)

Outline the key features and applications of Blockchain technology and distributed ledgers in accountancy.	C8 (d)
Define cyber security and identify the key risks to data that cyber-attacks bring.	C8 (e)
Identify and describe features for protecting the security of IT systems and software within business.	C8 (f)

Exam context

In this chapter we move to the main elements of internal control systems that organisations operate. Controls must be linked to organisational objectives and the main risks that organisations face. In addition, internal control systems do not just consist of the controls themselves but also the control environment within which controls operate.

Internal audit is a key part of the control system of larger companies and the external audit function exists to review controls and report on the financial statements.

Organisations are becoming increasingly reliant on computerised information systems. It is vital therefore to ensure these systems are secure – to protect the information held on them, to ensure operations run smoothly, to prevent theft and to ensure compliance with legislation.

Security and legal issues are likely to crop up regularly in the examination. There were three Section A questions in the specimen exam relating to this chapter. Part of one of the Section B questions also related to the content covered in this chapter.

Chapter overview

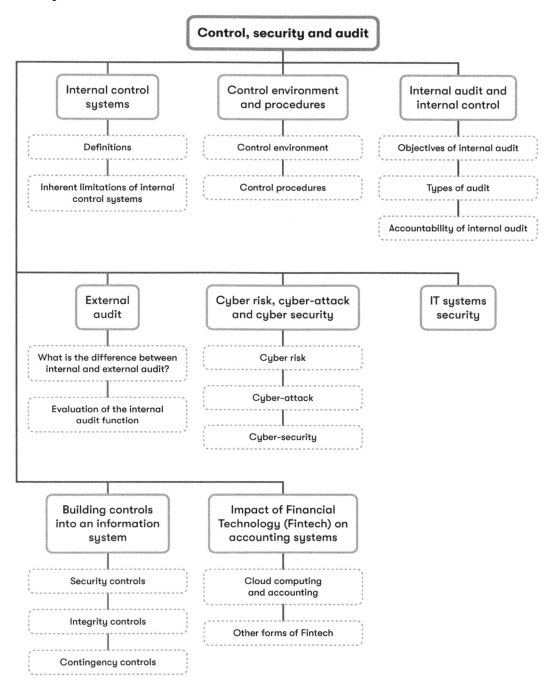

1 Internal control systems

1.1 Definitions

KEY TERM

Internal control system: This comprises the control environment and control procedures.

Control environment: The overall attitude, awareness and actions of directors and management regarding internal controls and their importance in the entity. The control environment encompasses the management style, and corporate culture and values shared by all employees. It provides the background against which the various other controls are operated.

Control procedures: The detailed controls in place, usually more formally explained and implemented.

Internal control systems include all the **policies** and **procedures** adopted by the directors and management of an entity to assist in achieving their objectives. Internal controls may be incorporated within computerised accounting systems. However, the internal control system extends beyond those matters which relate directly to the accounting system.

In order for internal controls to function properly, they have to be well directed across the entire organisation. Managers and staff will be more able (and willing) to implement controls successfully if it can be demonstrated to them what the objectives of the control systems are, while objectives provide a yardstick for the board when they come to monitor and assess how controls have been operating. Staff also need to understand them and what they are trying to achieve.

Activity 1: Purposes of internal control

What are the purposes of controls in an organisation?

A suitable **framework for controls** (such as the **FRC** Guidance on Risk management, Internal Control and related Financial and Business Reporting) would consist of **information** and **communication** processes, as well as **monitoring** their **continuing effectiveness** via measures such as **internal audit** which we shall discuss later in this chapter.

1.2 Inherent limitations of internal control systems

There are **inherent limitations of an internal control system**. A sound system of internal control can only provide the directors with **reasonable assurance** that their objectives are reached and may simply reduce, but not eliminate, the possibilities of:

- poorly judged decisions
- fraud
- human error
- deliberate circumvention of controls
- management override of controls
- unforeseeable circumstances.

Systems will provide **reasonable (not absolute) assurance** that the company will not be hindered in achieving its business objectives and in the orderly and legitimate conduct of its business but will not provide certain protection against all possible problems. The costs associated with certain controls may outweigh the benefits they deliver, which can also make controls less effective.

2 Control environment and procedures

We explained earlier that internal control systems can be split into

- The control environment
- Control procedures

2.1 Control environment

The following are elements of a strong **control environment**.

- Clear strategies for dealing with the significant risks that have been identified
- The company's culture, code of conduct, human resource policies and performance reward systems supporting the business objectives and risk management and internal control systems
- Senior management demonstrating values through its actions and policies commitment to competence, integrity and fostering a climate of trust within the company
- Clear definition of authority, responsibility and accountability so that decisions are made and actions are taken by the appropriate people
- Communication to employees of what is expected of them and scope of their freedom to act
- People in the company having the knowledge, skills and tools to support the achievements of the organisation's objectives and to manage effectively its risks

However, a strong control environment does not, by itself, ensure the effectiveness of the overall internal control system although it will have a major influence on it.

The control environment will have a major impact on the establishment of business objectives, the structuring of business activities and dealing with risks.

2.2 Control procedures

You may find **control procedures** classified in different ways; these are considered below. Classification of controls can be important because different classifications of control are tested in different ways.

Classification	Detail
Administration	These are concerned with achieving the objectives of the organisation and with implementing policies. These controls relate to channels of communication and reporting responsibilities.
Accounting	These controls aim to provide accurate accounting records and to achieve accountability. They apply to recording transactions and establishing responsibilities for records, transactions and assets.
Prevent	These are controls designed to prevent errors from happening in the first place. For example, checking invoices from suppliers against goods received notes before paying the invoices.
Detect	These are designed to detect errors once they have happened. Examples include bank reconciliations and physical checks of inventory against inventory records.
Correct	These are designed to minimise or negate the effect of errors. An example would be a back-up of computer input at the end of the day.

Essential reading

There are other classifications in Chapter 10 Section 1 of the Essential reading.

The Essential reading is available as an Appendix of the digital edition of the Workbook.

A useful framework for effective financial control procedures is (**SPAMSOAP**):

Segregation of duties - for example, the chair/chief executive roles should be split

Physical - these are measures to secure the safe custody of assets

Authorisation and approval - all transactions should require authorisation or approval by an appropriate responsible person; limits for the authorisations should be specified

Management - provide control through analysis/review of accounts, such as variance analysis

Supervision - ensures everyone is aware of work checks, reducing the risk of falsification or errors

Organisation - by identifying reporting lines, levels of authority and responsibility, this ensures everyone is aware of their control (and other) responsibilities

Arithmetical and accounting - such as reconciliations and the use of trial balances

Personnel - attention should be given to selection, training and qualifications of personnel, as well as personal qualities; the quality of any system is dependent on the competence and integrity of those who carry out control operations

Internal controls should not be confused with **internal checks**, which have a more restricted definition.

KEY
TERM

> **Internal checks:** Scrutiny of day-to-day transactions whereby the work of one person is proved independently or is complementary to the work of another, the object being the prevention or early detection of errors and fraud. It includes matters such as the delegation and allocation of authority and the division of work, the method of recording transactions and the use of independently ascertained totals, against which a large number of individual items can be proved.

Essential reading

You can read more about internal checks in Chapter 10 Section 2 of Essential reading.

The Essential reading is available as an Appendix of the digital edition of the Workbook.

Activity 2: Characteristics of internal control

What are the characteristics of a good internal control system?

Solution

3 Internal audit and internal control

Internal audit is **one part of an organisation's internal control system** but it plays a unique role.

KEY TERM

> **Internal audit:** An independent appraisal activity established within an organisation which functions by examining and evaluating the adequacy and effectiveness of other controls. The investigative techniques developed are applied to the analysis of the effectiveness of all parts of an entity's operations and management.

3.1 Objectives of internal audit

The internal audit department should seek to add value and monitor all aspects (not just accounting) of the business. Their work may cover the following broad areas:

(a) **Review systems** of accounting and internal control for both financial and non-financial controls (this includes reviewing the design of the systems, monitoring the operation of the systems by risk assessment and detailed testing and recommending cost-effective improvements)

(b) **Examination of information** – both financial and operating, including detailed testing of transactions, balances and procedures

(c) Review of the **economy, efficiency and effectiveness** of operations

(d) Review of **compliance** with laws, regulations and other external requirements and with internal policies and directives

(e) Review of **safeguarding of assets**

(f) Review of **implementation** and **communication** of corporate objectives

(g) Identification of significant **business risks**, monitoring overall risk management policy and monitoring risk management strategies for effectiveness

(h) **Special investigations** into particular areas, for example suspected fraud or how well the business complies with social and/or environmental matters.

Internal auditors' work on risk management is crucial to the way the organisation counters risk and forms part of the overall risk management procedures in place. The areas that auditors will concentrate on will depend on the **scope** and **priority** of the assignment and the **risks identified**. Where the risk management framework is insufficient, auditors will have to rely on their own **risk assessment** and will focus on **recommending an appropriate framework**. Where a framework for risk management and control is embedded in operations, auditors will aim to use **management assessment of risks** and concentrate on **auditing the risk management processes**.

There are two **key features** of any internal audit function that are central to them achieving their objectives:

- **Independence** – Although an internal audit department is part of an organisation, it should still be independent of the line management whose sphere of authority it may audit.

- **Appraisal** – Internal audit is concerned with the appraisal of work done by other people in the organisation, and internal auditors should not carry out any of that work themselves.

3.2 Types of audit

Internal auditors can get involved in virtually anything that the organisation requires them to do. This could involve a review of **social** or **environmental activity** of both employers and employees, as well as performing certain **investigations**.

However, there are three specific **types of audit** that you do need to be aware of.

3.2.1 Operational audits

This type of audit monitors management's performance and is sometimes known as 'management', 'efficiency' or 'value for money' audit.

3.2.2 Systems audits

Systems audits test and evaluate internal controls. Typically, there are two types of test:

- **Compliance testing**: evidence that the internal controls are being applied as prescribed
- **Substantive testing**: are there any errors or omissions from specific transactions?

If compliance tests reveal that internal controls are working satisfactorily then the amount of substantive testing can be reduced, and the internal auditor can concentrate the audit effort on those areas where controls do not exist or are not working satisfactorily.

Real life example

Suppose a department within a company processes travel claims which are eventually paid and recorded on the general ledger.

When conducting **compliance tests**, the internal auditor is **looking at the controls** in the travel claim section to see if they are working properly. This is not the same as looking at the travel claims themselves. For example, one of the internal controls might be that a clerk checks the addition on the travel claim and initials a box to say that they have done so. If they fail to perform this arithmetic check, then there has been a control failure – regardless of whether the travel claim had, in fact, been added up correctly or incorrectly.

When conducting **substantive tests**, the internal auditor is examining figures which they have extracted directly from the company's financial records. For this sort of test, the auditor is concerned only with establishing whether or not the figure in the ledger is correct. They are not concerned as to how it got there.

3.2.3 Transactions audits

A **transactions audit** aims to detect fraud within an accounting system's records and uses only substantive tests. Sometimes the term 'probity' is used to describe the need for honesty in this context, meaning that internal auditors are looking for instances of records that are not a fair reflection of what has actually happened.

3.3 Accountability of internal audit

Ideally the internal audit department should **report to the audit committee** of the board of directors as it is then free to access all parts of the organisation and report on all levels of management which ensures that its recommendations are implemented. (The role of the audit committee was discussed in Chapter 8)

The UK Corporate Governance Code (FRC, 2018) states that companies without an internal audit function should provide an **explanation for the absence**, describe how **internal assurance is achieved**, and how this affects the work of **external audit**.

The need for internal audit will depend on:

- The **scale, diversity** and **complexity** of the company's activities
- The number of employees
- Cost-benefit considerations
- **Changes** in the organisational structures, reporting processes or underlying information systems
- **Changes** in **key risks**
- **Problems** with **internal control systems**
- An **increased number** of **unexplained** or **unacceptable** events

Given an acceptable line of responsibility and clear terms of authority, it is vital that the internal auditor **is and is seen to be independent**. Internal audit requires a highly professional approach which is objective, detached and honest. Independence is a fundamental concept of auditing and this applies just as much to the internal auditor as to the external auditor. The internal auditor should not install new procedures or systems; neither should they engage in any activity which they would normally appraise, as this might compromise their independence.

Essential reading

In Chapter 10 Section 3 of Essential reading, you will find an activity which tests how well you have understood the role that internal audit plays in an internal control system.

The Essential reading is available as an Appendix of the digital edition of the Workbook.

4 External audit

> **External audit:** A periodic examination of the books of account and records of an entity carried out by an independent third party (the auditor) to ensure that they have been properly maintained, are accurate and comply with established concepts, principles, accounting standards and legal requirements and give a true and fair view of the financial state of the entity.

The **primary purpose** of an external audit is to review the books and records in order to give a **professional opinion** on whether the financial statements represent a **true and fair view** of the organisation. It is usually a legal requirement and for listed companies, an essential part of complying with the stock market's regulations.

4.1 What is the difference between internal and external audit?

The key differences between internal and external audit are:

	Internal	External
Reason	Add value and improve organisation's operations	Express an opinion on the financial statements
Reporting to	Board of directors (or similar, such as an audit committee)	Shareholders or members of the company
Work relating to	Operations of the organisation	Financial statements
Relationship with company	Employees of the company (can be outsourced though)	Independent of the company and its management

The table above shows that whilst some of the work may be similar, the whole basis and reasoning for their work is fundamentally different. This is emphasised by the difference in objectives with internal audit having a much wider scope than the narrow 'true and fair view' that external auditors are responsible for providing an opinion on

There should be **co-ordination** between the external and internal auditors to ensure that duplication of work is minimised and controls enhanced. This can be achieved via meetings and shared access to testing techniques and working papers.

4.2 Evaluation of the internal audit function

If external auditors can rely to an extent on the work of the internal audit department they will have to do less testing themselves. To make this judgement they will consider:

- **Organisational status** - Internal audit's specific status in the organisation and the effect this has on its ability to be objective
- **Scope of internal audit functions** - The nature and extent of the assignments which internal audit performs and whether management and the directors act on internal audit recommendations

- **Technical competence** - Whether internal audit work is performed by persons having adequate technical training and proficiency
- **Due professional care** - Whether internal audit work is properly planned, supervised, reviewed and documented

In relation to audited financial statements, the **Financial Reporting Review Panel** is responsible for monitoring the use of accounting standards in published financial statements and for examining and questioning the departure from accounting standards by large companies.

5 Cyber risk, cyber-attacks and cyber security

> **Cyber risk:** This is a term that covers a number of organisational risks which are possible consequences of a cyber-attack.
>
> **Cyber-attacks:** Deliberate attempts to damage an organisation by using the Internet to take advantage of poor security controls and system integrity.
>
> **Cyber security:** The protection of computer systems from the risk of cyber-attack through the use of hardware and software security procedures and controls.

5.1 Cyber risk

Cyber risk factors could include the following:

- **Financial losses** (including fines from non-compliance with relevant laws and regulations)
- **Reputational damage** (including loss of custom)
- **Operational disruption** (such as simply being unable to trade online)

5.2 Cyber-attacks

These can include the following:

- **Phishing** – The cyber-attacker sends emails to the victim which appear to be from a trusted source, for example a bank, leading the victim to divulge sensitive information under false pretences.
- **Pharming** – The cyber-attacker targets an organisation's website by automatically redirecting visitors from the organisation's website to a bogus website and collecting their data without their knowledge or approval.
- **Hacking** – The cyber-attacker uses specialist software and other tools to gain unauthorised access to an organisation's computer system, either to obtain data or to stop the system working altogether.
- **Distributed Denial of Service (DDoS) attack** – The cyber-attacker attempts to disrupt an organisation's online activities by preventing people from accessing the organisation's website. Botnets (large numbers of individual computers which have been taken over without the user knowing) are instructed to overwhelm the organisation's website with a wave of internet traffic so that the system is unable to handle it and may cause it to crash.
- **Webcam manager** – The cyber-attacker uses software to take control of the user's webcam.
- **File hijacker/ransomware** – The cyber-attacker gains access to the user's system to hijack their files and hold them to ransom.
- **Keylogging** – The cyber-attacker plants software onto the user's computer to record what the user types onto their keyboard. The objective is to learn passwords and user details to gain access to confidential information.
- **Screenshot manager** – The cyber-attacker obtains information from the victim by installing software onto the user's computer to enable screenshots of the user's computer screen to be taken. Like other cyber-attacks, the purpose can be to steal information, funds, or may even be to perform corporate espionage.

- **Ad clicker** – The cyber-attacker plants a program on the victim's machine that directs it to automatically click on specific adverts on a website to earn commission for the website's owner.

5.3 Cyber security

This is the protection of computer systems from the risk of cyber-attack through the use of hardware and software security procedures and controls. Common cyber security measures include:

Cyber security method	Description
Access control	These are physical and network procedures to restrict access to a system.
Boundary firewalls and internet gateways	Firewalls and internet gateways are software protection that intercept data being transmitted in and out of a system.
Malware and virus protection	Malware protection software prevents installation and removes suspicious programs (such as Trojans) and viruses from a system.
Patch management	This is a system procedure rather than a hardware or software solution (sometimes known as a 'bug-fix'). The organisation should ensure that the latest software updates are installed on the system when available.
Secure configuration	The organisation should have a policy which states that systems should be set up with cyber security as a priority.

PER alert

PER performance objective PO4 requires you to contribute to the effective governance of an organisation and raise awareness of risk. The material covered in this chapter will help you achieve this.

These cyber controls also highlight the need for a broader selection of IT system controls.

6 IT systems security

Activity 3: Threats to systems and data

Suggest some physical environmental threats to IT systems and data.

It is important that IT systems are secure and protect the data and information that they process and store. Security refers to **technical** issues related to the computer system, psychological and **behavioural** factors in the organisation and its employees, and protection against the unpredictable occurrences of the **natural world.** Security can be categorised as follows:

- **Prevention.** It is in practice impossible to prevent all threats cost effectively.
- **Detection.** Detection techniques are often combined with prevention techniques: a log can be maintained of unauthorised attempts to gain access to a computer system.
- **Deterrence.** As an example, computer misuse by personnel can be made grounds for disciplinary action.

- **Recovery procedures**. If the threat occurs, its consequences can be contained (for example checkpoint programs).
- **Correction procedures**. These ensure the vulnerability is dealt with (for example, by instituting stricter controls).
- **Threat avoidance**. This might mean changing the design of the system.

Physical access controls seek to prevent intruders accessing the IT system and include:

- Security and other staff who can act as 'gatekeepers'
- Door locks
- Keypad or card entry systems (being able to detect someone's identity from their biometrics is ideal, but that can be very expensive)
- Intruder alarms

Computer theft is an increasing problem as equipment becomes smaller and more portable. Whilst the loss of the physical asset is a concern, the loss of the data stored on the computer may cause a bigger problem.

Activity 4: Security measures (1)

You are the chief accountant at your company. Your department, located in an open-plan office, has five networked desktop PCs and three laser printers.

You have just read an article suggesting that the best form of security is to lock hardware away in fireproof cabinets, but you feel that this is impracticable.

Required

Recommend alternative security measures which you could adopt to protect the hardware in your department.

7 Building controls into an information system

Controls can be built into an IT system and they can be classified as follows:

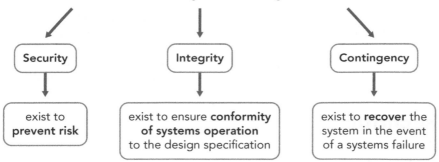

7.1 Security controls

Activity 5: Security measures (2)

Give an example for each of the **security risks** given below and suggest a suitable control.

Risk	Example	Control
Human error		
Malfunctioning hardware or software		

Natural disasters		
Deliberate actions		
Commercial espionage		
Malicious damage		
Industrial action		

7.2 Integrity Controls

7.2.1 Input controls

These ensure the accuracy, completeness and validity of input data by:

- **Data verification** – ensure the data is correct eg checking a password is correct, or a date is the correct date by asking a manager
- **Data validation** – ensures the data is reasonable by means of a variety of techniques: the number of characters in a password, an agreed batch total or a limit on the acceptable range of values that can be entered

7.2.2 Data processing controls

These also exist to ensure **accuracy and completeness** but focus on the processing of data **once it has been input.**

Outputs are verified by the following:

- Investigation and follow-up of error reports and exception reports
- Batch controls to ensure all items processed and returned
- Controls over distribution/copying of output

7.2.3 Back-up controls

These aim to maintain system and data integrity by ensuring that the most recent copy of the data can be recorded and restored in the event of loss or corruption to the primary storage media.

A well planned **back up and archive strategy** should include:

- **Off-site storage** and back up (including in the cloud)
- **Regular back up** of critical data
- **Archiving** plans (the process of moving data from primary storage, such as a hard disk, to tape or other portable media for long-term storage)
- **Disaster recovery plans** (we will discuss this next in relation to contingency controls)
- Regular **testing** to verify back up data can be successfully restored

7.2.4 Administrative controls

These should include the following:

- Careful personnel selection for senior IT roles
- Segregation of duties for other IT roles
- Passwords: Virtually all computer installations use passwords. Failed access attempts may be logged. Passwords are not fool proof.
- Standard system passwords (such as 1234 or 0000) when a device or user is first active must be changed to something that cannot be guessed.
- Passwords must never be divulged to others and must never be written down.
- Passwords must be changed regularly – and changed immediately if it is suspected that the password is known by others.
- Obvious passwords must not be used.

Other higher-level passwords are used by administrators to control access rights for the reading, modifying and deleting functions.

To keep track of how controls evolve over time, an **audit trail** may be used.

Audit trail: A record showing who has accessed a computer system and what operations they have performed.

Audit trails are useful both for maintaining security and for recovering lost transactions.

Accounting systems include an audit trail component that is able to be output as a report.

Essential reading

Chapter 10 Section 4 of the Essential reading covers various systems integrity issues for PCs and networks that you should be familiar with.

The Essential reading is available as an Appendix of the digital edition of the Workbook.

7.3 Contingency Controls

Contingency controls include the creation of a disaster recovery plan to ensure that the system recovers as fully and as soon as possible in the event of a disaster.

Disaster recovery plans provide for:

(a) **Standby procedures** so that some operations can be performed while normal services are disrupted
(b) **Recovery procedures** once the cause of the breakdown has been discovered or corrected
(c) **Personnel management** policies to ensure that (a) and (b) above are implemented properly

A **disaster recovery plan** must cover all activities, from the initial response to a 'disaster' through to damage limitation and full recovery.

Responsibilities must be clearly spelt out for all tasks.

8 Impact of Financial Technology (Fintech) on accounting systems

Cloud computing and accounting, automation, artificial intelligence, big data, data analytics, Blockchain and distributed ledger technology have all impacted on accounting systems and the work of accountants and auditors.

They are often referred to using the term financial technology or Fintech.

8.1 Cloud computing and accounting

> **Cloud computing:** This involves the provision of computing as a consumable service instead of a purchased product. It enables system information and software to be accessed by computers remotely as a utility through the Internet.
>
> **Cloud accounting:** The provision of accountancy software through the cloud. Users log in to the accountancy software to process financial transactions and produce management reports in the same way as if the software was installed on their own machine.

A cloud service can be private or public. A **public cloud** sells services to anyone on the Internet. (such as Amazon Web Services and Dropbox). A **private cloud** is a proprietary network or a data centre that supplies hosted services to a limited number of people. When a service provider uses public cloud resources to create their private cloud, the result is called a **virtual private cloud**. Private or public, the goal of cloud computing is to provide easy, scalable access to computing resources and IT services. In the UK, Sage, Quickbooks and Xero (as well as others) provide **cloud accounting services**.

The benefits of cloud accounting include:

- System data is automatically refreshed and kept up-to-date.
- Data is made is available to multiple users simultaneously and globally.
- System errors and inconsistencies are eliminated as only one set of data is held
- Data is stored in one offsite location and users simply access the information when required (plus there is no need to transmit the data between users over the internet or by USB stick, increasing data security).
- Multiple users mean key people can access financial and customer details easily.
- Reduces the cost and complexity of keeping backups of the data as this is done by the cloud service provider.
- Reduces the cost and time involved in upgrading the software.
- Improves support as the service provider can access the user's information to help resolve issues.

Despite these benefits, cloud accounting does increase the risk of cyber-attacks and therefore the loss of, or damage to data. Users are reliant on cyber security and back-ups being taken by the service provider. There is also a need for organisations to ensure subscriptions and corporate accounts for cloud services are kept up-to-date because there have been instances of data loss where organisations have failed to pay for the service or update payment details which have changed and this has led to services to be withdrawn and data deleted.

Developments in cloud accounting technology have increased the need for staff training in accountancy firms to use the new systems. It has also created a need for new guidance and procedures on using cloud-based infrastructures to be created and for new infrastructures to be developed to make best use of cloud-based systems.

8.2 Other forms of Fintech

> **Automation:** The ability of systems to perform routine activities and processing of data without the input of a human.
>
> **Artificial intelligence:** Also known as AI, this is the ability of a computer system to assist a human operator to make business decisions or help solve problems.
>
> **Big data:** Sets of data of such size that traditional databases are unable to store, manage or analyse them.
>
> **Data analytics:** The collection, management and analysis of large data sets (such as big data) with the objective of discovering useful information, such as customer buying patterns, that an organisation can use for decision making.

> **Distributed ledger technology (Blockchain):** Technology that allows organisations and individuals who are unconnected to share an agreed record of events, such as ownership of an asset.

Distributed ledger technology (also known as **Blockchain**) is a technology that eliminates the need for data and information to be stored and managed centrally.

Furthermore, this technology allows an accurate, up-to-date, single, trusted and transparent record to be shared between numerous organisations. The concept of Blockchain is best explained through its practical uses.

Real life example

The diamond industry uses a Blockchain system named Everledger to help prevent fraud and the transfer of stolen goods. All diamonds have unique characteristics (similar to how humans have individual fingerprints). The Everledger system creates an identity for every diamond by recording these unique characteristics. Every time a diamond is bought or sold, the sale is recorded by the system on the Blockchain so that the diamond's ownership can be traced.

Another example is in relation to the cryptocurrency Bitcoin. Bitcoins are created by individuals or organisations processing data and solving problems (known as mining).

Once mined, Bitcoins become the property of the miner and can be traded or transferred. Every transaction is recorded on a Blockchain. The Blockchain stores the transaction history of all Bitcoins, enabling the assurance that only legitimate owners of Bitcoins can spend or transfer them.

It also prevents Bitcoins being copied or being illegally generated.

For accountants and auditors, distributed ledgers and Blockchains allow for **increased clarity** and **transparency** in the recording of business transactions.

This is because transactions can also be posted to a public ledger on a Blockchain. This extra information means that there are more resources available for business planning and valuation, especially in relation to **measuring the value of assets** (since transactions concerning assets will have an indelible record).

Distributed ledgers also reduce the need for auditors to audit transactions and **verify the ownership of assets** because they have a source of information about the assets that they can trust.

Essential reading

For further information on all these types of Fintech, you should read Chapter 10 Section 5 of Essential reading.

The Essential reading is available as an Appendix of the digital edition of the Workbook.

Activity 6: Fintech

Explain (and provide examples) of how the various types of Fintech listed below might improve the effectiveness of the work undertaken by accountants and auditors.

Type of Fintech	Explanation
Automation	

Type of Fintech	Explanation
Artificial intelligence	
Big data and data analytics	
Distributed ledger technology	

Chapter summary

Control, security and audit

Internal control systems

Definitions
- Consists of control environment and control procedures
- Policies and procedures adopted by the directors and management
- Purpose is to achieve objectives and comply with laws and regulations
- Purpose is also to safeguard assets and allow quality internal and external reporting
- Assists with risk management

Inherent limitations of internal control systems
- Poorly judged decisions
- Fraud and error
- Management override
- Unforeseen events
- Cannot provide absolute levels of assurance, only reasonable assurance

Control environment and procedures

Control environment
- Clear demonstration of leadership through strategies adopted
- Demonstrated by culture
- Values including authority, responsibility and accountability
- Communication of key expectations from management

Control procedures
- Administration
- Accounting
- Prevent
- Detect
- Correct
- Internal checks
- For financial control procedures, use SPAMSOAP:
  - Segregation of duties
  - Physical
  - Authorisation and approval
  - Management
  - Supervision
  - Organisation
  - Arithmetic and accounting
  - Personnel

Internal audit and internal control

Objectives of internal audit
- Independent appraisal activity for evaluating adequacy and effectiveness of controls
- Reviewing systems, including their economy, efficiency and effectiveness
- Reviews for compliance, safeguarding assets, risks and other investigations
- Work includes independence and appraisal

Types of audit
- Operational audits (sometimes known as 'management', 'efficiency' or 'value for money' audits)
- Systems audits testing controls via compliance and substantive testing
- Transactions audits of items in the accounts (not controls)

Accountability of internal audit
- Internal audit accountable to management and/or audit committee
- Need for internal audit depends on organisational factors such as size, complexity, change and risk
- Independence is fundamental

External audit

What is the difference between internal and external audit?

- External audit only responsible for true and fair opinion (internal audit could be asked to do anything)
- External audit reports to shareholders (internal audit report to either board or audit committee)
- External audit focuses on the financial statements (internal audit focus is anywhere)
- External audit must be independent of the company (internal audit is usually employed by the company)

Evaluation of the internal audit function

- Organisational status
- Scope and authority of the internal audit function
- Technical competence
- Due professional care (planning, supervision, review)

Cyber risk, cyber-attack and cyber security

Cyber risk

- Financial losses (including fines from non-compliance with relevant laws and regulations)
- Reputational damage (including loss of custom)
- Operational disruption (such as simply being unable to trade online)

Cyber-attack

- Phishing (gaining access to data via false pretences)
- Pharming (collecting data by redirecting users to a bogus website)
- Hacking (illegally accessing data)
- Distributed denial of service (DDoS) attack (deliberately flooding a website with more traffic than it can handle to put it out of business)
- Webcam manager (taking control of a webcam to access images)
- File hijacker/ransomware (withholding access to files unless a ransom is paid)
- Keylogging (tracking keyboard entries to attempt to identify passwords)
- Screenshot manager (used as a form of espionage to steal data and other information)
- Ad clicker (directing users to a bogus website)

Cyber-security

- Access controls to block network access
- Firewalls and gateways to act as protective boundaries
- Malware and virus protection
- Patch management ('bug fixes')
- Secure configuration policy

IT systems security

- Threats can include fire, flood, adverse weather conditions, terrorism and even just accidents
- Security procedures can include prevent/detect/correct controls, as well as deterrence, recovery and threat avoidance
- Physical access controls can also be used (security staff, locked doors and intruder alarms)

BPP
LEARNING
MEDIA

Building controls into an information system

Security controls
- Monitoring and anti-virus software, control systems, segregation of duties and back-ups

Integrity controls
- Input controls to verify and validate data as it is being input
- Processing controls to ensure data is accurate and complete
- Output controls (such as error and exception reporting)
- Back-up controls to protect from data getting lost
- Administrative controls such as passwords, segregation of duties and the appointment of appropriate management

Contingency controls
- Standby procedures in the event of disruption
- Recovery procedures to restore data and systems
- Personnel management to enable these controls to work effectively
- Disaster recovery plans

Impact of Financial Technology (Fintech) on accounting systems

Cloud computing and accounting
- Cloud computing allows IT services to be accessed via the internet rather than onsite
- Cloud accounting uses cloud-based financial systems to record and process transactions and other activity
- Significant cost savings from using the cloud BUT there is a risk of using a third party for sensitive data

Other forms of Fintech
- Automation refers to the ability of systems to perform routine activities and processing of data without the input of a human
- Artificial intelligence refers to the ability of a computer system to make business decisions or help solve problems
- Big data describes sets of data of such size that traditional databases are unable to store, manage or analyse them
- Data analytics is the collection, management and analysis of large data sets (such as big data) with the objective of discovering useful information
- Distributed ledger technology (Blockchain) allows unconnected individuals and organisations to share an agreed record of events

Knowledge diagnostic

1. Internal controls

Internal controls should help organisations counter risks, maintain the quality of reporting and comply with laws and regulations. They provide reasonable assurance that the organisations will fulfil their objectives and consist of the control environment and control procedures.

2. Control environment

The **control environment** is influenced by **management's attitude** towards control, the **organisational structure** and the **values** and **abilities** of employees.

3. Control procedures

Control procedures can be classified in various ways including **administrative** and **accounting; prevent, detect** and **correct; discretionary** and **non-discretionary; voluntary** and **mandated; manual** and **automated.** The mnemonic **SPAMSOAP** can be used to remember the main types of control.

4. Internal audit

The role of internal audit will **vary** according to the **organisation's objectives** but is likely to include review **of internal control systems, risk management, legal compliance** and **value for money. Internal auditors** are **employees** of the organisation whose work is designed to **add value** and who report to the **audit committee.**

5. External audit

External auditors are from **accountancy firms** and their role is to **report on the financial statements to shareholders.**

6. IT security

Security, in information management terms, means the **protection of data** from accidental or deliberate threats which might cause unauthorised modification, disclosure or destruction of data, and the **protection of the information system** from the degradation or non-availability of services.

7. Fintech

Cloud computing and accounting, automation, artificial intelligence, big data, data analytics, Blockchain and **distributed ledger technology** have all impacted on accounting systems and the work of accountants and auditors. They are examples of financial technology.

Further study guidance

Question practice

Now try the following from the Further question practice bank [available in the digital edition of the Workbook]:

Number			
Q43	Exam Section A	2	2 mins
Q44	Exam Section A	2	2 mins
Q45	Exam Section A	2	2 mins
Q46	Exam Section A	2	2 mins
Q47	Exam Section A	2	2 mins
Q48	Exam Section B	4	5 mins

Further reading

There is an article on the ACCA website entitled 'Internal controls' that is relevant to material in this chapter.

Own research

Try and get hold of a set of audited financial statements (they are usually available on a company's website under headings such as 'Investors' or 'Governance') and find the independent auditor's report to understand what the external auditor is responsible for creating.

If your organisation has an internal audit department, try and obtain some of its reports to see exactly what they have been involved in.

Cyber security is often in the news so stay alert to stories which focus on this evolving topic.

For a deeper insight into one aspect of Fintech, try listening to the podcast *The Missing Cryptoqueen* which follows the real-life story of a new cryptocurrency and its enigmatic founder.

Activity answers

Activity 1: Purposes of internal control

Purposes of controls:

- Facilitate the business's **effective** and **efficient operation** and achieve its objectives
- Respond appropriately to significant **business, operational, financial, compliance** and other risks
- **Safeguarding of assets** from inappropriate use or from loss and fraud
- Help ensure the **quality** of **internal** and **external reporting**, requiring the **maintenance of proper records and processes** that generate a flow of **timely, relevant and reliable information** from within the organisation and from external sources
- Help ensure **compliance with applicable laws and regulations**
- **Guide** behaviour
- Highlight **inconsistencies**

Activity 2: Characteristics of internal control

A clearly defined organisation structure:

(1) **Different operations must be separated** into appropriate divisions and subdivisions.

(2) Officers must **be appointed to assume responsibility** for each division.

(3) **Clear lines of responsibility** must exist between each division and subdivision and the board.

(4) There must be overall **co-ordination of the company's activities** (through corporate planning).

Adequate internal checks:

(1) **Separation of duties** for **authorising** a transaction, **custody** of the assets obtained by means of the transaction and **recording** the transaction.

(2) **'Proof measures'** such as control totals, pre-lists and bank reconciliations should be used.

Acknowledgement of work done: persons who carry out a particular job should acknowledge their work by means of signatures, initials, rubber stamps, and so on

Protective devices for **physical security:**

Formal documents should acknowledge the transfer of responsibility for goods. When goods are received, a goods-received note should be used to acknowledge receipt by the storekeeper.

Pre-review: the authorisation of a transaction (for example a cash payment, or the purchase of an asset) should not be given by the person responsible without first checking that all the proper procedures have been carried out

A clearly defined **system for authorising transactions** within specified spending limits:

Post-review: completed transactions should be reviewed after they have happened; for example, monthly statements of account from suppliers should be checked against the purchase ledger accounts of those suppliers.

There should be **authorisation, custody** and **re-ordering** procedures.

(1) Funds and property of the company should be kept under **proper custody**. Access to assets (either direct or by documentation) should be **limited to authorised personnel**.

(2) Expenditure should only be incurred after authorisation and all expenditures are properly accounted for.

(3) All revenue must be properly accounted for and received in due course.

Personnel should have the capabilities and qualifications necessary to carry out their responsibilities properly.

An **internal audit** department should be able to verify that the control system is working and to review the system to ensure that it is still appropriate for current circumstances.

Activity 3: Threats to systems and data

Fire

Fire is the **most serious hazard** to computer systems. Destruction of data can be even more costly than the destruction of hardware.

A fire safety plan is an essential feature of security procedures in order to prevent fire, detect fire and put out the fire.

Water

Water is a serious hazard. Flooding and water damage are often encountered following firefighting activities elsewhere in a building.

This problem can be countered by the use of waterproof ceilings and floors together with the provision of adequate drainage.

Weather

Wind, rain and storms can all cause substantial **damage to buildings**. In certain areas the risks are greater, for example the risk of typhoons in parts of the Far East. Many organisations make heavy use of prefabricated and portable offices, which are particularly vulnerable.

Lightning

Lightning and electrical storms can play havoc with power supplies, causing power failures coupled with power surges as services are restored.

Power failure can be protected against by the use of a **separate generator** or rechargeable battery. It may be sufficient to maintain power only long enough to close down the computer system in an orderly manner.

Terrorist activity

Political terrorism is the main risk, but there are also threats from individuals with **grudges**.

In some cases, there is very little that an organisation can do: its buildings may just happen to be in the wrong place and bear the brunt of an attack aimed at another organisation or intended to cause general disruption. **Physical access** to buildings should be controlled.

Accidental damage

People are a physical threat to computer installations: there can be few of us who have not at some time spilt a cup of coffee over a desk covered with papers or tripped and fallen doing some damage to ourselves or to an item of office equipment.

Combating accidental damage is a matter of having a good office layout and eliminating hazards, such as trailing cables.

Activity 4: Security measures (1)

'Postcode' all pieces of hardware. Invisible ink postcoding is popular, but visible marking is a better deterrent. Heated soldering irons are ideal for imprinting postcodes onto objects with a plastic casing.

Mark the equipment in other ways. Some organisations spray their hardware with permanent paint, perhaps in a particular colour (bright red is popular) or using stencilled shapes.

Hardware can be bolted to desks. If bolts are passed through the desk and through the bottom of the hardware casing, the equipment can be rendered immobile.

Ensure that the organisation's standard security procedures (magnetic passes, keypad access to offices, signing in of visitors, etc) are followed.

Activity 5: Security measures (2)

Don't worry if your suggestion is not in the solution - these are just illustrations to give you an idea of the sort of thing you would see when considering IT security risks and controls.

Risk	Example	Control
Human error	Input error when recording an invoice	System limitations on acceptable entries
Malfunctioning hardware or software	Breakdown due to poor treatment	Proactive maintenance and user education
Natural disasters	Fire in an office containing systems and data	Off-site back-up and physical controls (such as Halon gas)
Deliberate actions	Fraud by staff	Segregation of duties
Commercial espionage	Insider dealing	Systems monitoring
Malicious damage	Viruses or other malware	Anti-virus software and user education on emails
Industrial action	Strike action	Maintain good relations with staff

Activity 6: Fintech

Again, your explanation may not exactly match the ones used in the solution, but as long as you have a good, general understanding of each term, you should be prepared.

Type of Fintech	Explanation
Automation	Accounting software can automatically download transactions from an organisation's online bank account. This saves the accountant time and frees them up to focus on more value-adding activities (such as analysis).
Artificial intelligence	Artificial intelligence (AI) in accounting software can assign transactions to appropriate nominal codes and record the transactions appropriately in the accounts. This intelligence is achieved by the accountant recording the transactions manually a few times before the system learns what types of transactions should be assigned to which nominal codes.
	Auditors can use AI systems that perform complete checks on financial data held, allowing 100% of transactions to be audited automatically on a continuous basis, removing the need for an auditor to perform routine audit checks to verify transactions.
Big data and data analytics	Predictive analytics helps auditors better target their work on key risks, improving the relevance of audits, for example it can be used by an auditor to find all sales transactions recorded near to or over the materiality level.
Distributed ledger technology	Blockchain is an example of a distributed ledger. For accountants and auditors, distributed ledgers and Blockchain allow for increased clarity and transparency in the recording of business transactions. This is because transactions are posted to a public ledger on a Blockchain. Distributed ledgers also reduce the need for auditors to audit transactions and verify the ownership of assets because they have a source of information about the assets that they can trust (this is due to records being encrypted and as such, secure).

Identifying and preventing fraud

Learning outcomes

On completion of this chapter you should be able to:

	Syllabus reference no.
Explain the circumstances under which fraud is likely to arise.	C7 (a)
Identify different types of fraud in the organisation.	C7 (b)
Explain the implications of fraud for the organisation.	C7 (c)
Explain the role and duties of individual managers in the fraud detection and prevention process.	C7 (d)
Define the term money laundering.	C7 (e)
Give examples of recognised offences under typical money laundering regulations.	C7 (f)
Identify methods for detecting and preventing money laundering.	C7 (g)
Explain how suspicions of money laundering should be reported to the appropriate authorities.	C7 (h)

Exam context

This chapter considers the various types of fraud that an organisation may be prone to and which may have to be investigated by internal audit. It is important that you are able to identify signs of fraud in different circumstances.

You also need to have a good knowledge of both how fraud is prevented and detected. Although there may be significant costs involved in implementing a good system of fraud prevention, the consequences of successful fraud may be very serious, both for the reputation of the organisation and the position of its directors. Money laundering represents a serious problem, but systems can be set up to help detect and prevent this.

The practical aspects of fraud (where it might occur and how it can be detected) are the most likely areas to be examined, as shown by the specimen exam where there was one Section A question on the topic and part of one of the Section B questions featured the issue of internal controls and fraud.

Chapter overview

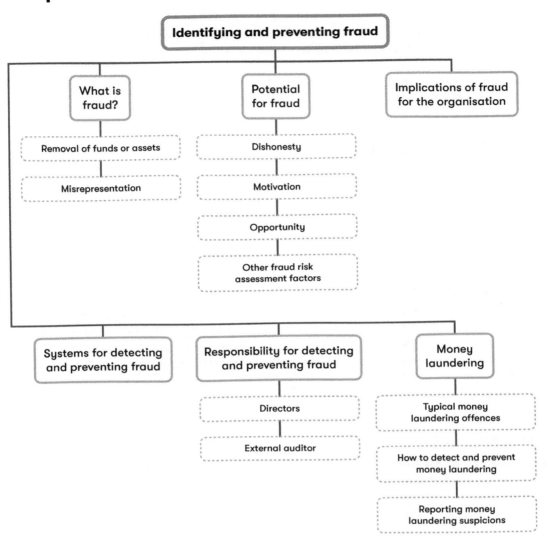

1 What is fraud?

> **KEY TERM**
>
> **Fraud:** Fraud is defined as a false representation of fact made with the knowledge of its falsity, or without belief in its truth, or recklessly careless, whether it be true or false.

In a corporate context, fraud can fall into one of two main categories:

- Removal of funds or assets
- Misrepresentation

1.1 Removal of funds or assets

Removal of funds or assets from a business includes the following:

- Theft of cash, such as petty cash, or inventory (ranging from insignificant items of stationery up to more high value items)
- Payroll fraud, for example claiming overtime for hours which they did not really work, inflating someone's rate of pay or even setting up a ghost employee and paying their wages to a different bank account
- Teeming and lading (eg using one customer's payments to cover theft from another account)
- Dispatching inventory to fictitious customers and then writing off the debt or colluding with customers, such as charging a lower amount than is appropriate (in both these cases, the fraudster has to have access to more than one aspect of the company's operations)
- Bogus supply of goods or services or paying for goods not received (again, these would require an insider to manipulate the amounts payable outside the organisation, so the extra amounts spent are shared between supplier and fraudster)
- Misuse of assets, such as raiding pension funds, or disposal of assets to employees for a value significantly below market price

1.2 Misrepresentation

Intentional misrepresentation of the financial position of the business is often caused by a desire to overstate or understate profits. This could include:

- Over-valuation of inventory (via inventory count records / returns not recorded accurately)
- Irrecoverable debt policy may not be enforced, leading to inflated trade receivables
- Fictitious sales
- Manipulation of year end events via credit notes, invoices and goods inwards/outwards records (this is sometimes called window-dressing)
- Understating expenses by failing to record certain amounts
- Manipulation of depreciation figures via inaccurate lifetimes or inappropriate policies.

Activity 1: Sales fraud

Suggest three ways of generating fictitious sales transactions or sales values.

Solution

2 Potential for fraud

There are generally three preconditions that are a prerequisite for fraud to occur.

2.1 Dishonesty

Honesty is a subjective quality, interpreted according to various ethical, cultural and legal norms. That said, we may define dishonesty as a predisposition to act contrary to accepted ethical, social and legal norms for fair and honest dealing. This tendency may arise from:

- Personality factors: a high need for achievement, status or security; a competitive desire to gain advantage over others; low respect for authority.
- Cultural factors: national or familial values, which may be more 'flexible' or anti-authority than the law and practice prevailing in the organisation. (Cultural values about the ethics of business 'bribes' (or 'gifts'), for example, vary widely. 'Lying' is also a very fluid concept: some cultures value 'saving face' (or agreeing) over giving strictly truthful responses.)

2.2 Motivation

In addition to a general predisposition or willingness to act dishonestly, should the opportunity arise, the individual needs a specific motivation to do so. Broadly, this involves a **calculation** of whether a given action is worthwhile. Individuals weigh up:

The potential rewards of an action...	...versus the potential sanctions
This considers the satisfaction of some need, or the fulfilment of some goal.	By contrast, this considers the deprivations required to carry it through.

The individual's goal or motive for fraudulent behaviour may be:

- Financial needs or wants, or envy of others (in the case of theft or fraud for monetary gain)
- A desire to exercise negative power over those in authority
- A desire to avoid punishment (in the case of cover ups, say).

2.3 Opportunity

Even if a person is willing to act dishonestly, and has a motive for doing so, they must still find an opportunity or opening to do so; a 'loophole' in the law or control system that:

- Allows fraudulent activity to go undetected, or
- Makes the risk of detection acceptable, given the rewards available.

An individual will have a high incentive to commit fraud if they are predisposed to **dishonesty** and the **rewards** for the particular fraud are high and there is an **opportunity** to commit fraudulent action with **little chance of detection** or with insignificant sanctions if caught.

Activity 2: Fraud strategies

Considering the three prerequisites, what immediate control strategies can prevent fraud?

Solution

2.4 Other fraud risk assessment factors

Signs of **high fraud risk** include indications of general factors such as:

- Lack of integrity
- Excessive pressures
- Poor control systems
- Unusual transactions
- Lack of audit evidence

A number of factors tend to crop up time and time again as issues that might indicate potential fraud.

Attention should be drawn to them if any of these factors come to light when assessing external and internal risks.

External factors	Internal factors
• The marketplace as a whole, (eg the trend to delayer may reduce the degree of supervision) • The industry in which the firm operates, (eg the building industry may be particularly prone to the risk of theft of raw materials, the travel industry may face risks due to the extensive use of agents and intermediaries and the retail industry must be vigilant to the abuse of credit cards). • In a competitive industry, fraud may be a tempting way of keeping up with the rest of the market.	Having considered the big picture, the next step is to apply the same logic at company level. Focus on the general and specific risks in the firm itself. Be alert to circumstances that might increase the risk profile of a company. • Changed operating environment • New personnel • New or upgraded management information systems • New overseas operations • Rapid growth • New technology • New products • Corporate restructuring • The prevalence of cash sales.

Types of risk to be considered include:

- **Business risk**, such as profits deviating significantly from the industry norm or an unusually complex corporate structure
- **Personnel risk**, including the behaviour and actions of staff
- **Computer risk**, such as the ease with which a hacker can gain access to an organisation's systems (compounded by a general lack of training or awareness among staff about this kind of risk)
- **Organisational risks**, such as extensive authority given to dominant managers, unclear structures of responsibility or a lack of supervision of remote locations
- **Strategic risks**, such as a lack of a business strategy or great emphasis being placed on reward by results.

Activity 3: Fraud behaviour

What behavioural evidence could suggest that fraud is being committed?

3 Implications of fraud for the organisation

Fraud often leads to the **removal of funds or assets** from a business which has the following impacts:

- Immediate financial implications of reductions in profits and/or cash
- Long-term effects on company performance, leading to possible collapse
- Intentional misrepresentation of the business's financial position or performance which can mask its true condition and affect future strategy.

If results are **overstated** the impact is demonstrated by:

- Excessive distribution of profits which can compromise financial stability
- Retained profits will be lower than believed
- Incorrect decisions will be made based on incorrect data
- Adverse impact on stakeholders (both investors and suppliers).

If results are **understated** the impact is demonstrated by:

- Negative publicity and an adverse impact on reputation among investors
- Legal consequences if fraud is uncovered by the authorities.

Real life example

During 2020, the auditors of German payments company **Wirecard** refused to sign-off the company's financial statements due to an inability to find sufficient appropriate audit evidence for substantial cash balances that made up around a quarter of its financial position. At the time of writing, there have been allegations of widespread fraud within the company which have led to investigations by the authorities in Germany as well as the loss of over 80% of the company's quoted value on the German Dax stock exchange.

(Source: 'Wirecard shares slump over missing €1.9 bn', BBC News https://www.bbc.co.uk/news/business-53093305).

---

4 Systems for detecting and preventing fraud

Prevention of fraud must be an integral part of corporate strategy and a control system has to be designed to detect and investigate fraud (such as that described in the chapter on **internal audit**).

General fraud prevention policies could include the following.

- **Emphasising ethics** can decrease the chances of fraud. Several businesses have formal codes of ethics which employees are required to sign covering areas such as gifts from customers. Management can also ensure that they set a good example.
- **Personnel controls** are a very important means of preventing fraud. Thorough **interviewing** and **recruitment procedures** including obtaining references can be an effective screening for dishonest employees. **Appraisal** and grievance systems can prevent staff demotivation.
- **Training and raising awareness** can be important. There are many examples of frauds taking place where people who were unwittingly close were shocked that they had no idea what was happening. **Fraud awareness education** should therefore be an integral part of the training programme, particularly for managers and staff in **high-risk areas** such as procurement, and staff with key roles in fraud prevention and detection, for example human resources.

The primary aim of internal controls should be to **prevent fraud**, but it is equally important that the controls support **frauddetection**. Controls discussed in the previous chapter should be selected and implemented with key risks in mind. Two key controls that are most useful in combating fraud are **segregation of duties** and the proactive use of **internal audit**.

Essential reading

For a thorough list of more specific controls that could be introduced to combat fraud, you should read Chapter 11 Section 1 of the Essential reading.

The Essential reading is available as an Appendix of the digital edition of the Workbook.

5 Responsibility for detecting and preventing fraud

5.1 Directors

Directors' responsibilities should aim to achieve the following.

- Ensure that the **activities** of the entity are conducted honestly and that its **assets** are safeguarded
- Establish arrangements to **deter** fraudulent or other dishonest conduct and to **detect** any that occurs
- Ensure that, to the best of their knowledge and belief, **financial information**, whether used internally or for financial reporting, is reliable.

It is therefore the responsibility of the **directors** to take reasonable steps to **detect** and **prevent** fraud.

5.2 External auditor

The **external auditor** is responsible for expressing an **opinion** on whether the financial statements give a true and fair view of the company's financial situation and results. In order to achieve this, the auditor should design audit procedures so as to have a **reasonable expectation** of detecting **material misstatements** arising from **fraud or error**. It should be emphasised that, in the case of a sophisticated fraud, which has been designed to escape detection by the auditors, a **reasonable expectation** is all that they can have.

If the auditors become aware during the audit that fraud or error may exist, they should **document their findings** and **report them to management**.

In the case of fraud, the auditors should then consider whether the matter should be **reported** to an appropriate authority in the public interest. If they decide that this is the case, they request that **the directors** make the report. If the directors do not do so, or if the fraud casts doubt on the integrity of the directors, the auditors should make the report themselves.

If the auditors take the view that the financial statements are materially affected by fraud or error, they should issue a **qualified opinion** within their auditor's report.

6 Money laundering

> **Money laundering:** Money laundering constitutes any financial transactions whose purpose is to conceal the origins of the proceeds of criminal activity.

The process of money laundering usually consists of three stages:

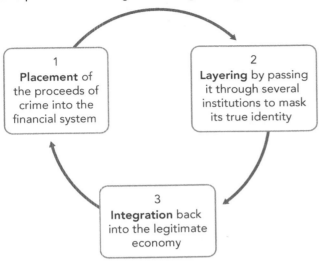

1
Placement of the proceeds of crime into the financial system

2
Layering by passing it through several institutions to mask its true identity

3
Integration back into the legitimate economy

- **Placement of proceeds** into the financial system – refers to how proceeds of criminal activity are placed into the legitimate financial system – for example, many criminal organisations operate legitimate cash-based businesses as fronts and inflate their revenues from these businesses with the proceeds of the criminal activity. These are paid into the business bank account.
- **Layering** – funds are transferred from one bank account to another, and then another, in a chain, to hide the origin of the original funds. Holders of bank accounts used in layering are offered a commission to accept and then pass on the funds. **Layering** - funds are transferred from one bank account to another, and then another, in a chain, to hide the origin of the original funds. Holders of bank accounts used in layering are offered a commission to accept and then pass on the funds.
- **Integrate back** into the legitimate economy – the funds are used by the criminals for whatever purpose they decide (eg buying yachts or expensive cars).

6.1 Typical money laundering offences

In essence there are three main types of offence:

- Having any **contact with the proceeds of crime** (whether deliberate or accidental)
- **Failing to report any suspicions** of criminal activity regarding money laundering to the appropriate authority
- Tipping off – in other words, warning a client that money laundering suspicions about them are going to be reported

Activity 4: Money laundering

Why should a professional adviser not give a warning to a client whom they suspect of money laundering?

6.2 How to detect and prevent money laundering

Before starting any commercial relationship with a prospective client, the law usually requires some kind of formal **identification**: for an individual, this could be a passport and a utilities bill; for an organisation, it could be their financial statements or other formal records regarding their existence.

Such a procedure is now so widespread that it serves as a deterrent against anyone attempting to use a business or personal relationship simply for the purposes of money laundering. This is another example of risk assessment and is known as **customer due diligence**.

Once this process is complete and any initial funds are considered legitimate, the individual or organisation is monitored to ensure they do not attempt to exploit this new relationship. This may take the form of gaining an understanding of the nature of any business activity and their associated cash flows in order to spot suspicious activity in future.

6.3 Reporting money laundering suspicions

It is usually a requirement of laws and regulations across the world for an organisation to employ someone who is responsible for dealing with any suspicions that money laundering might be taking place. In the UK, this person is known as a **Money Laundering Reporting Officer** (MLRO) or **Nominated Officer** and all suspicions are supposed to be reported (in the strictest confidence) to this MLRO. They will then decide whether to escalate the suspicion and alert the relevant authority (in the case of the UK, this is the **National Crime Agency** or NCA).

Essential reading

There is a more detailed overview of the various responsibilities associated with money laundering within Chapter 11 Section 2 of the Essential reading.

The Essential reading is available as an Appendix of the digital edition of the Workbook.

PER alert

PER performance objective PO4 requires you to contribute to the effective governance of an organisation and raise awareness of risk. The material covered in this chapter will help you achieve this.

Chapter summary

Identifying and preventing fraud

What is fraud?

Removal of funds or assets
- Theft of cash or inventory
- Payroll fraud
- Teeming and lading
- Dispatch or invoice fraud
- Misuse of assets

Misrepresentation
- Over-valuation of inventory
- Manipulation of irrecoverable debts
- Fictitious sales
- Manipulation of year end events
- Understating expenses
- Manipulation of depreciation figures

Potential for fraud

Dishonesty
- Very subjective – tendency to act contrary to fair and honest dealing
- May come from personality factors
- May be more of a reaction to society and/or culture

Motivation
- A balance between reward and consequences
- May stem from a financial need or a need to exercise power
- May even be a desire to avoid some form of punishment

Opportunity
- Usually presented by a loophole or gap in a set of controls

Other fraud risk assessment factors
- External factors (such as the competitiveness of the industry or the way that things are generally done)
- Internal factors (such as changes to technology, staff and systems, or the reliance on cash sales)
- Any combination of business, personnel, computer, organisational or strategic risk

Implications of fraud for the organisation

- Detrimental financial impacts on cash and/or sales
- Possible financial collapse or masking of true position
- Overstatements create a false sense of security, leading to poor decisions
- Understatement leads to poor reputation among stakeholders

Systems for detecting and preventing fraud

- Emphasising the importance of ethics
- Good systems of recruitment and appraisal
- Greater training and risk awareness
- Prevention and detection via a combination of segregation of duties and internal audit

Responsibility for detecting and preventing fraud

Directors

- Activities are conducted honestly and assets are safeguarded
- Arrangements to deter fraudulent or other dishonest conduct and to detect any that occurs
- Ensure reliable and trustworthy financial information

External auditor

- Opinion on financial statements regarding material misstatements whether due to fraud or error
- Any indication of fraud uncovered during the audit should be reported to management
- Opinion of reasonable assurance (not absolute) communicated via auditor's report

Money laundering

- Placement of criminal property in the banking system
- Layering via many different financial institutions to mask its true origin
- Placement back in the hands of the money launderer to imply some form of legitimacy

Typical money laundering offences

- Having any contact with the proceeds of crime
- Failure to report any suspicions
- Tipping off

How to detect and prevent money laundering

- Formal identification procedures on initial contact
- Regular monitoring of cash flows to understand nature of business
- Known as customer due diligence

Reporting money laundering suspicions

- Prompt reporting of suspicions to delegated person before possible escalation to regulator
- In the UK, the MLRO acts in this role and decides whether or not to inform the NCA

Knowledge diagnostic

1. Types of fraud

The practical aspects of fraud (where it might actually occur, how it can be detected) are the most likely topics to be examined. Common frauds include payroll frauds, conspiracy with other parties and stealing assets. More subtle measures including teeming and lading and manipulation of bank reconciliations and cashbooks to conceal theft.

2. Fraud preconditions

There are three broad prerequisites or 'preconditions' that must exist in order to make fraud a possibility: dishonesty, motivation and opportunity. Signs of high fraud risk include indications of lack of integrity, excessive pressures, poor control systems, unusual transactions and lack of audit evidence.

3. Fraud indicators

A number of factors tend to crop up frequently as indicators of potential fraud situations; these can be categorised under business and personnel risks. In order to prevent fraud, managers must be aware of the risks and signs of fraud.

4. Fraud controls

Prevention policies include emphasis on ethics and personnel and training procedures. Controls within particular business areas, such as segregation of duties and documentation requirements, are also significant. Controls must be developed in a structured manner, taking account of the whole spectrum of risk and focusing on the key risks identified in each area of the business.

5. Fraud responsibilities

Managers and staff should be aware of their responsibilities to help in detecting fraud. Fraud detection is also helped by having information readily available and allowing whistleblowing. Organisations should establish a fraud response plan, setting out how the method and extent of the fraud and possible suspects should be investigated. It is the responsibility of the directors to take such steps as are reasonably open to them to prevent and detect fraud.

6. Money laundering

The growth of globalisation has created more opportunities for money laundering which governments and international bodies are trying to combat with legislation. In the UK, there are various offences relating to money laundering, including tipping off a money launderer (or suspected money launderer) and failing to report reasonable suspicions. Reporting in the UK should be via the MLRO (or NO) to the National Crime Agency.

Further study guidance

Question practice

Now try the following from the Further question practice bank [available in the digital edition of the workbook]:

Number			
Q49	Exam Section A	1	1 min
Q50	Exam Section A	2	2 mins
Q51	Exam Section A	1	1 min
Q52	Exam Section A	2	2 mins
Q53	Exam Section A	2	2 mins
Q54	Exam Section A	2	2 mins
Q55	Exam Section A	4	5 mins

Further reading

You should keep looking online to see if any new articles on fraud have been published.

Own research

Fraud and money laundering are (sadly) regularly in the news, so you should keep an active eye on the media for stories related to this. Here are some examples that are fairly recent (and one that is not!):

*   Wirecard
*   Patisserie Valerie
*   Lehman Brothers
*   Tesco
*   Enron

Activity answers

Activity 1: Sales fraud

The following are just three obvious suggestions, but others will exist:

(1) Generation of false invoices

(2) Overcharging customers for goods or services

(3) Selling goods to friends (with a promise of buying them back at a later date).

Activity 2: Fraud strategies

Dishonesty

Don't employ people with predispositions to **dishonesty**, if possible: undertake legitimate and appropriate background and CV checks when carrying out recruitment and selection. (The more opportunity for fraud there is in the job, the more carefully dishonesty should be screened.)

Motivation

Reduce **motivations** for fraud. This is highly subjective, but the organisation should give attention to such matters as ensuring equity in pay and rewards; monitoring employees for signs of financial difficulty and its possible causes (eg gambling addiction) and offering counselling and support where required; providing generally good and equitable working terms and conditions; and establishing clear rules and strong sanctions for fraudulent behaviour.

Opportunity

Reduce **opportunities** for fraud. This is the function of a range of internal checks and controls, separating duties so no one person has sole control over a system; requiring authorisations for expenses/timesheets, cheques, and so on; using data security measures such as passwords; security checks; identification on office equipment to deter theft; and so on.

Activity 3: Fraud behaviour

Here are some common examples of the type of behaviour that a fraudster would typically display:

- Secretive behaviour
- Extravagant lifestyle
- Reluctance to take holidays
- Refusal to share information
- Excessive working hours

Activity 4: Money laundering

Tipping off a suspected money launderer is an offence. Alerting the suspect would be likely to hamper any subsequent investigation by the authorities as the suspect would most likely destroy any incriminating evidence and the case against them would collapse.

Skills checkpoint 3

Approaching corporate governance questions

Chapter overview

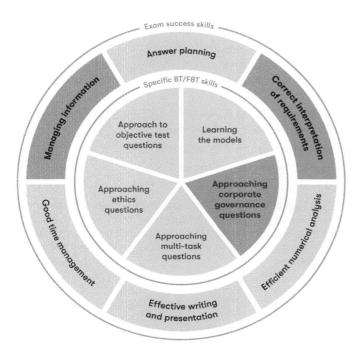

Introduction

Corporate governance is introduced in the BT/FBT exam. It is included in many of the subsequent ACCA exams, especially the auditing exams and the strategic business leader exam. The examiner has reported that candidates generally do well on the simpler knowledge based questions, but find the application type questions more difficult. This skills section therefore aims to improve your approaches to these questions. In this chapter we focus on the skills needed to answer the exams rather than covering the theory of corporate governance again. The skills covered here are transferable and could be applied to a number of other topics.

Corporate governance - key knowledge

There are quite a few principles or rules to learn in the syllabus relating to corporate governance. On the exam day itself, you may encounter a question which covers a particular detail that you can't remember. Remembering the following 'key points' of corporate governance may guide you to a more informed answer:

- **Agency problem** - the **directors of a company** (the agents) **act on behalf of the shareholders** and **other stakeholders** of a company (the principals). Their **objectives may conflict**. Corporate governance aims to ensure that the directors act in the interests of the stakeholders rather than in their own interests.

- Good corporate governance will mean that **no individual** or **group of individuals** becomes too powerful, because if they do they may make bad decisions. **Non-executive directors** are a key control to avoid this, by **challenging** and **scrutinising** the actions of the executive directors. The **roles of chair and chief executive should also be separated**, with the chair being a non-executive director.
- **Risk management** is a key issue of corporate governance. The **board of directors should take ultimate responsibility** for **managing the risks** that the company is taking on.
- The **audit committee** is **responsible** for the **system of internal controls** and **overseeing the internal and external auditors**. In order to allow auditors to discuss any concerns openly, the **committee should be made up entirely of independent non-executive directors**.
- The **remuneration committee** is responsible for setting the **remuneration policies** of the company. This committee should also be made up of **non-executive directors**, to avoid the situation where directors set their own pay.

Approach to questions

Exam questions on corporate governance could appear in both sections of the exam. In both sections, you may be given a short scenario. Typically, the situation in the scenario will challenge good corporate governance practices and you would be required to think about what should be done. A good approach to such questions is:

STEP 1 **Read the requirement.** What do you have to do? Be sure to note the instructions carefully, making sure you don't miss important words such as '**NOT**'. Don't read the options at this stage.

STEP 2 **Read through the scenario.** Think about the following as you read through it:
- Why does the situation present a threat for good corporate governance?
- What should/could be done to reduce the threat?

STEP 3 **Read the options:** (While there are many different types of OT question, most involve choosing one or more items). Are there any options that can be eliminated straight away? Perhaps they describe things that you know are not done in the real world, or perhaps they are unrealistic. After this, you will need to rank the remaining options in terms of which you think are the most likely, or most effective in achieving the corporate governance principles summarised above.

Exam success skills

The following question is an example of the sort of question you could see in your exam.

For this question, we will also focus on the following exam success skills:
- **Managing information.** Where there is information provided in the scenario you need to be able to absorb this quickly. Begin by reading the requirements so that you know what you are looking for in the scenario. While the scenario for each individual question may not look significant, given the number of questions you have to answer, any inefficiencies in reading will add up.
- **Correct interpretation of requirements.** Make sure that you note what you have to do carefully.
- **Good time management** - by actively reading the scenarios and knowing what you are looking for you will be using your exam time more effectively.

Skill activity

Question: Source: ACCA F1 examiner's report Dec 2014

Max is an independent non-executive director of PLK Company, a private company in which 75% of the equity is owned by members of one family. At a recent board meeting, Max was informed that the executives had entered into a one-year contract with VCV Company, a new supplier. Although the executives did not know this, Max's sister is an executive director of VCV Company.

Which of the following statements is correct?

○ Max should resign from the company as he can no longer be truly independent

○ Max should disclose his family connection with VCV Company immediately

○ Max needs to do nothing, as PLK Company is a private company

○ Max should have been consulted about the contract before it was signed

Applying the steps suggested above to this question:

B is the correct answer. C is incorrect as good corporate governance does not just apply to listed companies. In the case of PLK, 25% of the shares are owned by people who are not members of the family that owns the majority of the shares, and these shareholders would appreciate an independent non-executive director who would look after their interests.

STEP 1 The requirement. "Which of the following statements is correct?" All we know at the moment is that we will have to choose one statement. It is a multiple choice question. We don't read the options yet.

STEP 2 Read through the scenario.

- Is there a threat to good corporate governance? Max is an independent non-executive director. The fact that the company has entered into a contract with VCV could potentially threaten Max's independence, since Max's sister is an executive director of VCV. However, given that the contract has already been signed by the executive directors, without Max actually being aware of it does suggest that the contract has been made on normal commercial terms. The directors were unaware of Max's connection with VCV. It would NOT therefore appear to be a significant threat to Max's independence.

- What should be done to remove or reduce the threat? Let's assume that you don't know what should be done, so you will have to read the options and use a process of elimination to identify it.

STEP 3 Read the options:

(a) Max should resign from the company as he can no longer be truly independent

(b) Max should disclose his family connection with VCV Company immediately

(c) Max needs to do nothing, as PLK Company is a private company

(d) Max should have been consulted about the contract before it was signed

Are there any options that you can eliminate straight away?

- Option A would appear to be rather extreme. As discussed in Step 2, the contract would not appear to present a significant threat to Max's independence.

- Option D also appears unlikely. Contracts with suppliers are negotiated as part of the course of doing business. It would not usually be necessary to gain approval of commercial contracts from non-executive directors. The executive directors were not aware of Max's connection to VCV.

Having eliminated two options we are left with B and C. Intuitively, B would perhaps appear as the most sensible. By disclosing his family connection and presumably avoiding voting on any matters relating to the contract, should there be any, he can maintain his independence. So B would be the best guess.

B is the correct answer. C is incorrect as good corporate governance does not just apply to listed companies. In the case of PLK, 25% of the shares are owned by people who are not members of the family that owns the majority of the shares, and these shareholders would appreciate an independent non-executive director who would look after their interests.

Exam success skills diagnostic

Every time you complete a few questions, use the diagnostic below to assess how effectively you demonstrated the exam success skills in answering the questions. The table has been completed below for the above activity to give you an idea of how to complete the diagnostic.

Exam success skills	Your reflections/observations
Managing information	Did you read the requirements first? Reading the requirement before you read the scenario ensures that, when you read the scenario, you are focussed on what information you are looking for.
Correct interpretation of requirements	In the question above, there should have been little difficulty in interpreting what is required, but do ensure you read all requirements carefully.
Efficient numerical analysis	Not generally applicable to BT/FBT questions.
Good time management	On average you should be spending 1.2 minutes per mark. It does not make sense to time every question you do - some questions do take longer than this and some take less. Time yourself for groups of questions instead to give yourself an idea of whether you are working at the correct pace.
Most important action points to apply to your next question	

Summary

Being able to answer scenario-based questions which require application of your knowledge is important in the BT/FBT exam. Key skills to focus on throughout your studies will therefore include:

- As you read a scenario, ask yourself what the problem with the current situation is.
- What should be done about it?
- Read the options in the question and eliminate those that are clearly not correct.
- Look at the remaining options and choose which would be most likely based on your analysis of the scenario above.

12 Leading and managing

Learning outcomes

On completion of this chapter you should be able to:

	Syllabus reference no.
Define leadership, management and supervision and explain the distinction between these terms.	D1 (a)
Explain the nature of management. (a) Scientific/classical theories of management – Fayol, Taylor (b) The human relations school – Mayo (c) The functions of a manager – Mintzberg, Drucker	D1 (b)
Explain the areas of managerial authority and responsibility.	D1 (c)
Explain the situational, functional and contingency approaches to leadership with reference to the theories of Adair, Fiedler, Bennis, Kotter and Heifetz.	D1 (d)
Describe leadership styles and contexts using the models of Ashridge, and Blake and Mouton.	D1 (e)

Exam context

The first part of this chapter deals with the issues of management and considers a variety of different theories – you should note that the theories discussed in this chapter are noted specifically in the syllabus Study Guide, and hence are eminently examinable – and it's fair to say that the major challenge of this topic is learning the detail of the various theories. We then go on to consider the difference between managers and leaders. Popular exam topics include leadership style models, the difference between management and leadership and the difference between trait theories, style theories and contingency approaches. There were four questions in the specimen exam on topics covered in this chapter.

Chapter overview

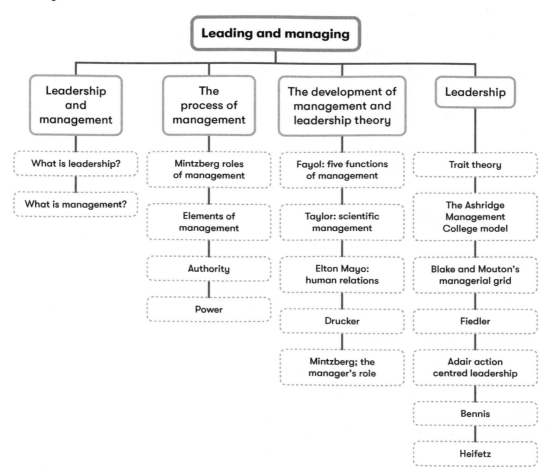

1 Leadership and management

1.1 What is leadership?

Leadership is the process of influencing others to work willingly towards goals, to the best of their capabilities, perhaps in a manner different to that which they would otherwise have chosen.

A leader exercises acts of influence frequently and persistently.

Key leadership skills include:

(a) Entrepreneurship

(b) Interpersonal skills

(c) Decision-making and problem solving

(d) Time management and personal organisation

(e) Self development

1.2 What is management?

Management is the process of getting activities completed efficiently and effectively, with and through other people.

> **Management:** Management is responsible for using the organisation's resources to meet its goals. It is accountable to the owners: shareholders in a business, or government in the public sector.

An organisation has been defined as 'a social arrangement for the controlled performance of collective goals.' This definition suggests the need for management.

(a) Objectives have to be set for the organisation.

(b) Somebody has to monitor progress and results to ensure that objectives are met.

(c) Somebody has to communicate and sustain corporate values, ethics and operating principles.

(d) Somebody has to look after the interests of the organisation's owners and other stakeholders.

Activity 1: Management structure

John, Paul, George and Ringo set up in business together as repairers of musical instruments. Each has contributed $5,000 as capital for the business. They are a bit uncertain as to how they should run the business and, when they discuss this in the pub, they decide that attention needs to be paid to planning what they do, reviewing what they do and controlling what they do.

Required

Suggest two ways in which John, Paul, George and Ringo can manage the business assuming no other personnel are recruited.

Solution

Different organisations have different structures for carrying out management functions. For example, some organisations have separate strategic planning departments. Others do not.

In a **private sector business**, managers act, ultimately, on behalf of shareholders. In practical terms, shareholders rarely interfere, as long as the business delivers profits year on year.

In a **public sector organisation**, management acts on behalf of the government. Politicians in a democracy are in turn accountable to the electorate. More of the objectives of a public sector organisation might be set by the 'owners' – ie the government – rather than by the management. The government might also tell senior management to carry out certain policies or plans, thereby restricting management's discretion.

Essential reading

See Chapter 12 Section 1 of the Essential reading for more detail on leading and managing.

The Essential reading is available as an Appendix of the digital edition of the Workbook.

2 The process of management

2.1 Mintzberg: three key management roles:

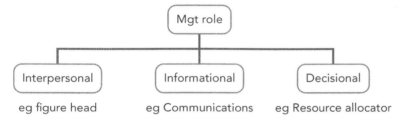

We shall be looking at this in more detail in Section 3, but for now the important point is to be aware of the range of tasks that a manager has to take care of.

2.2 Elements of management

A manager is an integral part of the organisational structure and therefore has:

(a) Authority – the **right** to do something
(b) Responsibility – the **obligation** to get something done
(c) Accountability – the **readiness to accept responsibility**, judgement by others
(d) Power – the **ability** to do something.

Delegation enables management to allocate **responsibility** and **authority** to subordinates, whilst retaining overall accountability.

It is the role of the manager to **take responsibility** and **organise people** to get things done. This involves the use of **authority** and **power** and implies a hierarchy in which power is delegated downwards while accountability is rendered upwards.

These elements are important, and we need to go into these in more detail in the following sections. Make sure you understand the concepts and can differentiate between them.

2.3 Authority

> **Authority:** The right to do something; in an organisation it is the right of a manager to require a subordinate to do something in order to achieve the goals of the organisation.

A person's (or office's) authority can come from a variety of sources, including from above (supervisors) or below (if the position is elected). Managerial authority thus has three aspects.

- Making decisions within the scope of one's own managerial authority
- Assigning tasks to subordinates
- Expecting and requiring satisfactory performance of these tasks by subordinates

Weber (1947) put the kind of authority we see in organisations into a wider context, proposing that there were three ways in which people could acquire legitimate power (or authority).

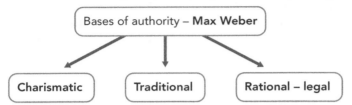

(a) **Charismatic authority** arises from the personality of the leader and their ability to inspire devotion through, for example, sanctity, heroism

(b) **Traditional authority** rests on established belief in the importance of immemorial tradition and the status it confers.

(c) **Rational-legal authority** arises from the working of accepted normative rules, such as are found in organisations and democratic governments.

2.4 Responsibility and accountability

Responsibility is the liability of a person to discharge duties. Responsibility is the obligation to do something; in an organisation, it is the duty of an official to carry out assigned tasks.

With responsibility, we must associate **accountability**. Managers are accountable to their superiors for their actions and are obliged to report to their superiors how well they have exercised the authority delegated to them.

Delegation of authority occurs in an organisation where a superior **gives a subordinate** the **discretion** to make decisions within a certain sphere of influence. This can only occur if the superior initially possesses the authority to delegate.

When a superior delegates authority to a subordinate, the **subordinate is accountable** to the superior. However, the superior remains fully accountable to their superiors; responsibility and accountability cannot be abdicated by delegation.

As well as being essential for running an organisation, **delegation** brings a number of other **benefits**.

(a) **Training**. Subordinates gain experience of problems and responsibility, which helps to prepare them for promotion and contributes to the avoidance of crises of management succession.

(b) **Motivation**. Herzberg found that responsibility was an important factor in job satisfaction and motivation.

(c) **Assessment**. Subordinates' performance in relation to delegated responsibility can be used as a measure of their need for further training and experience and their readiness for promotion.

(d) **Decisions**. Delegation brings decisions closer to the situations that require them, potentially improving them by having them made by those with most knowledge of the problems and factors involved.

Activity 2: Delegation

You have a large complex spreadsheet which requires a large amount of data to be manually input onto the spreadsheet on a monthly basis.

Required

Suggest three reasons why you may not want to delegate this piece of work.

Solution

Real life example

Probably the most often mentioned example of a leader with charismatic authority is Alexander the Great. He was personally able to motivate his army through his actions and behaviour because he, like them, was a soldier – his men trusted him and supported him through a long, bloody and ultimately successful campaign against the Persian Empire. The chief drawback of charismatic authority is that it is very difficult to pass onto anyone else; within thirty years of his death, his vast empire stretching from the Mediterranean to India was almost gone.

Bringing things up to date, Queen Elizabeth II became head of the United Kingdom at the young age of 27 because she was the eldest daughter of a king who left no male heir, and as such, she inherited his title, and therefore had traditional authority.

An elected government would be said to have rational legal authority, if it has followed the accepted normative rules. A government that has rigged an election to win would be lacking in authority and would find it more difficult to impose any form of control over the population of that country. Notice that in this situation, the government, lacking authority, would rely instead on *power* to influence the people, perhaps through intimidation or coercion.

2.5 Power

KEY TERM

Power: Power is distinct from authority but is often associated with it. While authority is the right to do something, power is the ability to do it.

2.5.1 Sources of power – French and Raven

French and Raven (1959) identified the following sources of power within organisations:

Power	
Physical power	This is the power of superior force.
Resource power	This is the control over resources which are valued by the individual or group.

Power	
Coercive power	This is power based on fear of punishment.
Reward power	This is related to resource power. Senior managers may have the power to grant pay increases to subordinates.
Position power or legitimate power	This is the power which is associated with a particular job in an organisation. It is more or less the same as authority.
Expert power	This is power which is based on expertise, although it only works if others acknowledge that expertise.
Referent power	This power lies in the personal qualities of the individual.
Negative power	This is the use of disruptive attitudes and behaviour to stop things from happening.

Activity 3: Power

What kind of power is used by a manager who promises a pay increase if productivity rises?

- O Position power
- O Resource power
- O Reward power
- O Referent power

Essential reading

See Chapter 12 Section 2 of the Essential reading for more detail on the process of management.

The Essential reading is available as an Appendix of the digital edition of the Workbook.

3 Development of management and leadership theory

We now move on to consider a number of writers who have addressed the issue of how best to manage workers. Notice that here we are discussing *theories* – it is notoriously difficult to forecast how people will react in a certain set of circumstances, and many theories have been developed to explain employees' motivations and expectations in the workplace. Below, we begin by giving a timeline showing when some of the most influential theories were developed.

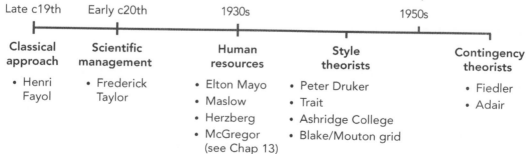

Late c19th	Early c20th	1930s		1950s
Classical approach	Scientific management	Human resources	Style theorists	Contingency theorists
• Henri Fayol	• Frederick Taylor	• Elton Mayo • Maslow • Herzberg • McGregor (see Chap 13)	• Peter Druker • Trait • Ashridge College • Blake/Mouton grid	• Fiedler • Adair

BPP
LEARNING
MEDIA

We shall look through some of these theories in more detail. These theorists are usually categorised under three headings:

(a) Classical (or Scientific) theories of management – (i) Fayol, and (ii) Taylor
(b) Human relations school – Mayo
(c) The functions of managers – (i) Drucker and (ii) Mintzberg

3.1 Henri Fayol: five functions of management

Fayol (1967) classified five **functions of management** which apply to any organisation.

Function	
Planning	Determining **objectives**, and strategies, policies, programmes and procedures for achieving those objectives, for the organisation and its sub-units
Organising	Establishing a **structure of tasks** which need to be performed to achieve the goals of the organisation; grouping these tasks into jobs for individuals or teams; allocating jobs to sections and departments; **delegating** authority to carry out the jobs; and providing **systems of information** and communication, for the co-ordination of activities
Commanding	Giving **instructions** to subordinates to carry out tasks, for which the manager has authority (to make decisions) and responsibility (for performance)
Co-ordinating	**Harmonising** the goals and activities of individuals and groups within the organisation. Management must reconcile differences in approach, effort, interest and timing in favour of overall (or 'super-ordinate') shared goals.
Controlling	**Measuring** and **correcting** the activities of individuals and groups, to ensure that their performance is in accordance with plans. Deviations from plans are identified and corrected

You may be struck by two key 'omissions' from Fayol's classification, from a more modern viewpoint.

(a) **'Motivating'** is not mentioned. It is assumed that subordinates will carry out tasks when 'commanded' or instructed to do so, regardless of whether or how far they may 'want' to.

(b) **'Communicating'** is not mentioned, although it is implied by the process of commanding (giving instructions), co-ordinating (sharing information) and controlling (giving feedback).

Fayol's classification reflects the classical view that saw the act of management as the controlling of resources and processes. The idea that management is an **interpersonal process**, involving communication and the ability to influence and motivate, is a more recent concept.

3.2 F W Taylor: scientific management

Frederick W Taylor pioneered the scientific management movement in the US.

Taylor was an engineer and sought the most efficient methods.

He was among the first to argue that management should be based on 'well recognised, clearly defined and fixed principles, instead of depending on more or less hazy ideas.' Taylor was a very skilled engineer and took an engineering efficiency approach to management.

The principles of scientific management (*Taylor, 1911*) include the following.

(a) The development of a true science of work. 'All knowledge which had hitherto been kept in the heads of workmen should be gathered and recorded by management. Every single subject, large and small, becomes the question for scientific investigation, for reduction to law.'

(b) The scientific selection and progressive development of workers. Workers should be carefully trained and given jobs to which they are best suited.

BPP LEARNING MEDIA

(c) The application of techniques to plan, measure and control work for maximum productivity

(d) The constant and intimate co-operation between management and workers: 'the relations between employers and men form without question the most important part of this art'

In practice, scientific management techniques included the following key elements.

(a) Work study techniques were used to analyse tasks and establish the most efficient methods to use. No variation was permitted in the way work was done, since the aim was to use the 'one best way'.

(b) Planning and doing were separated. It was assumed that the persons who were intellectually equipped to do a particular type of work were probably unlikely to be able to plan it to the best advantage: this was the manager's job.

(c) Jobs were micro-designed: divided into single, simple task components which formed a whole specialised 'job' for an individual, rather than permitting an individual to perform whole or part-task processes. (Task 'meaning' and 'significance', now considered essential to job satisfaction, had not yet emerged as important values.)

(d) Workers were paid incentives on the basis of acceptance of the new methods and output norms; the new methods greatly increased productivity and profits. Pay was assumed to be the only important motivating force.

Scientific management as practised by Taylor and contemporaries such as Gilbreth and Gantt was very much about manual work. However, elements of scientific management are still practised today, whenever there is a concern for productivity and efficiency.

3.3 Elton Mayo: human relations

The main principles of the Human Relations school (*Mayo 1933*) are:

(a) Individuals seek more than financial satisfaction from their jobs.

(b) Individuals can often perform better if they are allowed control over their work.

(c) Group interaction is an important element in determining the behaviour of an organisation.

The human relations school of theorists has made a number of contributions to management thought including:

(a) There are benefits in looking after and involving employees.

(b) Individual workers cannot be treated in isolation but must be seen as members of a group.

(c) The need to belong to a group and have status within it is more important than monetary incentives or good physical working conditions.

(d) Informal groups exercise a strong influence on worker behaviour.

(e) Supervisors and managers must manage group operations rather than individuals.

Real life example

Mayo and his colleagues first thought that the level of lighting influenced output, so to test this out, they increased the level of lighting in one of the production rooms of a factory, with the result that productivity increased significantly. To have a comparison, they then reduced the lighting to a level below the original level, expecting that output would fall.

It did not.

It stayed high. This was a shock, and so for completeness, they returned the lighting back to the level it was before; the output stayed high.

Finally it was realised that the employees weren't performing more effectively because of the lighting – it was because they were aware they were being studied. Not out of fear of being found to be lazy, but because they felt special – management was interested in them. *That* was the motivator.

3.4 Style theories

Writers in the last fifty years have taken a more **flexible view**:

- The search for efficiency continues with work study and industrial engineering, whilst specific techniques have been developed for project management.
- Human relations theory has been expanded through industrial psychology.
- Much writing has focussed on the managers' task.

We shall now look at the work of a number of writers in this area, and again, it is important that you know what they were talking about. If there is a diagram given, then it is recommended that you learn it.

3.5 Drucker

Peter Drucker, an Austrian professor, believed that management has three basic functions (*Drucker 1993*):

(a) Managing a business. The purposes of the business are:

- To create a customer
- Innovation

(b) Managing managers. The requirements here are:

- Management by objectives (MbO)
- Proper structure of managers' jobs
- Creating the right spirit in the organisation
- Making a provision for the managers of tomorrow
- Arriving at sound principles of organisation structure

(c) Managing worker and work

A manager's performance in all areas of management, including management of the business, can be enhanced by a study of the principles of management, the acquisition of organised knowledge (eg management techniques) and systematic self-assessment.

Drucker suggested that management could also be broken down into five categories:

Setting objectives for the organisation. Managers decide what the objectives of the organisation should be and quantify the targets of achievement for each objective. They must then communicate these targets to other people in the organisation.

Organising the work. The work to be done in the organisation must be divided into manageable activities and manageable jobs. The jobs must be integrated into a formal organisation structure, and people must be selected to do the jobs.

Motivating employees and communicating information to them to enable them to do their work.

The job of **measurement**. Management must:

(a) Establish objectives or yardsticks of performance for all personnel

(b) Analyse actual performance, appraise it against the objectives or yardsticks which have been set, and analyse the comparison

(c) Communicate the findings and explain their significance both to subordinate employees and to superiors

Developing people. The manager 'brings out what is in them or he stifles them. He strengthens their integrity or he corrupts them'.

Every manager performs all five functions listed above, no matter how good or bad a manager they are. However, a bad manager performs these functions badly, whereas a good manager performs them well. Unlike Fayol, Drucker emphasised the importance of communication in the functions of management.

3.6 Mintzberg: the manager's role

Henry Mintzberg described managerial roles, arguing that management is a disjointed, non-systematic activity. *Mintzberg (1989)* did a study of a small sample of US corporations. He suggests that in their daily working lives managers fulfil three types of managerial role.

Role category		
Interpersonal Based on manager's formal authority or position	**Figurehead** (or ceremonial) **Leader** Liaison	A large part of a Chief Executive's time is spent representing the company at dinners, conferences, and so on. Hiring, firing and training staff, motivating employees, and reconciling individual goals with the objectives of the organisation. Making contacts outside the vertical chain of command. Some managers spend up to half their meeting time with their peers rather than with their subordinates.
Informational Based on managers' access to: • Upward and downward channels • Many external contacts	**Monitor** **Spokesperson** Disseminator	The manager monitors the environment, and receives information from subordinates, superiors and peers in other departments. Much of this information is of an informal nature, derived from the manager's network of contacts. The manager provides information on behalf of the unit and/or organisation to interested parties. The manager disseminates relevant information to subordinates.
Decisional Based on the manager's formal authority and access to information, which allow him or her to take decisions relating to the work of the department as a whole.	**Entrepreneur** Disturbance handler **Resource allocator** **Negotiator**	A manager initiates projects to improve the department or to help it react to a changed environment. A manager has to respond to unexpected pressures, taking decisions when there is deviation from the plan. A manager takes decisions relating to the mobilisation and distribution of limited resources to achieve objectives. Both inside and outside the organisation, negotiation takes up a great deal of management time.

Mintzberg's research challenged the classical view of the manager as separate to, or above, the routine demands of day-to-day work.

(a) Managers are not always able to be reflective, systematic planners.

(b) Managerial work is disjointed and discontinuous.

(c) Managers do have routine duties to perform, especially of a ceremonial nature (receiving important guests) or related to authority (signing cheques as a signatory) – contrary to the myth that all routine work is done by juniors.

(d) Managers prefer verbal and informal information to the formal output of management information systems. Verbal information is 'hotter' and probably easier to grasp.

(e) Management cannot be reduced to a science or a profession. According to Mintzberg, managerial processes cannot be analysed scientifically or codified into an examinable body of theory.

Mintzberg states that general management is, in practice, a matter of judgement and intuition, gained from experience in particular situations rather than from abstract principles. 'Fragmentation and verbal communication' characterise the manager's work.

Activity 4: Developing people

Who suggested that a primary managerial role is 'developing people'?

O   Handy

O   Taylor

O   Herzberg

O   Drucker

4 Leadership

There are three basic 'schools of leadership theory':

School	Comment
Trait theories	Based on analysing the personality characteristics or preferences of successful leaders
Style theories	Based on the view that leadership is an interpersonal process whereby different leader behaviours influence people in different ways. More or less effective patterns of behaviour (or 'styles') can therefore be adopted
Contingency theories	Based on the belief that there is no 'one best way' of leading, but that effective leaders adapt their behaviour to the specific and changing variables in the leadership context: the nature of the task, the personalities of team members, the organisation culture, and so on

4.1 Trait theory

Trait theories of leadership attempt to identify the distinguishing characteristics of successful leaders. Most studies single out the following traits:

(a) Intelligence – above average but not genius level

(b) Initiative – independence and inventiveness, the capacity to perceive a need for action and the urge to do it

(c) Self-assurance

(d) The helicopter factor – ability to rise above the particulars of a situation and perceive it in relation to the overall environment

Other studies mention: enthusiasm, sociability, integrity, courage, imagination, decisiveness, determination, energy, faith, virility, good health, above average height or well below it.

In general, criticisms of trait theory are:

(a) Possession of all traits becomes an impossible ideal.

(b) Too many exceptions to the rule.

(c) If reduced to the useful minimum they become at best necessary but not sufficient

(d) Traits are not well defined and not much use in practice for recruitment of leaders.

Trait theory has been more or less discredited.

(a) The premise that certain traits (or qualities) are absolutely necessary for effective leadership has never been substantiated.

(b) The lists of traits proposed for leaders have been vast, varied and contradictory.

(c) Trait theories ignore the complexities of the leadership situation, and not everybody with leadership 'traits' turns out to be a good leader.

Real life example

One trait that is often claimed for leaders is that they are tall; of the thirty presidential elections between 1900 and 2016, the taller candidate won two thirds of the time. However, there are notable exceptions to the theory that leaders should be tall – Napoleon Bonaparte was only average height, Winston Churchill was only five foot six, Nicolas Sarkozy is five foot five. That's the trouble with Trait theory – no matter which trait you use, there are always lots of exceptions.

4.2 Style theories of leadership

There are various classifications of leadership style. Although the labels and definitions of styles vary, style models are often talking (broadly) about the same thing – a continuum of behaviours from:

(a) Wholly task-focused, directive leadership behaviours (representing high leader control) at one extreme; and

(b) Wholly people-focused, supportive/relational leadership behaviours (representing high subordinate discretion) at the other.

Key style models include:

- The **Ashridge Model**: tells, sells, consults, joins
- **Blake and Mouton's Managerial Grid**: concern for task, concern for people

4.2.1 The Ashridge Management College model

This model distinguishes four different styles:

Tight   **Loose**

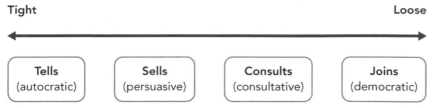

(a) **Tells (autocratic)**

The 'tells' style is where the **leader makes all of the decisions** and issues instructions which must be obeyed without question. Quick decisions can be made when speed is required but it does not encourage initiative and commitment from subordinates.

(b) **Sells (persuasive)**

This style is where the leader still makes all of the decisions but believes that **subordinates have to be motivated** to accept them and carry them out properly. Employees are made aware of the reasons for decisions but they may not accept the decisions.

(c) **Consults**

This style is where the **leader confers with subordinates** and takes their views into account but retains the final say. This encourages motivation and employees can contribute their knowledge but it may take much longer to reach decisions.

(d) **Joins (democratic)**

This style is where the leader and followers make the decision on the **basis of consensus**. This can provide high motivation and commitment from employees but decision making might become a very long process.

The Ashridge studies found that:

(a) In an ideal world, **subordinates preferred the 'consults' style** of leadership.

(b) **People led by a 'consults'** manager had the **most favourable attitude** to their work.

(c) **Most** subordinates **feel they are being led by a 'tells' or 'sells'** manager.

(d) In practice, **consistency** was **far more important** to subordinates than any particular style. The least favourable attitudes were found among subordinates who were unable to perceive any consistent style of leadership in their superiors.

Essential reading

See Chapter 12 Section 3 of the Essential reading for more detail on management theory.

The Essential reading is available as an Appendix of the digital edition of the Workbook.

Activity 5: Leadership style

Consider two situations:

(1) Due to external factors, the budget for your department has been reduced and 25% of your staff must be made redundant. Records of each employee's performance are available.

(2) There is a recurring administrative problem which is minor, but irritating to everyone in your department. Several solutions have been tried in the past, but without success. You think you have a workable remedy , but unknown problems may arise, depending on the decisions made.

Required

Suggest an appropriate style of leadership for each of the two situations. Think about your reasons for choosing each style in terms of the results you are trying to achieve, the need to secure commitment from others, and potential difficulties with both.

4.2.2 Blake and Mouton's managerial grid

Blake and Mouton's managerial grid (*Blake et al. 1964*) looks at the two basic criteria for leadership:

- Concern for task being achieved
- Concern for people/staff carrying out the task

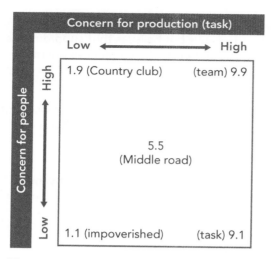

The extreme cases shown on the grid are:

(a) 1.1 **impoverished:** the manager is lazy, showing little interest in either staff or work.

(b) 1.9 **country club:** the manager is attentive to staff needs and has developed satisfying relationships. However, there is little attention paid to achieving results.

(c) 9.1 **task management:** almost total concentration on achieving results. People's needs are virtually ignored.

(d) 5.5 **middle of the road** or the **dampened pendulum:** adequate performance through balancing the necessity to get the task done with importance of team morale.

(e) 9.9 **team: high** work accomplishment through 'leading' committed people who identify themselves with the organisational aims.

The managerial grid was intended as an appraisal and management development tool. It recognises that a balance is required between concern for task and concern for people, and that a high degree of both is possible (and highly effective) at the same time.

 ## Activity 6: Managerial Grid

Which position on Blake and Mouton's grid do you think each of the following statements represents?

Statement	Position on grid
I attend because it is expected. I either go along with the majority position or avoid expressing my views.	
I try to come up with good ideas and push for a decision as soon as I can get a majority behind me. I don't mind stepping on people if it helps a sound decision.	
I like to be able to support what my boss wants and to recognise the merits of individual effort. When conflict rises, I do a good job of restoring harmony.	

4.3 Contingency theories

Contingency theories see effective leadership as being dependent upon a number of variable factors; there are a number or theorists in this area whose work is specifically mentioned in the syllabus and we look at these in turn here – perhaps the best approach would be to learn the key variables that each of the theorists focuses on in order to be able to recognise which one is being referred to in a question. While it is perhaps the case that Fiedler and Adair are the most widely known of the contingency theorists, it would be unwise to ignore the others, as they are specifically mentioned in the syllabus.

4.3.1 Fiedler

Fiedler (1967) identified two variables in leadership:

- Favourability of the situation for the manager
- Proximity of manager to their team

Where the 'favourability of situation to manager' (favourable, unfavourable or in the middle) determines the 'psychological proximity of manager' to their team (close or distant)

- If the situation for the manager is in the extremes the manager needs to be distant from their team, eg things are going really well, the manager should adopt a distant stance, or may be accused of favouritism when give out bonus.

  Or if things going really badly and need to make employees redundant, then better to be distant.

- Only if the situation is in the middle does the manager benefit from being close to team. For example, motivating them to meet targets which are almost in reach.

Situational factors include:

- Task structure
- Power of the leader
- Trust

4.3.2 John Adair - action centred leadership

The 'action-centred' or 'functional' leadership model *(Adair, 1973)* is part of the contingency school of thought, because it sees the leadership process in a context made up of three interrelated variables: task needs, the individual needs of group members and the needs of the group as a whole. These needs must be examined in the light of the whole situation, which dictates the relative priority that must be given to each of the three sets of needs.

Effective leadership is a process of identifying and acting on that priority, exercising a relevant cluster of roles to meet the various needs.

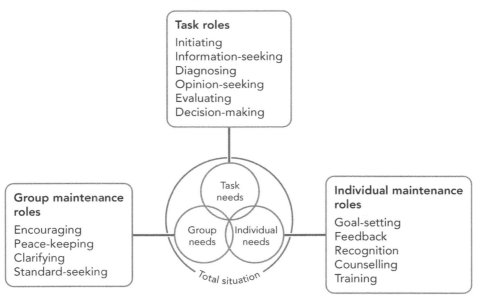

Adair's theory is often known as 'action centred leadership'. Action in one area will impact the other areas. Managers must therefore balance their attention between the three variables.

Managers need to develop their leadership skills to:

(a) Energise and support change

(b) Secure commitment from their staff

(c) Set direction

(d) Develop people

4.3.3 Bennis

Warren Bennis puts forward some specific differences between the role of the manager and the role of the leader.

(a) The manager administers and maintains, by focusing on systems and controls and the short term.

(b) The leader innovates, focuses on people and inspires trust, and holds a long-term view.

As a further distinction, Bennis distinguishes between the manager as someone who 'does things right' and the leader who 'does the right thing'.

Bennis studied leadership by examining leaders of every description in the hope of finding some common characteristics and concluded that there is no one right way to lead, but it does set out common competencies displayed by leaders. *Bennis (1985)* calls them:

(a) The management of attention: a compelling cause or vision, to give focus

(b) The management of meaning: the ability to communicate

(c) The management of trust: being consistent and honest

(d) The management of self: being aware of personal weaknesses and strengths

Other tasks of the leader that Bennis sees as important are:

(a) Constantly reminding people why their work is important

(b) Creating an atmosphere of trust

(c) Encouraging curiosity and risk taking in the organisation culture

(d) Fostering an atmosphere of 'hope' which can be particularly helpful when things go wrong

Bennis believes that leadership in the modern age is a shared task, with power spread around rather than centralised. It could be that the most important role of modern leaders is deciding who will be in their teams.

4.3.4 Heifetz: dispersed leadership

This approach recognises the importance of social relations, the need for a leader to be accepted and the fact that nobody will be an ideal leader in every circumstance. Also referred to as 'informal' or 'emergent', it proposes that individuals at all organisational levels can exert a 'leadership influence'.

Heifetz (1994) distinguishes between the exercise of 'leadership' and the exercise of 'authority'. This separates leadership from the formal organisational hierarchy and traditional positions of 'power'. The leader can only be identified by examining relationships with the 'followers' in the group – they could quite easily be someone who 'emerges', rather than someone who has been predefined as the leader from the outset.

This approach is more sociological and political in its basis than traditional management thinking, drawing as it does upon the prevailing organisational culture and context. A leader's individual qualities are less important than the leadership process, and the relationships created and sustained within it.

Essential reading

See Chapter 12 Sections 3 of the Essential reading for more detail on Leadership.

The Essential reading is available as an Appendix of the digital edition of the Workbook.

Chapter summary

Leading and managing

Leadership and management

What is leadership?
- Entrepreneurship
- Interpersonal skills
- Decision making and problem solving
- Time management and personal organisation
- Self development

What is management?
- Set objectives
- Monitor progress and results
- Corporate values
- Interests of owners and stakeholders

The process of management

Mintzberg roles of management
- Interpersonal
- Informational
- Decisional

Elements of management
- Authority
- Responsibility
- Accountability
- Power

Authority
- Charismatic authority
- Traditional authority
- Rational legal authority
- Responsibility and accountability

Power
- Physical
- Resource
- Coercive
- Reward
- Legitimate
- Expert
- Referent
- Negative

The development of management and leadership theory

Fayol: five functions of management
- Planning
- Organising
- Commanding
- Co-ordinating
- Controlling

Taylor: scientific management
- Development of science of work
- Scientific selection and development
- Techniques to plan, measure and control work
- Constant co-operation between management and workers

Elton Mayo: human relations
- More than financial satisfaction
- Control over work
- Group interaction

Drucker
- Objective setting
- Work organisation
- Motivation
- Measuring performance and control
- Developing people

Mintzberg; the manager's role
- Interpersonal
- Informational
- Decisional

Leadership

Trait theory
- Aim to identify distinguishing characteristics of successful leaders
- Many exceptions to rules so not useful

The Ashridge Management College model
- Tells
- Sells
- Consults
- Joins

Blake and Mouton's managerial grid
- Two basic criteria concern for task and concern for people
- Extreme cases:
  - Impoverished
  - Country club
  - Task management
  - Team

Fiedler
- Task structure
- Power of the leader
- Trust

Adair action centred leadership
- Needs of the task
- Needs of the individual
- Needs of the group

Bennis
- Manager v leader

Heifetz
- Distinguishes between leader and authority
- Leaders may emerge from group

BPP
LEARNING
MEDIA

Knowledge diagnostic

1. Management

Management is the process of **getting things done**. Leadership on the other hand is about providing **direction** and **influencing** others to follow that direction. Supervisors are lower level managers who are more hands on and **day-to-day** and are less likely to have line responsibility for staff.

2. Mintzberg's managerial functions

Mintzberg identifies managerial functions as interpersonal, informational and decisional roles. We can distinguish **authority, responsibility, accountability** and **power.** Ideally they should all coincide however that is not always the case.

3. Delegation

Delegation is the process of passing down responsibility and authority whilst retaining accountability

4. Development of management and leadership theory

Management theory has developed over time. Classical – Fayol's Management functions; Planning, Organising, Commanding, Coordinating and Controlling. Scientific – Taylor's four principles. Human Relations – Elton Mayo (emphasised group dynamics and concern for individual motivation).

Style – Drucker's three basic functions

5. Leadership theory

Trait Theory which looks at a wide range of personality factors and so has had much criticism.

Style – Ashridge (tell, sell, consult and join), and **Blake & Mouton's** grid.

Contingency theory – Fiedler (situation and proximity) and **Adair** (task, group and individual). This approach suggests that the appropriate style depends on a range of factors.

Further study guidance

Question practice

Now try the following from the Further question practice bank [available in the digital edition of the workbook]:

Number			
Q56	Exam Section A	2	2 mins
Q57	Exam Section A	2	2 mins
Q58	Exam Section A	2	2 mins
Q59	Exam Section A	2	2 mins
Q60	Exam Section A	2	2 mins

Further reading

There is an article on the ACCA website entitled 'Theories of leadership style' that is relevant to material in this chapter. You are strongly advised to read this article in full as part of your preparation for the FBT exam.

Activity answers

Activity 1: Management structure

The purpose of this exercise has been to get you to separate the issues of management functions from organisational structure and hierarchy. John, Paul, George and Ringo have a number of choices. Here are some extreme examples.

(1) All the management activities are the job of one person.

   In this case, Paul, for example, could plan, direct and control the work and the other three would do the work.

(2) Division of management tasks between individuals could be carried out (repairing drums **and** ensuring plans are adhered to would be Ringo's job, and so on).

(3) Management by committee. All of them could sit down and work out the plan together, etc. In a small business with equal partners this is likely to be most effective.

Activity 2: Delegation

Reasons to delegate:

- Fear of being undermined if the junior discovers a quicker way to input the data
- Frustration – quicker to do it yourself
- Lack of confidence in a junior's ability
- Loss of power, whilst not the biggest issue in this example, in certain situations the manager may not like to relinquish power over this spreadsheet.

(Only three were required)

Activity 3: Power

The correct answer is: Reward power

Reward power is an aspect of resource power so, while Option 2 is not incorrect, it is not as good an answer as Option 3.

Activity 4: Developing people

The correct answer is: Drucker

Activity 5: Leadership style

Appropriate style of leadership:

(1) You may have to 'tell' here: nobody is going to like the idea and, since each person will have their own interests at heart, you are unlikely to reach consensus. You could attempt to 'sell', if you can see a positive side to the change in particular cases: opportunities for retraining, say.

(2) You could 'consult' here: explain your remedy to staff and see whether they can suggest potential problems. They may be in a position to offer solutions – and, since the problem affects them too, they should be committed to solving it.

Activity 6: Managerial Grid

Statement, position on grid:

Statement	Position on grid
I attend because it is expected. I either go along with the majority position or avoid expressing my views.	1.1: low task, low people

Statement	Position on grid
I try to come up with good ideas and push for a decision as soon as I can get a majority behind me. I don't mind stepping on people if it helps a sound decision.	9.1: high task, low people
I like to be able to support what my boss wants and to recognise the merits of individual effort. When conflict rises, I do a good job of restoring harmony.	1.9 high people, low task

13

Recruitment and selection

Learning outcomes

On completion of this chapter you should be able to:

	Syllabus reference no.
Explain the importance of effective recruitment and selection to the organisation.	D2 (a)
Describe the recruitment and selection process and explain the stages in this process.	D2 (b)
Describe the roles of those involved in the recruitment and selection processes.	D2 (c)
Describe the methods through which organisations seek to meet their recruitment needs.	D2 (d)
Explain the advantages and disadvantages of different recruitment and selection methods.	D2 (e)
Explain the purposes and benefits of diversity and equal opportunities policies within the human resources plan.	D2 (f)
Explain the practical steps that an organisation may take to ensure the effectiveness of its diversity and equal opportunities policy.	D2 (g)

Exam Context

This part of the syllabus is a rich source of potential questions. There were two questions from the specimen exam relating to this topic.

Chapter overview

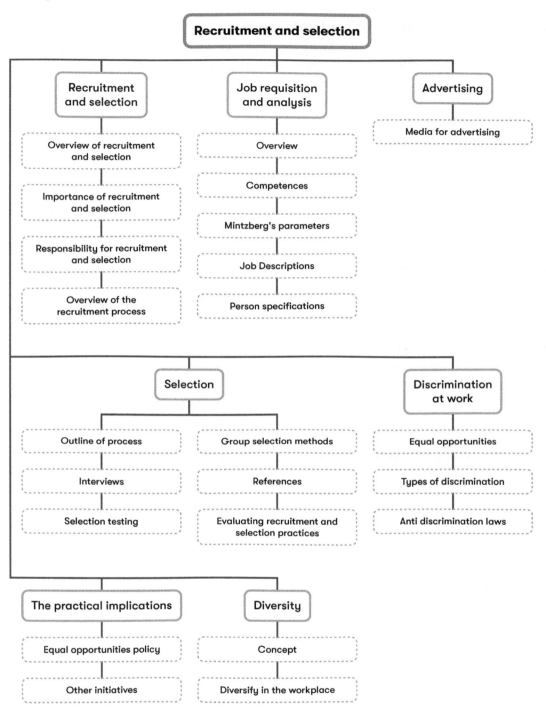

Recruitment and selection

- Recruitment and selection
  - Overview of recruitment and selection
  - Importance of recruitment and selection
  - Responsibility for recruitment and selection
  - Overview of the recruitment process

- Job requisition and analysis
  - Overview
  - Competences
  - Mintzberg's parameters
  - Job Descriptions
  - Person specifications

- Advertising
  - Media for advertising

- Selection
  - Outline of process
  - Interviews
  - Selection testing
  - Group selection methods
  - References
  - Evaluating recruitment and selection practices

- Discrimination at work
  - Equal opportunities
  - Types of discrimination
  - Anti discrimination laws

- The practical implications
  - Equal opportunities policy
  - Other initiatives

- Diversity
  - Concept
  - Diversify in the workplace

BPP LEARNING MEDIA

1 Recruitment and selection

1.1 Overview of recruitment and selection

The aim of the recruitment and selection process is to obtain the **quantity and quality of employees** needed to fulfil the organisation's objectives. It comprises three main stages:

(a) Defining the requirements

(b) Attracting applicants

(c) Selecting the right candidates

Recruitment : The part of the process concerned with finding applicants: it is a positive action by management, going into the labour market (internal and external), communicating opportunities and information, and generating interest.

Selection: The part of the employee resourcing process which involves choosing between applicants for jobs: it is largely a 'negative' process, eliminating unsuitable applicant.

1.2 Importance of recruitment and selection

Human resources management (HRM) believes that employees are a scarce and crucial resource and so recruitment and training issues are key to achieving the organisation's strategy.

- There may be skills shortages in key areas
- In modern "knowledge based" economies, people with the right aptitudes are essential.

Detailed **human resource planning** defines what resources the organisation needs to meet its objectives, and what sources of labour (internal and external) are available. The organisation's skill requirements may be met through recruitment – but there may also be plans for reducing staff numbers, redeployment, training and development, promotion, retention (to reduce loss of skills through staff turnover), and so on.

1.3 Responsibility for recruitment and selection

Numerous people may be included in the recruitment and selection process:

(a) Senior managers (for senior positions and HR planning)

(b) Human Resources (HR) department

(c) Line managers

(d) Recruitment consultants

Activity 1: Recruitment consultants

Suggest three advantages and three disadvantages of using external recruitment consultants.

Solution

1.4 Overview of the recruitment process

The recruitment process can be summarised by the following diagram:

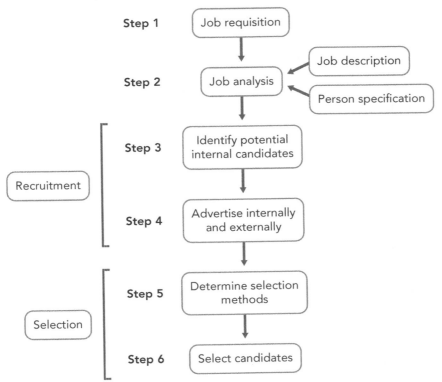

2 Job requisition and analysis

2.1 Overview

Job requisition is a process to ensure all vacancies are valid and authorised.

Job analysis is the process of collecting, analysing and setting out information about the content of jobs. This leads to two documents:

- **Job description** – tasks and duties, skills and knowledge
- **Person specification** – personal attributes required of job-holder

2.2 Competences

Competences are commonly used during the process of defining job descriptions:

KEY
TERM

> **Competence:** An individual's capacity that leads to behaviour that meets the job demands within the parameters of the organisational environment and that, in turn, brings about desired results.

Different categories of competence include:

- Behavioural/ personal - eg ability to relate well to others
- Work based/ occupational competences - eg ability to produce financial statements
- Generic competences are competences that are not specific to any one particular job eg problem solving.

2.3 Mintzberg's parameters

Mintzberg (1989) proposes three parameters of job design:

(a) **Job specialisations:**

    (i) How many different tasks are contained within the job and how multi-skilled do the job holders need to be?

    (ii) To what extent does the worker have control over the work?

(b) **Regulation of behaviour** - how does the organisation control the behaviour to ensure co-ordination.

(c) **Training** in skills and indoctrination in organisational values.

2.4 Job descriptions

Job descriptions (or job specifications) are detailed accounts of the **job role** of the individual or groups of workers of a particular type. The contents of a job description include:

(a) Job title and job grade

(b) Department/section and location

(c) Wage salary/range

(d) Function of department and main purpose of job

(e) Duties and responsibilities

(f) Specific limits to authority

(g) Responsible to and for

(h) Date prepared and Reference number

2.5 Person specifications

A **person specification** is a set of role-specific **attributes** used to attract applications and used as a benchmark against which to compare candidates' actual attributes when making the selection decision. These may be derived from analysis of attributes of known high-performing job holders in similar roles.

2.5.1 Rodger's seven-point plan

One method that has been used for the selection process is **Alec Rodger's Seven Point Plan** (Rodger, A (1952)):

Point	Examples
Physical make-up	Strength, appearance, health
Attainments	Qualifications, career achievements
General intelligence	Average, above average
Special aptitudes	Manual dexterity, mental sharpness
Interests	Mechanical, people-related
Disposition	Calm, independent
Circumstances	Location, car owner

Essential reading

See Chapter 13 Section 1 of the Essential reading for more detail on recruitment and job design.

The Essential reading is available as an Appendix of the digital edition of the Workbook.

3 Advertising

3.1 Objectives of advertising

The objective of advertising vacancies is to **attract suitable applications** from people likely to fit job and person specifications and job advertisements should aim to:

(a) Clearly describe the job on offer.

(b) Provide information about the company.

(c) Arouse interest from readers.

(d) Deter unsuitable persons from applying.

(e) Hold reader's attention.

3.2 Media for advertising

Media for recruitment advertising include:

(a) Informal (word of mouth, staff recruit others)

(b) In house (magazine, notice board, memo to managers)

(c) Publications (trade journals, local and national press)

(d) Careers service (schools, job centre, Professional & Executive register)

(e) Recruitment fairs ('milk round', local business groups)

(f) Specialist Agencies (Secretarial Bureau, 'head-hunter')

(g) Local radio, television and cinema

(h) Internet including social media

4 Selection

Outline of process:

Step 1 Deal with responses to adverts (application forms and CVs)

Step 2 Assess each application against criteria

Step 3 Sort applications

Step 4 Invite candidates for interview

Step 5 Selection testing

Step 6 Contact applications: Provisional offer or rejection

4.1 Interviews

4.1.1 Objectives of interviews

Most organisations use **interviews** as a basis for selection and interviews should be a **two-way process** to achieve the following:

(a) Find the best person

(b) Ensure applicants understand the job

(c) Give the best possible impression of the organisation

(d) Offer fair treatment to all applicants

Real life example

We have all been in an interview, and we all know how scary it can be. Some interviews are well conducted and allow both parties to see if they can work with the other, so they can make a decision – the interviewer deciding if they want to hire the candidate in front of them, and the interviewee deciding if this job is something they believe will help them achieve their long term career goals – but often interviews fall short. In this section we consider the different types of interviews, the features that interviews should (in theory) possess, and conclude with a discussion of the pros and cons of interviews as a technique for identifying appropriate potential employees. As you're reading through it, try to relate it to your experiences of good and bad interviews.

4.1.2 Types of interviews

There are three types of interview:

(a) **Individual** (one to one or face to face) interviews

(b) **Panel** interviews - two or three people interview the candidate (eg and HR specialist and the manager of the department where the successful candidate will work

(c) **Selection boards -** A large panel interviews the candidate

4.1.3 Advantages of interviews

Advantages of interviews include:

(a) Personal information assessed more easily

(b) Allows more flexible approach

(c) Can put applicant on the spot

4.2 Limitations of interviews

Problem	Comment
Scope	An interview is too **brief** to 'get to know' candidates in the kind of depth required to make an accurate prediction of work performance.
Artificiality	An interview is an **artificial situation**: candidates may be on their best behaviour or, conversely, so nervous that they do not do themselves justice. Neither situation reflects what the person is really like.
The halo and horns effects	The tendency for people to make an **initial general judgement** about a person (either positive or negative) based on a single obvious attribute, such as how they are dressed or their size. This single attribute will colour later perceptions, and make an interviewer mark the person up or down on every other factor in their assessment.
Contagious bias	The interviewer changes the behaviour of the applicant by **suggestion**. The applicant might be led by the wording of questions, or non-verbal cues from the interviewer, to change what they are doing or saying in response.
Stereotyping	Stereotyping groups together people who are assumed to share certain characteristics (women, say, or vegetarians), then attributes certain traits to the group as a whole. It then assumes that each individual member of the supposed group will possess that trait.
Incorrect assessment	Qualitative factors such as motivation, honesty or integrity are very difficult to define and assess objectively.

Problem	Comment
Logical error	For example, an interviewer might decide that a young candidate who has held two or three jobs in the past for only a short time will be unlikely to last long in any job. (This isn't necessarily the case.)
Inexperienced interviewers	Inexperienced or unskilled interviewers may undermine the process through: • Inability to evaluate information about a candidate properly • Failure to compare a candidate against the job description or person specification • Failure to take control of the direction and length of the interview • Using inappropriate question types to elicit data or put candidates at ease • A reluctance to probe into facts or challenge statements where necessary

Essential reading

See Chapter 13 Section 2 of the Essential reading for more detail on interviews.

The Essential reading is available as an Appendix of the digital edition of the Workbook.

4.3 Selection testing

Selection testing involves submitting applicants to formal tests to identify:

- Degree of competence in performing required skills
- Attributes such as intelligence and personality

4.3.1 Types of testing

(a) **Psychometric testing:**

    (i) Personality assessed against known scales (introversion/extroversion, Belbin types, cognitive style etc)

    (ii) Resulting profile compared to *norm tables* – ie profiles of good performers in similar roles

    (iii) Used to select candidates and to pinpoint areas for personal development

(b) **Proficiency and attainment testing:**

    (i) Intelligence tests – seeks to assess basic IQ or verbal reasoning

    (ii) Aptitude/skills testing (eg numerical, dexterity, spatio-visual ability)

    (iii) Job simulation/work sampling to test proficiency (eg typing speed, telesales role play)

4.3.2 Evaluation of selection testing:

(a) **Advantages**

    (i) Ensure fulsome coverage of all aspects of a candidate

    (ii) Test of ability not just blind acceptance of a CV

    (iii) Good accuracy record for some types of testing

(b) **Disadvantages**

    (i) Can be very time consuming

    (ii) Candidate might feel affronted

    (iii) High expense of buying tests or employing consultants/specialists

(iv)   Can measure current skills and not potential

(v)   Interpretation of tests results

4.4   Group selection methods

Group selection methods (sometimes known as 'assessment centres') are used for jobs requiring leadership and/or team working. It is a process involving small groups of participants undertaking a series of tests and exercises under observation with a view to assess their skills and competencies.

The above process often lasts several days ('country weekend') and may include:

(a)   Decision-making **simulations**

(b)   **Communication** exercises

(c)   **Structured interviews** and tests

(d)   Leadership and team **challenges**

Participants observed by **multiple assessors** who report back later on their overall assessment of each participant.

Activity 2: Assessment centre

Suggest three advantages and disadvantages of using assessment centre

Solution

4.5   References

References are used by employers mainly to verify straightforward factual information such as previous job details and the period of employment. Any information on the applicants' personality must make allowances for bias and blandness. References may be written or via the telephone:

(a)   **Advantages**

(i)   Independent opinion

(ii)   Honest feedback

(b)   **Disadvantages**

(i)   Bias for/against

(ii)   Bland (fear of being sued)

4.6   Evaluating recruitment and selection practices

To get a clear idea of how efficient their recruitment and selection practices are, firms can ask themselves these questions.

*   Can we identify human resources requirements from the business plans?

*   How fast do we respond to demands from line managers for human resources?

*   Do we give/receive good advice on labour market trends?

*   Do we select the right advertising media to reach the market?

*   How effective (and cost effective) is our recruitment advertising?

- How do our recruits actually perform – do we end up employing the right people?
- Do we retain our new recruits?

Recruitment and selection practices can be reviewed in various ways.

Review	Comment
Performance indicators	Each stage of the process can be assessed by performance indicators; for example, the time it takes to process an application. Data can be collected to check any deviation from standard.
Cost effectiveness	For example, number of relevant responses per recruitment ad, or cost of various advertising media per application elicited (or person employed).
Monitoring the workforce	High staff turnover, absenteeism and other problems (particularly among new recruits) may reflect poor recruitment and selection. Lack of workforce diversity may highlight discriminatory practices.
Attitude surveys	The firm can ask its recruits what they thought of the process.
Actual individual job performance	A person's actual performance can be compared with what was expected when they were recruited.

Real life example

Smith and Abrahamsen (1992) developed a scale that plots selection methods according to how accurately they predict a candidate's future performance in the job.

This is known as a **predictive validity** scale. The scale ranges from 1 (meaning that a method is right every time) to 0 (meaning that a method is no better than chance).

Method	% use by firms	Predictive validity
Interviews	92	0.17
References	74	0.13
Work sampling	18	0.57
Assessment centres	14	0.40
Personality tests	13	0.40
Cognitive tests	11	0.54
Biodata (biography analysis)	4	0.40
Graphology (handwriting analysis)	3	0.00

The results surprisingly show a pattern of employers relying most heavily on the **least** accurate selection methods. Interviews in particular seem not much better than tossing a coin.

5 Discrimination at work

5.1 Equal opportunities

Many countries have legislation to prevent discrimination (eg on the basis of gender, race or disability).

> **Equal opportunities:** An approach to the management of people at work based on **equal access** and **fair treatment**

Equal opportunities relates to **all aspects of employment**:

(a) Adverts

(b) Recruitment and selection

(c) Access to training

(d) Promotion

(e) Disciplinary procedures

(f) Redundancy and dismissal

(g) Pay and conditions

(h) Prohibiting discrimination on the ground of gender and marital status.

Activity 3: Benefits of equal opportunities

How does equal opportunities benefit organisations?

5.2 Types of discrimination

There are four main types of discrimination:

- **Direct discrimination** - one group is treated less favourable than another
- **Indirect discrimination** - a policy is fair in form but discriminatory in practice
- **Victimisation** - a person is penalised for giving information or taking action in pursuit of a claim of discrimination
- **Harassment** - the use of threatening, offensive or abusive language or behaviour.

Activity 4: Indirect discrimination

Suggest four examples of practices that would constitute indirect discrimination on the grounds of gender.

Solution

5.3 Anti-discrimination laws

Many countries have introduced various laws aimed to prohibit different types of discrimination:

Race Relations laws prohibit discrimination on the grounds of:

- Colour
- Race
- Nationality
- Ethnic or national origin

Other forms of discrimination laws:

- Rehabilitation of offenders
- Disability
- Sexual orientation
- Religious belief
- Age

6 The practical implications

6.1 Equal opportunities policy

One recommendation is that organisations should develop an equal opportunities policy. This should include policy statements and a code of practice on equal opportunities.

Setting up a successful **equal opportunities policy** requires:

(a) Secure support from top management: create senior accountabilities

(b) Set up a representative working party to produce a Code of Practice

(c) Formulate action plans and allocate resources to publicise/implement policy

(d) Implement monitoring and review of minority staff entering/progressing/leaving

(e) Plan and implement positive action initiatives to facilitate minority access to opportunities

6.2 Other initiatives

Some employers are doing more than the legal minimum by addressing the underlying causes of discrimination. **Positive action initiatives** include:

(a) **Flexible hours**/part time working

(b) **Career break** or return to work schemes

(c) **Putting equal opportunities higher on the agenda** (eg appointing equal opportunity manager) and positive action (to encourage applications from minorities)

(d) **Fast tracking** school leavers (as well as graduates)

(e) **Training** for women returnees

(f) **Awareness training**

(g) Counselling and **disciplinary policies**

7 Diversity

7.1 Concept

Diversity goes further than just providing equal opportunities in the workforce. Diversity's main thrust is to ensure, within a legally acceptable framework, the **composition of the workforce reflects the population** as a whole. Here **the rationale is that a diverse organisation will both understand and meet its customer's needs better.**

In order to reflect diversity and to **see it as an opportunity** not a hurdle, managers need to ensure that **organisational systems** also support diversity.

For example:

(a) Recruitment and selection

(b) Education and training

(c) Career development

(d) Communications methods and channels

(e) Work/life balance

7.2 Diversity in the workplace

Diversity in the workplace means:

(a) Managing co-operative working in diverse teams

(b) Tolerance of individual differences

(c) Communicating effectively with an ethnically diverse workforce

(d) Managing workers with diverse family structures and responsibilities

(e) Managing the adjustments to be made by an ageing workforce

(f) Managing diverse career paths and aspirations

(g) Confronting educational/qualification issues in an international workforce

The steps in implementing a diversity policy are:

Step 1 Analyse your business environment

Step 2 Define diversity and its business benefits

Step 3 Introduce the diversity policy into the corporate strategy

Step 4 Embed diversity into core HR processes and systems

Step 5 Involve staff at all levels

Step 6 Communicate, communicate, communicate

Step 7 Understand your company's needs

Step 8 Evaluate

Chapter summary

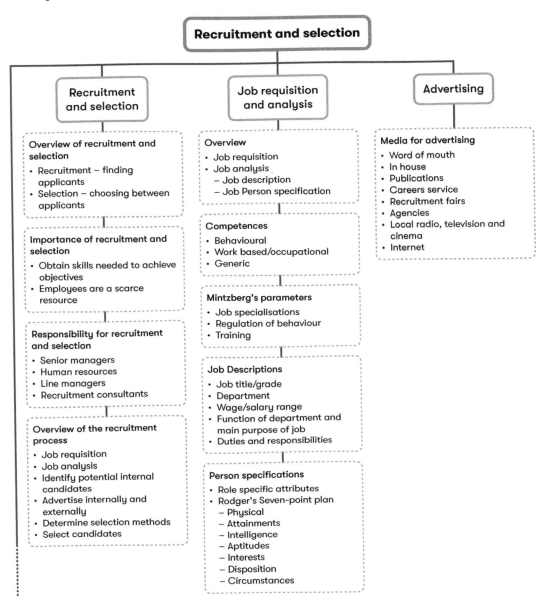

Recruitment and selection

Recruitment and selection

Overview of recruitment and selection
- Recruitment – finding applicants
- Selection – choosing between applicants

Importance of recruitment and selection
- Obtain skills needed to achieve objectives
- Employees are a scarce resource

Responsibility for recruitment and selection
- Senior managers
- Human resources
- Line managers
- Recruitment consultants

Overview of the recruitment process
- Job requisition
- Job analysis
- Identify potential internal candidates
- Advertise internally and externally
- Determine selection methods
- Select candidates

Job requisition and analysis

Overview
- Job requisition
- Job analysis
  - Job description
  - Job Person specification

Competences
- Behavioural
- Work based/occupational
- Generic

Mintzberg's parameters
- Job specialisations
- Regulation of behaviour
- Training

Job Descriptions
- Job title/grade
- Department
- Wage/salary range
- Function of department and main purpose of job
- Duties and responsibilities

Person specifications
- Role specific attributes
- Rodger's Seven-point plan
  - Physical
  - Attainments
  - Intelligence
  - Aptitudes
  - Interests
  - Disposition
  - Circumstances

Advertising

Media for advertising
- Word of mouth
- In house
- Publications
- Careers service
- Recruitment fairs
- Agencies
- Local radio, television and cinema
- Internet

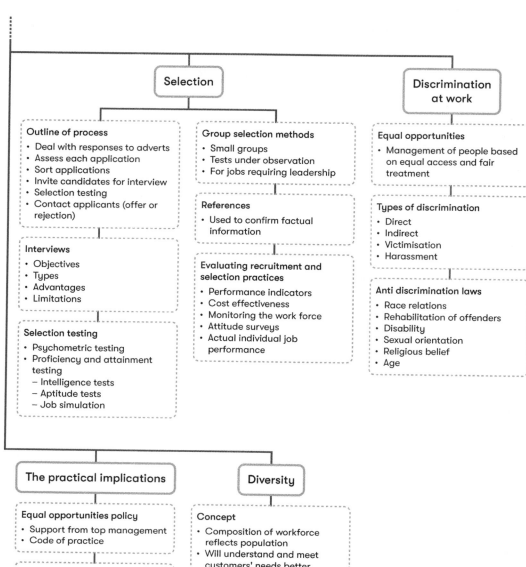

Selection

Outline of process
- Deal with responses to adverts
- Assess each application
- Sort applications
- Invite candidates for interview
- Selection testing
- Contact applicants (offer or rejection)

Interviews
- Objectives
- Types
- Advantages
- Limitations

Selection testing
- Psychometric testing
- Proficiency and attainment testing
  - Intelligence tests
  - Aptitude tests
  - Job simulation

Group selection methods
- Small groups
- Tests under observation
- For jobs requiring leadership

References
- Used to confirm factual information

Evaluating recruitment and selection practices
- Performance indicators
- Cost effectiveness
- Monitoring the work force
- Attitude surveys
- Actual individual job performance

Discrimination at work

Equal opportunities
- Management of people based on equal access and fair treatment

Types of discrimination
- Direct
- Indirect
- Victimisation
- Harassment

Anti discrimination laws
- Race relations
- Rehabilitation of offenders
- Disability
- Sexual orientation
- Religious belief
- Age

The practical implications

Equal opportunities policy
- Support from top management
- Code of practice

Other initiatives
- Flexible hours/part time working
- Return to work/career break

Diversity

Concept
- Composition of workforce reflects population
- Will understand and meet customers' needs better

Diversify in the workplace
- Analyse business environment
- Define diversity and benefits
- Introduce diversity policy
- Embed into core HR processes
- Ensure leaders implement
- Involve staff
- Communicate
- Understand company's needs
- Evaluate

Knowledge diagnostic

1. Recruitment and selection

The aim of the recruitment and selection process is to obtain the **quantity and quality of employees** needed to fulfil the organisation's objectives.

2. People involved in recruitment

Various people and groups may be included in the recruitment and selection process, including senior managers, the HR department, line managers, and recruitment consultants.

3. Approach to recruitment

Recruitment is the process of **attracting candidates** of the appropriate skill and calibre. Techniques include advertising, recruitment fairs and use of agencies. A systematic approach to recruitment will begin with a **job analysis** from which a **job description** and **person specification** will be drawn up.

4. Selection

Selection is the process of **choosing the appropriate candidate** from those who have been recruited.

5. Review

Recruitment and selection practices should be **reviewed** to ensure that they are appropriate.

6. Equal opportunities

Equal opportunities is about providing **equal access** to opportunities and treating people **fairly**. Legislation in some countries covers **discrimination** on the grounds of sex, race, age and disability. It is unlawful in these regimes to base decisions such as selection and pay on those factors.

7. Equal opportunities policy

Establishing an equal opportunities policy requires an organisation to undertake a number of steps which might include securing support from top management, and setting up a working party to produce a Code of Practice.

8. Diversity

Diversity management is about having systems and management approaches that **make the most of the diverse workforce** to better meet customer needs and the objectives of the organisation.

Further study guidance

Question practice

Now try the following from the Further question practice bank [available in the digital edition of the workbook]:

Number	Level	Marks	Approximate time
Q67	Exam Section A	2	2 mins
Q68	Exam Section A	1	1 min
Q69	Exam Section B	4	5 mins

Further reading

There is an article on the ACCA website entitled "Equal opportunities" that is relevant to material in this chapter. You are strongly advised to read this article in full as part of your preparation for the FBT exam.

Activity answers

Activity 1: Recruitment consultants

Advantages:

- Time savings for internal HR department
- Quality of service provided
- Can be used to screen candidates to eliminate unsuitable candidates

Disadvantages:

- Cost - usually at least two or three months' salary
- Risk - of unsuitable candidates being recruited
- Access to company information is shared with an external body

Activity 2: Assessment centre

Advantages:

- More time to assess candidates
- Wider range of skills can be tested
- Reduce bias in selection process

Disadvantages:

- Time
- Cost
- Candidates may modify their behaviour to 'pass'.

Activity 3: Benefits of equal opportunities

Benefits of equal opportunities to organisations:

- Retention of staff
- Company image/PR
- Motivation
- Reduced risk of litigation

Activity 4: Indirect discrimination

Here are four examples, but clearly the list is not exhaustive!

(1)   Advertising a vacancy in a primarily male environment, where women would be less likely to see it.

(2)   Offering less favourable terms to part-time workers (given that most of them are women).

(3)   Specifying age limits which would tend to exclude women who had taken time out of work for child-rearing.

(4)   Asking in selection interviews about plans to have a family (since this might be to the detriment of a woman, but not a man).

14

Individuals, groups and teams

Learning outcomes

On completion of this chapter you should be able to:

	Syllabus reference no.
Describe the main characteristics of individual and group behaviour.	D3 (a)
Outline the contributions of individuals and teams to organisational success.	D3 (b)
Identify individual and team approaches to work.	D3 (c)
Explain the differences between a group and a team.	D4 (a)
Explain the purposes of a team.	D4 (b)
Explain the role of the manager in building the team and developing individuals within the team. (a) Belbin's team roles theory (b) Tuckman's theory of team development	D4 (c)
List the characteristics of effective and ineffective teams.	D4 (d)
Describe tools and techniques that can be used to build the team and improve team effectiveness.	D4 (e)

Exam context

Relationships within a team and the management of teams often figure in the examinations, including named models such as Tuckman and Belbin. A question featured the work of Tuckman in the specimen exam.

Chapter overview

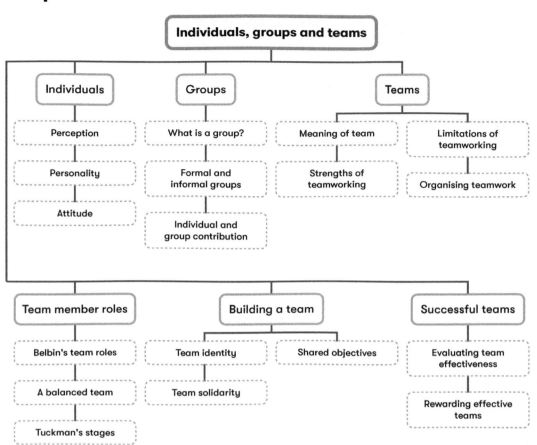

Individuals, groups and teams

- Individuals
  - Perception
  - Personality
  - Attitude
- Groups
  - What is a group?
  - Formal and informal groups
  - Individual and group contribution
- Teams
  - Meaning of team
  - Strengths of teamworking
  - Limitations of teamworking
  - Organising teamwork

- Team member roles
  - Belbin's team roles
  - A balanced team
  - Tuckman's stages
- Building a team
  - Team identity
  - Team solidarity
  - Shared objectives
- Successful teams
  - Evaluating team effectiveness
  - Rewarding effective teams

1 Individuals

Managers need to understand what motivates *individuals* within the groups and teams they control. Key variables include:

- Perception
- Personality
- Attitude

1.1 Perception

Perception is the process by which the brain selects and organises information in order to make sense of it. People behave according to what they perceive – not according to what really is.

Perception can therefore have an impact on how the individual approaches their work:

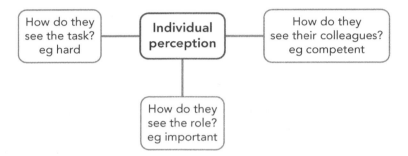

1.2 Personality

In order to identify, describe and explain the differences between people, psychologists use the concept of **personality**.

Personality is the total pattern of characteristic ways of thinking, feeling and behaving that constitute the individual's distinctive method of relating to the environment.

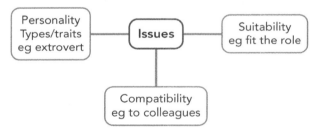

1.3 Attitudes

Attitudes are our general standpoint on things: the positions we have adopted in regard to particular issues, things and people, as we perceive them.

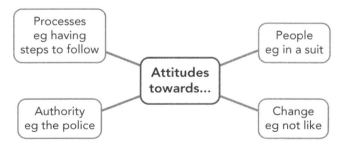

Activity 1: Individuals' behaviour

In what ways do you feel or behave differently at work compared to when you are with your family/social group/sports team?

Essential reading

See Chapter 14 Section 1 of the Essential reading for more detail on individuals.

The Essential reading is available as an Appendix of the digital edition of the Workbook.

2 Groups

2.1 What is a group?

A group is any collection of people who perceive themselves to be a group.

Groups have certain attributes that a random crowd does not possess.

(a) **A sense of identity**. There are acknowledged boundaries to the group which define who is in and who is out, who is us and who is them.

(b) **Loyalty to the group**, and acceptance within the group. This generally expresses itself as conformity or the acceptance of the norms of behaviour and attitudes that bind the group together and exclude others from it.

(c) **Purpose and leadership**. Most groups have an express purpose, whatever field they are in: most will, spontaneously or formally, choose individuals or subgroups to lead them towards the fulfilment of those goals.

2.2 Formal and informal groups

Informal groups will invariably be present in any organisation. Informal groups include workplace cliques, and networks of people who regularly get together to exchange information, groups of 'mates' who socialise outside work, and so on. They have a constantly fluctuating membership and structure.

Formal groups will be intentionally organised by the organisation, for a task for which they are held responsible – they are task oriented and become **teams**. Although many people enjoy working in teams, their popularity in the workplace arises because of their effectiveness in fulfilling the organisation's work.

Activity 2: Group support

What groups are you a member of in your study or work environment(s)? How big are these groups? How does the size of your class, study group, work team – or whatever:

(1) Affect your ability to come up with questions or ideas?

(2) Give you help and support to do something you couldn't do alone?

2.3 Individual and group contribution

People contribute different skills and attributes to the organisation as individuals than they do as group members because:

(a) Human behaviour is different in groups than in solo or interpersonal situations: **group dynamics** have an effect on performance.

(b)   Groups offer **synergy**: the pooling and stimulation of ideas and energies in a group can allow greater contribution than individuals working on their own. ('None of us is as smart as all of us', (quote ascribed to Kenneth Blanchard).)

(c)   Group dynamics and synergy may also be **negative**: distracting the individual, stifling individual responsibility and flair, and so on. Individuals may contribute more and better in some situations.

Individuals contribute:	Groups contribute:
A set of skills	A mix of skills
Objectives set by manager	Some teams can set their own objectives under the corporate framework
A point of view	A number of different points of view, enabling a swift overview of different ways of looking at a problem
Creative ideas related to the individual's expertise	Creative ideas arising from new combinations of expertise
'I can't be in two places at once'	Flexibility as team members can be deployed in different ways
Limited opportunity for self-criticism	Opportunity for exercising control

3 Teams

3.1 Meaning of team

A team is a group of people with complementary skills who have a **common purpose** and objectives for which they hold themselves accountable.

A **team** is more than a group. It has joint **objectives** and **accountability** and may be set up by the organisation under the supervision or coaching of a team leader, although **self-managed teams** are growing in popularity.

3.2 Strengths of teamworking

Teams are particularly well adapted to the following purposes:

Type of role	Comments
Work organisation	Teams combine the skills of different individuals. Teams are a co-ordinating mechanism: they avoid complex communication between different business functions.
Control	Fear of letting down the team can be a powerful motivator: team loyalty can be used to control the performance and behaviour of individuals.
Idea generation	Teams can generate ideas, eg through brainstorming and information sharing.
Decision-making	Decisions are evaluated from more than one viewpoint, with pooled information. Teams make fewer, but better evaluated, decisions than individuals.

3.3 Limitations of teamworking

Teams and teamworking are very much in fashion, but there are potential **drawbacks**.

(a)   Teamworking is not suitable for all jobs – although some managers do not like to admit this.

(b) Teamwork should be introduced because it leads to better performance, not because people feel better or more secure.

(c) Team processes (especially seeking consensus) can delay decision-making. The team may also produce the compromise decision, not the right decision.

(d) Social relationships might be maintained at the expense of other aspects of performance.

(e) Group norms may restrict individual personality and flair.

(f) 'Group think' (Janis, 1982): team consensus and cohesion may prevent consideration of alternatives or constructive criticism, leading the team to make risky, ill-considered decisions.

(g) Personality clashes and political behaviour within a team can get in the way of effective performance.

3.4 Organising teamwork

There are three basic approaches to the organisation of teamwork:

Multidisciplinary teams bring together individuals from different departments who **each have a particular skill** or specialism so that knowledge is pooled.

Multiskilled teams bring together individuals who **can perform any of the group's tasks**, allowing greater flexibility in the allocation of roles.

Virtual teams bring together individuals working in remote locations, reproducing the social, collaborative and information-sharing aspects of teamworking using Information and Communications Technology (ICT).

4 Team member roles

4.1 Belbin's team roles

Meredith Belbin (*Belbin 1993*) characterised the successful mix of team roles in an effective team as follows:

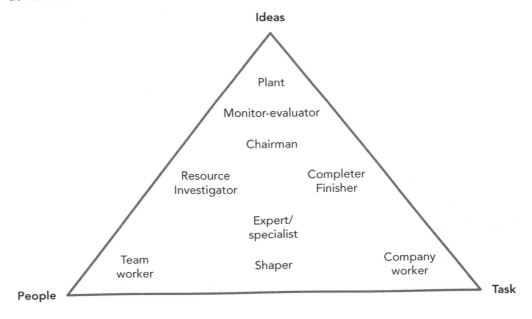

Role and description	Team-role contribution	Allowable weaknesses
Plant Creative, imaginative, unorthodox	Solves difficult problems	Ignores details, too preoccupied to communicate effectively
Resource investigator Extrovert, enthusiastic, communicative	Explores opportunities, develops contacts	Over-optimistic, loses interest once initial enthusiasm has passed
Co-ordinator (chair) Mature, confident, a good chairperson	Clarifies goals, promotes decision-making, delegates well	Can be seen as manipulative, delegates personal work
Shaper Challenging, dynamic, thrives on pressure	Has the drive and courage to overcome obstacles	Can provoke others, hurts people's feelings
Monitor-evaluator Sober, strategic and discerning	Sees all options, judges accurately	Lacks drive and ability to inspire others, overly critical
Teamworker Co-operative, mild, perceptive and diplomatic	Listens, builds, averts friction, calms the waters	Indecisive in crunch situations, can be easily influenced
Implementer (cmpny worker) Disciplined, reliable, conservative and efficient	Turns ideas into practical actions	Somewhat inflexible, slow to respond to new possibilities
Completer-finisher Painstaking, conscientious, anxious	Searches out errors and omissions, delivers on time	Inclined to worry unduly, reluctant to delegate, nitpicker
Specialist Single-minded, self-starting, dedicated	Provides knowledge and skills in rare supply	Contributes only on a narrow front, dwells on technicalities, overlooks the 'big picture'

4.2 A balanced team

These team roles are not fixed within any given individual. Team members can occupy more than one role, or switch to 'backup' roles if required, hence there is no requirement for every team to have nine members. However, since role preferences are based on personality, it should be recognised that:

- Individuals will be naturally inclined towards some roles more than others.
- Individuals will tend to adopt one or two team roles more or less consistently.
- Individuals are likely to be more successful in some roles than in others.

The nine roles are complementary, and Belbin suggested that an 'ideal' team should represent a mix or balance of all of them. If managers know employees' team role preferences, they can strategically select, 'cast' and develop team members to fulfil the required roles.

PER alert

Knowledge of these different roles may help you in leadership and management tasks under performance objective PO5, requiring you to 'show initiative within your team, working towards organisational goals, collaborating with and supporting others.'

Activity 3: Belbin

The following phrases and slogans project certain team roles:

(Examples are drawn from *Belbin (1993)*)

(1)   The small print is always worth reading.

(2)   Let's get down to the task in hand.

(3)   In this job you never stop learning.

(4)   Without continuous innovation, there is no survival.

(5)   Surely we can exploit that?

(6)   When the going gets tough, the tough get going.

(7)   I was very interested in your point of view.

(8)   Has anyone else got anything to add to this?

(9)   Decisions should not be based purely on enthusiasm.

Required

Identify which team role each slogan projects.

5 Team development

5.1 Tuckman's stages

Four stages in group development were identified by *Tuckman (1965)*.

Step 1	**Forming**
	The team is just coming together. Each member wishes to impress their personality on the group. The individuals will be trying to find out about each other, and about the aims and norms of the team. There will at this stage probably be a wariness about introducing new ideas. The objectives being pursued may as yet be unclear and a leader may not yet have emerged.
Step 2	**Storming**
	This frequently involves more or less open conflict between team members. There may be changes agreed in the original objectives, procedures and norms established for the group. If the team is developing successfully this may be a fruitful phase, as more realistic targets are set and trust between the group members increases.
Step 3	**Norming**
	A period of settling down: there will be agreements about work sharing, individual requirements and expectations of output. Norms and procedures may evolve which enable methodical working to be introduced and maintained.

| Step 4 | **Performing** |
| | The team sets to work to execute its task. The difficulties of growth and development no longer hinder the group's objectives. |

Later writers added two stages to Tuckman's model:

(a) **Dorming**. Once a group has been performing well for some time, it may get complacent, and fall back into self-maintenance functions, at the expense of the task.

(b) **Mourning/adjourning**. The group sees itself as having fulfilled its purpose – or, if it is a temporary group, is due to physically disband. This is a stage of confusion, sadness and anxiety as the group breaks up. There is evaluation of its achievements, and gradual withdrawal of group members. If the group is to continue, going on to a new task, there will be a renegotiation of aims and roles: a return to the forming stage.

Activity 4: Team formation stages

Read the following descriptions of team behaviour and decide to which category they belong (forming, storming, norming, performing, dorming).

(1) Two of the group arguing as to whose idea is best

(2) Progress becomes static

(3) Desired outputs being achieved

(4) Shy member of group not participating

(5) Activities being allocated

5.2 Shared objectives

Getting commitment to the team's shared objectives may involve a range of leader activity:

- Clearly setting out the objectives of the team
- Allowing the team to participate in setting objectives
- Giving regular feedback on progress and results with constructive criticism
- Getting the team involved in providing performance feedback
- Offering positive reinforcement (praise etc) for co-operative working and task achievement by the team as a whole (rather than just 'star' individuals)
- Championing the success of the team within the organisation.

6 Team building

In the previous section, we suggested that teams have a natural evolutionary life cycle, and that four stages can be identified. Not all teams develop into mature teams and might be stuck, stagnating, in any one of the stages.

So, it often falls to the supervisor or manager to build the team. There are three main issues involved in team building.

Issues	Comments
Team identity	Get people to see themselves as part of this group
Team solidarity	Encourage loyalty so that members put in extra effort for the sake of the team
Shared objectives	Encourage the team to commit itself to shared work objectives and to co-operate willingly and effectively in achieving them

Team development can be facilitated by active **team building** measures to support team identity, solidarity and commitment to shared objectives.

Activity 5: Team building exercises

The following are commonly used team building exercises:

(1)   Sending a project team (involved in the design of electronic systems for racing cars) on a recreational day out karting.

(2)   Sending two sales teams on a day out playing 'War Games', each being an opposing combat team trying to capture the other's flag, armed with paint guns.

(3)   Sending a project team on a conference at a venue away from work, with a brief to review the past year and come up with a vision for the next year.

Required

State why each of the exercises might be effective for team building.

Solution

6.1 Team identity

A manager might seek to reinforce the sense of identity of the group. Arguably this is in part the creation of boundaries, identifying who is in the team and who is not.

(a) **Name**. Staff at McDonald's restaurants are known as the Crew. In other cases, the name would be more official, describing what the team actually does (eg Systems Implementation Task Force).

(b) **Badge or uniform**. This often applies to service industries, but it is unlikely that it would be applied within an organisation.

(c) Expressing the team's **self-image**. Teams often develop their own jargon, especially for new projects.

(d) Building a team **mythology**. Over time, groups and teams build up their own history and character. Stories from the past may take on an almost mythical nature (mistakes as well as successes).

(e) **A separate space**. It might help if team members work together in the same or adjacent offices, but this is not always possible. (A team intranet page may perform this function for a virtual team.)

6.2 Team solidarity

Team solidarity implies cohesion and loyalty inside the team. A leader might be interested in:

(a) **Expressing** solidarity

(b) Encouraging **interpersonal relationships** – although the purpose of these is to ensure that work gets done

(c) **Dealing withconflict** by getting it out into the open; disagreements should be expressed and then resolved

(d) **Controlling competition** – the team leader needs to treat each member of the team fairly and to be seen to do so; favouritism undermines solidarity

(e) Encouraging some **competition with other groups,** if appropriate; for example, sales teams might be offered a prize for the highest monthly orders; London Underground runs best-kept station competitions.

Activity 6: Group cohesion

Can you see any dangers in creating a very close-knit group? Think of the effect of strong team cohesion on:

(1) What the group spends its energies and attention on

(2) How the group regards outsiders, and any information or feedback they supply

(3) How the group makes decisions.

What could be done about these dangerous effects?

Solution

7 Successful teams

7.1 Evaluating team effectiveness

The task of the team leader is to build a 'successful' or 'effective' team. The criteria for team effectiveness include:

(a) **Task performance**: fulfilment of task and organisational goals

(b) **Team functioning**: constructive maintenance of team working, managing the demands of team dynamics, roles and processes

(c) **Team member satisfaction**: fulfilment of individual development and relationship needs.

There are a number of factors, both quantitative and qualitative, that may be assessed to decide whether or how far a team is operating effectively. Some factors cannot be taken as evidence on their own but may suggest underlying problems – accident rates may be due to poor safety systems, for example – as well as poor morale and lack of focus due to team problems.

Some of the characteristics of **effective** and **ineffective** teams may be summarised as follows:

Quantifiable		
Labour turnover	Low	High
Accident rate	Low	High
Absenteeism	Low	High
Output and productivity	High	Low
Quality of output	High	Low
Individual targets	Achieved	Not achieved
Stoppages and interruptions to the workflow	Low	High (eg because of misunderstandings, disagreements)
Qualitative		
Commitment to targets and organisational goals	High	Low
Understanding of team's work and why it exists	High	Low
Understanding of individual roles within the team	High	Low
Communication between team members	Free and open	Mistrust
Ideas	Shared for the team's benefit	'Owned' (and hidden) by individuals for their own benefit
Feedback	Constructive criticism	Point scoring, undermining
Problem-solving	Addresses causes	Only looks at symptoms
Interest in work decisions	Active	Passive acceptance
Opinions	Consensus	Imposed solutions
Job satisfaction	High	Low
Motivation in leader's absence	High	'When the cat's away ...'

7.2 Rewarding effective teams

Organisations may try to encourage effective team performance by designing reward systems that recognise team, rather than individual, success. Indeed, **individual performance rewards** may act **against** team co-operation and performance.

(a)   They emphasise individual rather than team performance.

(b)   They encourage team leaders to think of team members only as individuals, rather than relating to them as a team.

BPP LEARNING MEDIA

For **team rewards** to be effective, the team must have certain characteristics.

- Distinct roles, targets and performance measures (so the team knows what it has to do to earn the reward)
- Significant autonomy and thus influence over performance (so the team perceives that extra effort will be rewarded)
- Maturity and stability
- Co-operation
- Interdependence of team members (so that the team manages member contribution, everyone 'pulls their weight', no one feels they could earn higher rewards on their own).

Reward schemes which focus on team (or organisation) performance include:

(a) **Profit sharing** schemes, based on the distribution of a pool of cash related to profit

(b) **Gain sharing** schemes, using a formula related to a suitable performance indicator, such as added value. Improvements in the performance indicator must be perceived to be within the employees' control, otherwise there will be no incentive to perform.

(c) **Employee share option** schemes, giving staff the right to acquire shares in the employing company at an attractive price.

Chapter summary

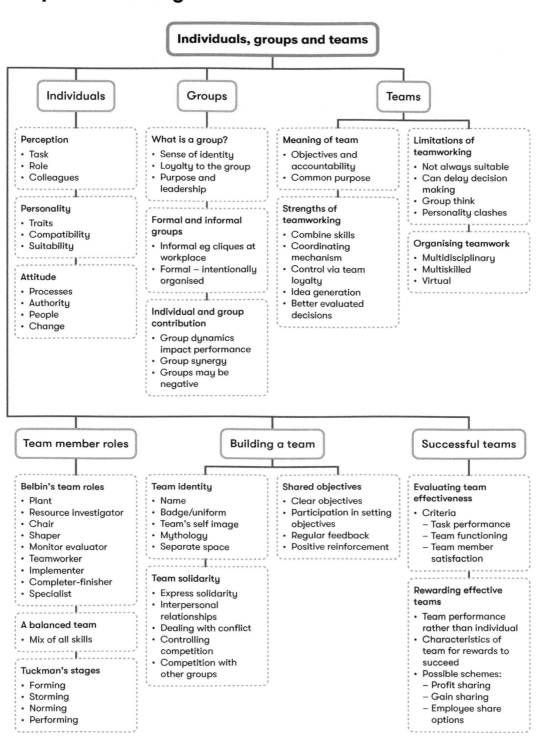

Individuals, groups and teams

Individuals

Perception
- Task
- Role
- Colleagues

Personality
- Traits
- Compatibility
- Suitability

Attitude
- Processes
- Authority
- People
- Change

Groups

What is a group?
- Sense of identity
- Loyalty to the group
- Purpose and leadership

Formal and informal groups
- Informal eg cliques at workplace
- Formal – intentionally organised

Individual and group contribution
- Group dynamics impact performance
- Group synergy
- Groups may be negative

Teams

Meaning of team
- Objectives and accountability
- Common purpose

Strengths of teamworking
- Combine skills
- Coordinating mechanism
- Control via team loyalty
- Idea generation
- Better evaluated decisions

Limitations of teamworking
- Not always suitable
- Can delay decision making
- Group think
- Personality clashes

Organising teamwork
- Multidisciplinary
- Multiskilled
- Virtual

Team member roles

Belbin's team roles
- Plant
- Resource investigator
- Chair
- Shaper
- Monitor evaluator
- Teamworker
- Implementer
- Completer-finisher
- Specialist

A balanced team
- Mix of all skills

Tuckman's stages
- Forming
- Storming
- Norming
- Performing

Building a team

Team identity
- Name
- Badge/uniform
- Team's self image
- Mythology
- Separate space

Team solidarity
- Express solidarity
- Interpersonal relationships
- Dealing with conflict
- Controlling competition
- Competition with other groups

Shared objectives
- Clear objectives
- Participation in setting objectives
- Regular feedback
- Positive reinforcement

Successful teams

Evaluating team effectiveness
- Criteria
  - Task performance
  - Team functioning
  - Team member satisfaction

Rewarding effective teams
- Team performance rather than individual
- Characteristics of team for rewards to succeed
- Possible schemes:
  - Profit sharing
  - Gain sharing
  - Employee share options

Knowledge diagnostic

1. Individuals

Managers need to understand the key variables that impact on individual behaviour – **perception, personality** and **attitude.**

2. Groups

A group is any collection of people within the organisation. These may be either **formal** and **informal** and individuals may be members of more than one group.

3. Teams

A team is a formal organised group with **common goals** and **complementary skills**. They may be **multidisciplinary** or **multiskilled**.

4. Belbin

Belbin described nine roles within a team: chair, shaper, plant, monitor- evaluator, company worker, resource investigator, teamworker, completer-finisher, and specialist.

5. Tuckman

Tuckman identified the stages of group development: forming, storming, norming and performing.

6. Team building

Managers may be required to build the team. Three issues to consider when building a team are how to create a **team identity**, how to encourage **team solidarity** and how to ensure that all members of the team are committed to the **shared objectives** of the team.

Further study guidance

Question practice

Now try the following from the Further question practice bank [available in the digital edition of the Workbook]:

Number	Level	Marks	Approximate time
Q70	Exam Section A	1	1 min
Q71	Exam Section A	2	2 mins
Q72	Exam Section A	2	2 mins
Q73	Exam Section A	2	2 mins

Further reading

There is an article on the ACCA website entitled 'The importance of teams' that is relevant to the material in this chapter. You are strongly advised to read this article in full as part of your preparation for the FBT exam.

Activity answers

Activity 1: Individuals' behaviour

Here are some possible answers:

- Strive towards an identifiable objective
- Actively seek to develop new skills
- Seek approval and recognition from colleagues and superiors
- Adopt a more formal approach/response
- Defer to colleagues at a higher level
- Conform to regulations and conventions
- Complain a lot
- Get more and more frustrated about the inadequate systems
- Stab people in the back – play power games.

Activity 2: Group support

Your primary groups are probably your tutor group or class. If at work, it would be the section in which you work. If the groups are large, you may feel reluctant to put forward ideas or ask questions, but even within a large group you should feel there is support and that help is at hand if you need it.

Activity 3: Belbin

Team roles:

(1) Completer-finisher
(2) Implementer/company worker
(3) Specialist
(4) Plant
(5) Resource investigator
(6) Shaper
(7) Teamworker
(8) Co-ordinator/chair
(9) Monitor-evaluator

Activity 4: Team formation stages

Categorising the behaviour of group members in the situations described results in the following: (a) storming, (b) dorming, (c) performing, (d) forming, (e) norming.

Activity 5: Team building exercises

Exercising effective for team building:

(1) Recreation helps the team to build informal relationships: in this case, the chosen activity also reminds them of their tasks, and may make them feel special, as part of the motor racing industry, by giving them a taste of what the end user of their product does.

(2) A team challenge forces the group to consider its strengths and weaknesses, to find its natural leader. This exercise creates an 'us' and 'them' challenge: perceiving the rival team as the enemy heightens the solidarity of the group.

(3) This exercise encourages the group to raise problems and conflicts freely, away from the normal environment of work and also encourages brainstorming and the expression of team members' dreams for what the team can achieve in the future.

Activity 6: Group cohesion

Problems may arise in an ultra-close-knit group because:

(1)   The group's energies may be focused on its own maintenance and relationships, instead of on the task.

(2)   The group may be suspicious or dismissive of outsiders and may reject any contradictory information or criticism they supply; the group will be blinkered and stick to its own views, no matter what; cohesive groups thus often get the impression that they are infallible: they can't be wrong – and therefore can't learn from their mistakes.

(3)   The group may squash any dissent or opinions that might rock the boat. Close-knit groups tend to preserve a consensus – falsely, if required – and to take risky decisions, because they have suppressed alternative facts and viewpoints.

This phenomenon is called '**group think**' (*Janis 1982*). In order to limit its effect, the team must be encouraged to:

(1)   Actively seek outside ideas and feedback

(2)   Welcome self-criticism within the group

(3)   Consciously evaluate conflicting evidence and opinions.

15

Motivating individuals and groups

Learning outcomes

On completion of this chapter you should be able to:

	Syllabus reference no.
Define motivation and explain its importance to the organisation, teams and individuals.	D5 (a)
Explain content and process theories of motivation: Maslow, Herzberg, McGregor and Vroom.	D5 (b)
Explain and identify types of intrinsic and extrinsic reward.	D5 (c)
Explain how reward systems can be designed and implemented to motivate teams and individuals.	D5 (d)

Exam context

Motivation is likely to appear regularly in the exam and so the various theories must be well understood. There was one question in the specimen exam which related to motivation.

Chapter overview

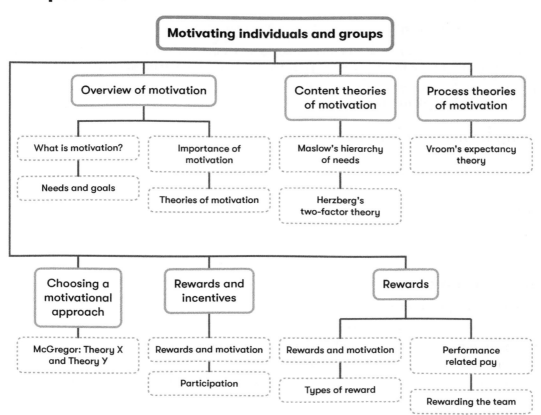

1 Overview of motivation

1.1 What is motivation?

Motivation is concerned with what causes people to act in a certain way, whether it be drinking a glass of water to reduce thirst or working hard to achieve a promotion at work.

If managers understand what motivates their staff, they can actively use this knowledge to drive towards the organisation's objectives.

Activity 1: What is motivation?

80% of respondents expressed the view that they would continue to work even if they had no economic need to do so.

Required

Discuss why people would work if they had no economic reason to do so.

1.2 Need and goals

The **basic assumptions of motivation** are that:

(a) People seek to satisfy their needs and goals

(b) Organisations can offer some of the satisfaction people seek

(c) Organisations can influence people's behaviour

(d) If people's needs and goals are met they will have job satisfaction and a positive attitude to work.

1.3 Importance of motivation

The impact of motivation and job satisfaction on **performance** is difficult to measure accurately.

(a) Motivation is about getting **extra** levels of commitment and performance from employees, over and above mere compliance with rules and procedures. If individuals can be motivated, by one means or another, they might work more efficiently (and productivity will rise) or they will produce a better quality of work.

(b) The case for job satisfaction as a factor in improved performance is not proven.

(c) The key is to work 'smarter' – not necessarily 'harder'.

The signs by which **low morale or dissatisfaction** are gauged are also ambiguous.

(a) **Low productivity** is not invariably a sign of low morale. There may be more concrete problems (eg with work organisation or technology).

(b) **High labour turnover** is not a reliable indicator of low morale: the age structure of the workforce and other factors in natural wastage will need to be taken into account. Low turnover, likewise, is no evidence of high morale: people may be staying because of a lack of other opportunities in the local job market, for example.

However, there is some evidence that satisfaction correlates with mental health, so symptoms of **stress** or psychological dysfunction may be a signal that all is not well. (Again, a range of non-work factors may be contributing.)

Motivation is a useful concept, despite the fact that the **impact** of motivation, job satisfaction and morale on performance are difficult to measure.

Activity 2: Demotivation

How does demotivation manifest itself in organisations?

1.4 Theories of motivation

There are two groups of theories that attempt to explain motivation and how people can be motivated:

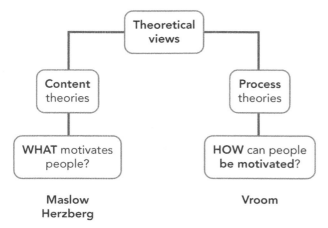

Maslow
Herzberg

Vroom

2 Content theories of motivation

2.1 Maslow's hierarchy of needs

Abraham **Maslow** (1908–1970), an American psychologist, produced his hierarchy of needs as follows (*Maslow, A.H. (1943)*):

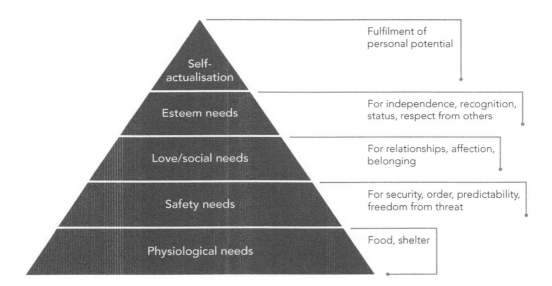

(a) An individual's needs can be arranged in a '**hierarchy** of relative pre-potency' (as shown). Each level of need is **dominant until satisfied**; only then does the next level of need become a motivating factor. A need which has been satisfied no longer motivates an individual's behaviour.

(b) The need for self-actualisation can rarely be satisfied.

(c) In addition, Maslow described:

(i) Freedom of enquiry and expression needs (for social conditions permitting free speech, and encouraging justice, fairness and honesty)

(ii) Knowledge and understanding needs (to gain knowledge of the environment, to explore, to learn).

Activity 3: Maslow's hierarchy of needs

Decide which of Maslow's categories the following fit into:

(1)   Receiving praise from your manager

(2)   A family party

(3)   An artist forgetting to eat

(4)   A man washed up on a desert island

(5)   A pay increase

(6)   Joining a local drama group

(7)   Buying a house

(8)   Being awarded a Nobel prize.

2.1.1   Key limitations to Maslow's hierarchy of needs

(a)   An individual's behaviour may be in response to several needs.

(b)   The same need may cause different behaviour in different individuals.

(c)   Not all needs manifest themselves in a hierarchical order.

2.2   Herzberg's two-factor theory

Frederick **Herzberg** produced his **two factor theories** of motivation *(Herzberg, F. et al (1959))*. He concluded that certain factors led to job satisfaction *(motivators)* and a different group led to dissatisfaction *(hygiene factors)*.

Motivators (yield job satisfaction)	Hygiene factors (yield dissatisfaction)
Recognition	Policies and administration
Responsibility	Supervision
Achievement	Salary
Advancement	Working conditions

A lack of motivator factors will encourage employees to concentrate on the hygiene factors. These, although they can be regarded as motivators in the very short term, will eventually dissatisfy.

Herzberg suggested that where there is evidence of poor motivation, such as low productivity, poor quality and strikes, management should not pay too much attention to hygiene factors, such as pay and conditions. Despite the fact that these are the traditional targets for the aspirations of organised labour, their potential for bringing improvements to work attitudes is limited. Instead, Herzberg suggested three types of **job design** which would offer job satisfaction through enhanced motivator factors.

* Job **rotation** - the planned transfer of staff from one job to another to increase staff variety.
  - Job **enlargement** - the attempt to widen jobs by increasing the number of operations in which a job holder is involved.
  - Job **enrichment** - planned, deliberate action to build greater responsibility, breadth and challenge of work into a job. Job enrichment is similar to **empowerment**.

Essential reading

See Chapter 15, Section 1 of the essential reading for more details about job design.

The Essential reading is available as an Appendix of the digital edition of the Workbook.

3 Process theories of motivation

3.1 Vroom's expectancy theory

Vroom's 'Expectancy Theory' *(Vroom, V. (1964))* is based on a simple calculation:

The expectancy equation may be stated as:

$F = V \times E \times I$

where:

F = the **force** or strength of the individual's motivation to behave in a particular way

V = **valence**: the strength of the individual's preference for a given outcome or reward

E = **expectancy**: the individual's perception that the behaviour will result in a particular

I = **instrumentality**, the individual's belief that achieving a particular performance goal will lead to a reward.

In this equation, the lower the values of valence, expectancy or instrumentality, the less the motivation. An employee may have a high expectation that increased productivity will result in promotion (because of managerial promises, say), but if they are indifferent or negative towards the idea of promotion (because they dislike responsibility), they will not be motivated to increase their productivity. Likewise, if promotion is very important to them – but they do not believe higher productivity will get them promoted (because they have been passed over before, perhaps), their motivation will be low.

Real life example

A colleague has told you that if you spend two hours every evening studying for your FIA/ACCA exams, you will pass your exams, and then you will get a promotion. Your motivation to study will depend on the following:

- Expectancy – your belief that studying two hours every evening will ensure that you pass your exams

- Instrumentality – your belief that if you pass your exams you will get the promotion

- Valence – how important is the promotion to you?

4 Choosing a motivational approach

4.1 McGregor Theory X and Theory Y

McGregor (1987) presented two opposing **assumptions** held by managers about employees, which affected how they managed and motivated them. These theories are *opposite ends of a continuum.*

Theory X assumes that individuals have an inherent dislike for work and will avoid it if they can. A Theory X employee:

(a) Prefers to be directed

(b) Has little ambition

(c) Is resistant to change, gullible

(d) Must be coerced and controlled

Theory Y asserts that work is as natural as play or rest. A Theory Y employee has:

(a) Self-direction

(b) Self-control

(c) An emphasis on self-actualising needs.

Theory X employees need a 'carrot and stick' approach whilst Theory Y employees need managers to encourage motivation by influencing the circumstances of work.

5 Rewards and incentives

5.1 Rewards and motivation

A **reward** is something given to an individual or team in recognition of contribution and success.

- **Intrinsic** rewards are related to the job itself, eg love being a nurse
- **Extrinsic** rewards are outside of the job role: eg financial (you like the pay), or non-financial (you like the hours/working environment).

An **incentive** is the *offer* of a reward designed to motivate current and future performance.

Motivation can come from the following areas:

- **Financial rewards** and incentive (extrinsic) can motivate (see Section 6).
- **Job satisfaction** (intrinsic) is a key motivator and is created through:

(a) Variety

(b) Task identity/clarity

(c) Autonomy/ownership

(d) Constructive feedback

(e) Task significance

5.2 Participation

Participation in decision making is usually perceived as a motivator.

Participation works as a motivator if the '**5 Cs**' are present:

(a) **Certainty** – participation should be genuine.

(b) **Consistency** – efforts to establish participation should be made consistently over a long period.

(c) **Clarity** – the purpose of participation is made clear.

(d) **Capacity** – the individual has the ability and information to participate effectively

(e) **Commitment** – the manager believes in and genuinely supports participation.

6 Reward

6.1 Rewards and motivation

Pay has a central – but ambiguous – role in motivation theory. It is not mentioned explicitly in any need list, but it offers the satisfaction of many of the various needs.

Individuals may also have needs unrelated to money, which money cannot satisfy, or which the pay system of the organisation actively denies (eg the need for leisure/family time – not overtime!) So to what extent is pay an inducement to better performance? Can pay be an effective motivator or incentive?

Maslow and Herzberg both recognise money as a means of satisfying some needs and symbolising worth. However, pay does not satisfy higher order needs and should thus be considered a hygiene factor.

6.2 Types of reward

An organisation may offer a range of rewards to employees, perhaps combined in a reward package. The range offered may include some or all of the following.

- Basic wages or salary
- Overtime payments (perhaps for employees paid a wage based on hours worked)
- Performance-related bonus
- Shares
- Share options (the opportunity to buy shares at a favourable price)
- Benefits in kind (for example personal use of a company vehicle)

- Pension contributions
- Service contracts and termination payments.

Packages for employees at different levels are likely to differ.

6.3 Performance-related pay

KEY
TERM

> **Performance related pay (PRP):** Pay that is related to output (in terms of the number of items produced or time taken to produce a unit of work), or results achieved (performance to defined standards in key tasks, according to plan).
> - The most common individual PRP scheme for wage earners is straight **piecework**: payment of a fixed amount per unit produced, or operation completed.
> - For managerial and other salaried jobs, a form of **management by objectives** will probably be applied. PRP is often awarded at the discretion of the line manager, although guidelines may suggest, for example, that those rated exceptional get a bonus of 10% whereas those who have performed less well only get, say, 3%.
> - For service and other departments, a PRP scheme may involve **bonuses** for achievement of key results, or **points schemes**, where points are awarded for performance of various criteria (efficiency, cost savings, quality of service, and so on). Certain points totals (or the highest points total in the unit, if a competitive system is used) then win cash or other awards.

6.3.1 Benefits of PRP

- Improves commitment and capability
- Improves focus on the business's performance objectives
- Encourages two-way communication
- Allows greater supervisory responsibility
- Recognises achievement when other means are not available.

6.3.2 Potential problems with PRP

- Subjectivity of awards for less measurable criteria (eg 'teamwork')
- Encouraging short-term focus and target-hitting (rather than improvements)
- Divisive/against teamworking (if awards are individual)
- Difficulties gaining union acceptance (if perceived to erode basic pay).

Activity 4: PRP

Why might PRP fail to motivate?

6.4 Rewarding the team

6.4.1 Group bonus schemes

Group incentive schemes typically offer a bonus for a team which achieves or exceeds specified targets. Offering bonuses to a whole team may be appropriate for tasks where individual contributions cannot be isolated, workers have little control over their individual output because tasks depend on each other, or where team building is particularly required. It may enhance team spirit and co-operation as well as provide performance incentives, but it may also create pressures within the group if some individuals are seen not to be pulling their weight.

6.4.2 Profit sharing schemes

Profit-sharing schemes offer employees (or selected groups) bonuses, directly related to profits or value added. Profit sharing is based on the belief that all employees can contribute to profitability, and that that contribution should be recognised. The effects may include profit-consciousness and motivation in employees, commitment to the future prosperity of the organisation, and so on.

The actual incentive value and effect on productivity may be wasted, however, if the scheme is badly designed.

Activity 5: Equitable pay

How can organisations ensure equitable pay?

Chapter summary

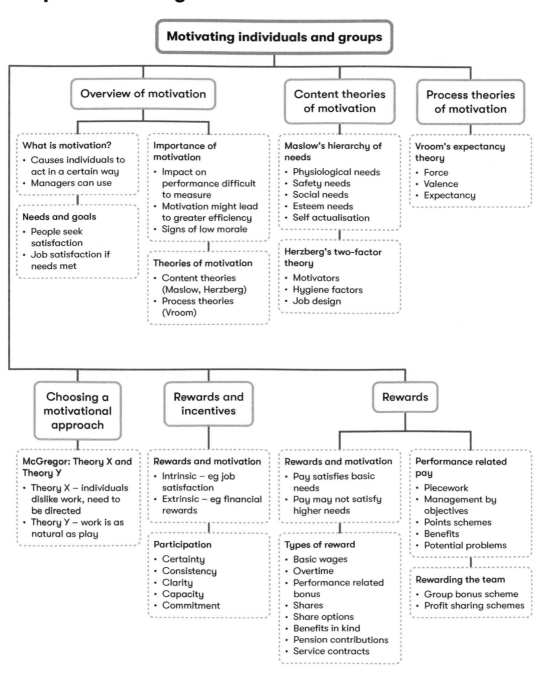

Motivating individuals and groups

Overview of motivation

What is motivation?
- Causes individuals to act in a certain way
- Managers can use

Needs and goals
- People seek satisfaction
- Job satisfaction if needs met

Importance of motivation
- Impact on performance difficult to measure
- Motivation might lead to greater efficiency
- Signs of low morale

Theories of motivation
- Content theories (Maslow, Herzberg)
- Process theories (Vroom)

Content theories of motivation

Maslow's hierarchy of needs
- Physiological needs
- Safety needs
- Social needs
- Esteem needs
- Self actualisation

Herzberg's two-factor theory
- Motivators
- Hygiene factors
- Job design

Process theories of motivation

Vroom's expectancy theory
- Force
- Valence
- Expectancy

Choosing a motivational approach

McGregor: Theory X and Theory Y
- Theory X – individuals dislike work, need to be directed
- Theory Y – work is as natural as play

Rewards and incentives

Rewards and motivation
- Intrinsic – eg job satisfaction
- Extrinsic – eg financial rewards

Participation
- Certainty
- Consistency
- Clarity
- Capacity
- Commitment

Rewards

Rewards and motivation
- Pay satisfies basic needs
- Pay may not satisfy higher needs

Types of reward
- Basic wages
- Overtime
- Performance related bonus
- Shares
- Share options
- Benefits in kind
- Pension contributions
- Service contracts

Performance related pay
- Piecework
- Management by objectives
- Points schemes
- Benefits
- Potential problems

Rewarding the team
- Group bonus scheme
- Profit sharing schemes

Knowledge diagnostic

1. Overview of motivation

Motivation is the **urge to do something** or avoid something. Knowledge of what motivates staff can help managers to improve performance.

2. Content and process theories

Content theories – such as **Maslow's** hierarchy of needs and **Herzberg's** two factor theorem – look at *what* motivates staff. **Vroom's** expectancy theory looks at *how* to motivate and so is a **process theory**.

3. McGregor

McGregor presented two types of employees – theory X, who dislike work, and therefore need to be controlled and directed, and theory Y who enjoy work, so should be given the opportunity to manage themselves. In reality most employees are somewhere between these two extremes.

4. Rewards and motivation

Rewards can be **intrinsic** or **extrinsic**. An **incentive** is the offer of a reward designed to motivate current and future performance. Extrinsic rewards such as pay may not motivate employees. Job design can lead to greater motivation, such as job rotation, job enlargement and job enrichment.

5. Profit related pay

Profit related pay may motivate employees to work towards the organisation's objectives. However, poorly thought out schemes, such as rewards based on subjective judgement of managers may fail to achieve this. Group bonus schemes and profit-sharing schemes may be used to motivate teams.

Further study guidance

Question practice

Now try the following from the Further question practice bank [available in the digital edition of the workbook]:

Number			
Q75	Exam Section A	1	1 min
Q76	Exam Section A	2	2 mins
Q77	Exam Section A	2	2 mins
Q78	Exam Section A	2	2 mins
Q79	Exam Section B	4	5 mins

Further reading

There are two articles on the ACCA website that are relevant to the material in this chapter. The first is entitled 'Let's get motivated' and the second is entitled 'Understanding Herzberg's motivational theory'. You are strongly advised to read these articles in full as part of your preparation for the FBT exam.

Activity answers

Activity 1: What is motivation?

Reasons cited were

- Interest or accomplishment (particularly amongst managerial class)
- To keep occupied (particularly amongst working class and farmers)

They said they would miss most

- Friends and contacts (31%)
- Feeling of doing something (25%)
- The kind of work they do (12%)

Activity 2: Demotivation

Demotivation can manifest itself in the following:

- Poor time keeping
- Absenteeism
- Staff turnover
- Missed targets
- Indifference

Activity 3: Maslow's hierarchy of needs

Maslow's categories:

(1) Esteem needs

(2) Social needs

(3) Self-actualisation needs overriding lower-level needs!

(4) Physiological needs

(5) Safety needs initially; esteem needs above a certain income level

(6) Social needs or self-actualisation needs

(7) Esteem needs

(8) Self-actualisation or esteem needs.

Activity 4: PRP

PRP might fail to motivate because:

(1) The rewards from PRP are often too small to motivate effectively. Anyhow, some employees may not expect to receive the rewards and hence will not put in the extra effort.

(2) It is often unfair, especially in jobs where success is determined by uncontrollable factors.

(3) If people are rewarded individually, they may be less willing to work as a team.

(4) People may concentrate on short-term performance indicators rather than on longer-term goals such as innovation or quality. In other words, people put all their energy into hitting the target rather than doing their job better.

(5) PRP schemes have to be well designed to ensure performance is measured properly, people consider them to be fair and there is consent to the scheme.

Activity 5: Equitable pay

Organisations can ensure equitable pay by:

- Benchmarking internally

- Benchmark externally
- Create pay scales linked to job descriptions.

Skills checkpoint 4

Approaching multi-task questions

Chapter overview

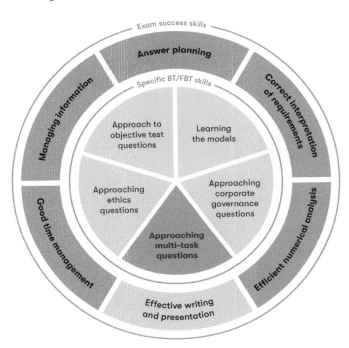

Introduction

MTQs in Section B comprise 24% of your exam (via six 4-mark questions, usually broken down into two parts of two marks each). It is therefore important that you give adequate revision time to practising these questions. The technical content is the same as in Section A of the exam, however the format and the mark allocation varies.

All syllabus areas will be covered by MTQS and there will be one question for each section of the syllabus as follows:

A	The business organisation, its stakeholders and the external environment
B	Business organisational structure, functions and governance
C	Accounting and reporting systems, compliance, control, technology and security
D	Leading and managing individuals and teams
E	Personal effectiveness and communication
F	Professional ethics in accounting and business

Types of question

In Section B, there is more variety in the types of question that can be used. You may see some or all of the following types of question in your exam:

- **Multiple response questions** with more than four options - for example, choose two items from six or four from eight.
- **Gap fill questions** - where you need to complete a paragraph by filling gaps that appear in the text. Responses are selected by clicking on the gap and selecting the correct response from a drop down menu.
- **Multi response matching** - where candidates select responses according to a grid of choices. Task 1 of the skills activity below is an example of multi response matching.
- **Hotspot questions** - where you have to clock on the relevant part of a symbol or diagram. For example, there may be a number of boxes where you are required to select the boxes that apply.
- **Number entry question** - where you will need to calculate a value and enter it into a box. Such questions will not be common in BT/FBT as most of the syllabus covers qualitative topics rather than quantitative.

The good news about Section B is that there will be partial marking. In a two mark multiple response question for example, which requires you to select two items from six, you would get one mark if only one of your answers was correct. In Section A, you only get marks for multi response questions if you all of your selections are correct.

Approach to multi-task questions

The following step by step approach is recommended:

STEP 1 **Read the requirements of all tasks.** There are usually two tasks worth 2 marks each in each Section B question.

STEP 2 **Recall relevant technical theory** that you will need to answer the question.

STEP 3 **Read the scenario** to identify the relevant information.

STEP 4 **Answer each task in turn** - doing the easier task first

Exam success skills

The following question is an example the sort of MTQ (multi-task question) you could see in Section B of your exam.

For this question, we will also focus on the following exam success skills:

(a) Managing information

There is a scenario associated with this MTQ which runs to around 320 words. It can feel daunting. It is important therefore to know what you are looking for when you read the scenario and this means reading the requirement of the task first, before you read the scenario. After reading the task, think about the technical knowledge you will need to answer the question. When you do read the scenario, you will be much more focussed on what you need to look for in the scenario.

(b) Correct Interpretation of requirements

Sometimes when you are focused on applying technical knowledge you have learned it is easy to misinterpret the requirements of a question. For example, giving the highest value when the lowest is asked for. Also, the order of the information given in the scenario may be different to the order of the information given in the part of the question where you give your answer.

(c) Good time management

You should be guided by the mark allocation in MTQs as the sub questions can have different requirements, there is no set format for these questions so you need to react to what is presented, however the rule of 1.2 minutes per mark still applies. You may have completed section A of the exam in less time, which is good news for Section B as the scenarios can be quite time consuming to read and digest. As with section A, the questions in Section B with shorter scenarios are usually quicker to attempt and may give you more time for the calculations. You do not have to answer the sub questions in order, you should play to your exam strengths, which means attempting the questions you are most confident about first.

Skill activity

The following question is from the ACCA web site, and is one of the additional multi-task questions provided alongside the specimen exam:

Go Car Co is a car sales company. The company employs four sales staff (Ahmed, Ben, Critica and Damla) at their largest branch. A new vacancy has arisen for an area sales manager for the region, based at the Head Office in another city.

The four people were asked to an interview by their own manager to review their own performance and to indicate whether they were motivated to apply for the new role and the following were part of their responses to the manager's question about that.

Person	
Ahmed	"I have all the skills for the role and wish to further my career and take on a more senior role. I think I will be successful because I trust the interview panel to act fairly and transparently, so I am reasonably confident that they will recognise me as the most suitable candidate."
Ben	"I have performed well over the last 12 months and have been rewarded with a very good performance bonus as a result. If I apply for the manager's role and am successful, I may not be better off financially because I would no longer get the sales commission or a performance bonus in my new role. Also, it would be more convenient for me personally to be based here than at Head Office, because of the extra travelling involved."
Critica	"I work extremely hard on training and developing myself in the sales role, but the training materials we are using do not seem to be very effective. When I use the suggested selling techniques, I don't seem to be able to sell any more cars, so I don't feel I am confident enough to apply for a promotion just yet."
Damla	"I am really keen to apply for the role and possess the relevant skills and a masters' degree in management. The problem I have with applying for the role is that I do not think I will be successful because I think the interview panel have already identified other people who they prefer for the role. I fear that however highly qualified I am and even if I perform well at the interview, I will not be successful."

Task 1:

Which of the following three elements of the Vroom theory of expectancy is MOST significant in affecting each of the candidates' motivational force regarding a potential application of the sales manager's role? (2 marks)

	Expectancy	Instrumentality	Valence
Damla			
Critica			
Ben			
Ahmed			

Task 2:

The manager of four other car sales staff at another branch of Go Cars Go (Alwyn, Bob, Chloe and Dumy) has been asked to complete a grid for Head Office to estimate the overall Vroom's motivational force of each of these sales people to apply for the vacant manager's role at Head Office.

The following scores out of 10 were given by the manager for the potential candidates, against each of the three elements of motivational force:

Element of motivational force	Alwyn	Bob	Chloe	Dumy
Expectancy	4	8	3	7
Instrumentality	8	6	7	2
Valence	7	3	7	8

Which candidate has the LOWEST motivational force, overall, to apply for the new role of manager at Head Office? (2 marks)

- ○ Dumy
- ○ Chloe
- ○ Bob
- ○ Alwyn

Approach

(a) **Read the requirement** of the two tasks. In the first task you have to identify which element of Vroom's theory is demonstrated by each of four people. In the second, you need to state which candidate has the LOWEST motivational force overall.

(b) **Recall the technical theory** - in this case, Vroom's expectancy theory:

    (i) Motivational force = Expectancy × instrumentality × valence

    (ii) Expectancy is the belief that effort will achieve a performance goal.

    (iii) Instumentality is the belief that achieving the goal will lead to a reward.

    (iv) Valence is the value that one places on the reward..

(c) **Now you know what you are looking for.** For task 1, you will need to decide which of the three variables (expectancy, instrumentality or valence) appears to be the most important for each person. For task 2 you need to do a calculation for each person to see who has the lowest motivation.

(d) You may have noticed that the scenario for task 2 is quite a bit shorter than that of task 1, so it would be better to do this task first. In this question, task 2 does not require any information from the scenario for task 1, so it is fine to do this.

(e) **Read the scenario** for task 2 - you just need to multiply the three scores for each individual, and the one with the lowest scores is the correct answer.

(f)   Read the scenario for task 1, remembering that what you need to know for the first task is which of the three variables is likely to be strongest for each candidate: After reading each candidate, put your answer for that candidate in the grid by highlighting the appropriate radio button. **BEWARE!** In the answer grid, the names of the four candidates are shown in a different order to how they are presented in the scenario.

Solutions

Task 1

	Expectancy	Instrumentality	Valence
Damla		✔	
Critica	✔		
Ben			✔
Ahmed		✔	

Justification:

- Damla does not believe that her effort (having the relevant skills) will result in the desired performance goal (getting offered the job). She is therefore focused on the expectancy variable.
- Critica believes that she has met a desired performance goal, as she has mastered all the training materials, but does not believe that these have helped her get the reward, which is making more sales. She is therefore focussing on instrumental.
- Ben is very focussed on rewards. He feels that the rewards of the job would do not make it attractive, but in his current job he does believe that the rewards are good. He is clearly motivated by the valence.
- Ahmed is motivated by the fact that he believes that having the right skills will lead to the reward - being offered the job. He is therefore focussing in the instrumental aspect.

Note. In task 1, the answers relating to Ahmed and Ben are more obvious that Damla and Critica. Even if you only got 2 out of the four correct, you would still get 1 mark out of 2, so all would not be lost.

Task 2

The overall scores achieved by multiplying the scores for each element by each other are as follows:

Alwyn: (4 × 8 × 7) = 224

Bob = 144

Chloe = 147

Dummy = 112

Dummy has the lowest score and therefore the lowest motivation.

Exam success skills diagnostic

Every time you complete a Section B MTQ, use the diagnostic below to assess how effectively you demonstrated the exam success skills in answering the questions. The table has been completed below for the question in this checkpoint to give you an idea of how to complete the diagnostic.

Exam Success Skill	Your reflections/observations
Managing information	Did you read the requirements before reading the detail in the scenario?

Correct Interpretation of requirements	Did you do what the requirement asked? (eg in task 2, state who has the **lowest** motivation rather than the **highest**)
	It would have been disappointing to get the answer correct, but fail to get the marks because you didn't follow the instructions given.
Answer planning	n/a
Efficient numerical analysis	n/a
Effective writing and presentation	n/a
Good Time Management	Did you manage to attempt the entire question in 5 minutes?
	Did you attempt the sub questions in the order set, or did you think about how long each one would take and devise an action plan to give you the most time for the calculation elements?
Most important action points to apply to your next question	
Make sure that you remember to practice MTQs as part of your exam preparation, endeavouring to attempt all elements in the time allowed (5 minutes)	

Summary

- Make sure that you remember to practice MTQs as part of your exam preparation, endeavouring to attempt all elements in the time allowed (5 minutes)

- Remember that you don't have to answer the tasks within a question in order and that the answer from one task will never be needed to answer the second one.

- Read the question carefully and use the mark allocation to guide how long it should take to answer and how complex it is likely to be.

- Next steps – Try question 30 from the further question practice in the workbook. Try to apply the techniques described above when you do this question, in particular, reading the requirements first, then thinking about the technical knowledge before reading the scenarios. Would you do task 1 first or task 2?

16

Training and development

Learning outcomes

On completion of this chapter you should be able to:

	Syllabus reference no.
Explain the importance of learning and development in the workplace.	D6 (a)
Describe the learning process: Honey and Mumford, Kolb.	D6 (b)
Describe the role of the human resources department and individual managers in the learning process.	D6 (c)
Describe the training and development process: identifying needs, setting objectives, programme design, delivery and validation.	D6 (d)
Explain the terms 'training', 'development' and 'education' and the characteristics of each.	D6 (e)
List the benefits of effective training and development in the workplace.	D6 (f)

Exam context

Training and development are very examinable topics, especially if linked to appraisal and performance management. There were two questions in the specimen exam relating to this chapter.

Chapter overview

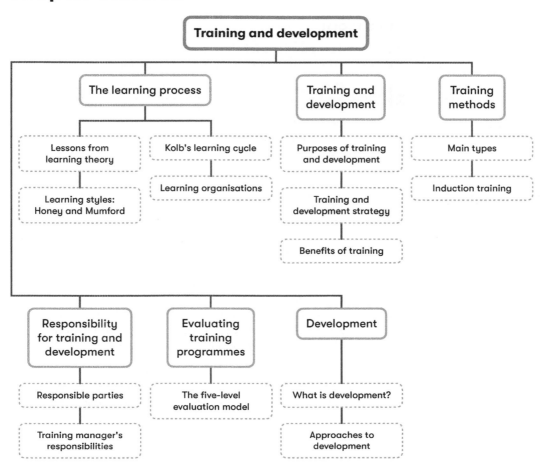

1 The learning process

1.1 Lessons from learning theory

Learning theory offers certain useful propositions for the design of **effective training programmes** and the role of the human resources department in developing such programmes.

Proposition	Comment
The individual should be **motivated** to learn.	The advantages of training should be made clear, according to the individual's motives – money, opportunity, valued skills or whatever.
There should be clear **objectives and standards** set, so that each task has some meaning.	Each stage of learning should present a challenge, without overloading trainees or making them lose confidence. Specific objectives and performance standards will help trainees in the planning and control process that leads to learning, and provide targets against which performance will constantly be measured.
There should be timely, relevant **feedback** on performance and progress.	This will usually be provided by the trainer and should be concurrent – or certainly not long delayed. If progress reports or performance appraisals are given only at the year end, for example, there will be no opportunity for behaviour adjustment or learning in the meantime.
Positive and negative **reinforcement** should be judiciously used.	Recognition and encouragement enhance individuals' confidence in their competence and progress: punishment for poor performance – especially without explanation and correction – discourages the learner and creates feelings of guilt, failure and hostility.
Active **participation** is more telling than passive reception (because of its effect on the motivation to learn, concentration and recollection).	If a high degree of participation is impossible, practice and repetition can be used to reinforce receptivity. However, participation has the effect of encouraging 'ownership' of the process of learning and changing – committing individuals to it as their own goal, not just an imposed process.

1.2 Learning styles: Honey and Mumford

*Honey and Mumford (1986)*identified four learning styles that people adopt. Knowledge of the style favoured by the learner helps to tailor learning activities.

(a) **Theorists** – seek to understand underlying theoretical concepts taking an intellectual, logical approach to actions.

(b) **Reflectors** – observe and consider phenomena then act at their own pace

(c) **Activists** – like to learn by doing something. They act first and consider the consequences afterwards.

(d) **Pragmatists** – study if there is a direct link to practical problems (on the job training). They like to learn how to do something rather than the underlying theory.

1.3 Kolb's learning cycle

The learning cycle (D. Kolb 1984) demonstrates that **experiential learning** involves trainees learning through experience.

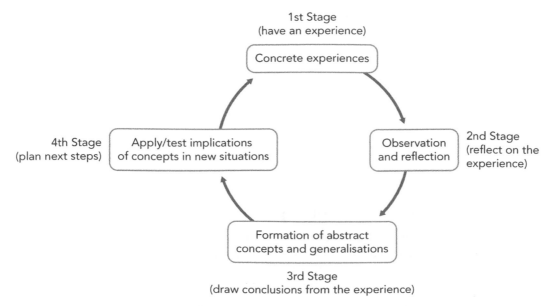

1st Stage
(have an experience)

Concrete experiences

2nd Stage
(reflect on the experience)

Observation and reflection

3rd Stage
(draw conclusions from the experience)

Formation of abstract concepts and generalisations

4th Stage
(plan next steps)

Apply/test implications of concepts in new situations

Suppose that an employee interviews a customer for the first time (concrete experience). They observe their own performance and the dynamics of the situation (observation) and afterwards, having failed to convince the customer to buy the product, the employee thinks about what they did right and wrong (reflection). They come to the conclusion that they failed to listen to what the customer really wanted and feared, underneath their general reluctance: they realise that the key to communication is active listening (abstraction/generalisation). They decide to apply active listening techniques in their next interview (application/testing). This provides them with a new experience with which to start the cycle over again.

1.4 Learning organisation

> **Learning organisation:** One that facilitates the learning of all its members by gathering and sharing knowledge, tolerating experience and solving problems analytically.

Learning organisations are good at:

- Experimentation, ie tolerate risk that things may go wrong
- Learning from past experience
- Learning from others
- Transferring knowledge quickly and efficiently throughout the organisation.

Activity 1: Learning organisation

Suggest some practical ways of becoming a learning organisation.

2 Training and development

2.1 Purposes of training and development

There are many factors affecting a person's performance at work. Training and development is one method by which an organisation may seek to improve the performance of its staff. The main **purpose** of training and development is to raise competence and therefore performance standards. It is also concerned with personal development, helping and motivating employees to fulfil their potential.

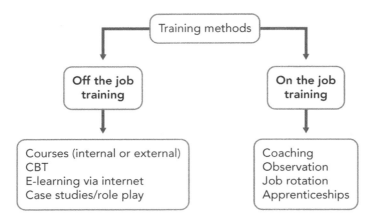

2.2 Training and development strategy

Organisations create **'training and development' strategies** to tie in with the overall business strategy. A **systematic approach** should be used to developing the strategy to ensure that the training undertaken meets the needs of the organisation.

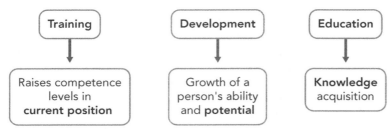

2.3 Benefits of training

Benefits of training for the **organisation** include:

(a) Improves **productivity** of staff

(b) **Reduces accidents** and errors at work (and associated costs)

(c) Improves **motivation and retention** of staff

(d) **Improves quality of staff** available internally for promotion

(e) **Attracts better staff** due to showing commitment and progression opportunities

(f) Enables **succession planning** and career development

(g) Source of competitive advantage through **innovation**

(h) Helps build **corporate culture**.

Benefits of training for the **employee** include:

(a) Enhances portfolio of **skills**

(b) **Psychological benefits** (helps self-esteem and confidence in future)

(c) **Social benefit** (can help satisfy 'social needs')

(d) **The job** (helps them do it successfully).

Essential reading

See Chapter 16 Section 1 of the Essential reading for more detail on evaluation of training needs.

The Essential reading is available as an Appendix of the digital edition of the Workbook.

3 Training methods

3.1 Types of training

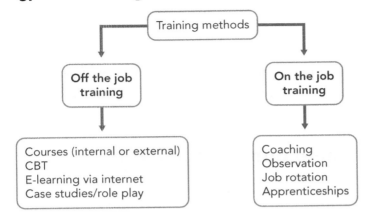

Activity 2: External courses

What are the pros and cons to the organisation of sending people on **off-site** courses using an **external** provider?

Solution

Activity 3: Internal training

What are the pros and cons to the individual of **on the job** training by an **internal** manager/employee?

Solution

3.2 Induction training

Induction training is the process whereby a person is formally introduced and integrated into an organisation or department. Inductions should be an 'ongoing' process that involves mentoring, coaching, training and monitoring.

Essential reading

See Chapter 16 Section 2 of the Essential reading for more detail on training methods.

The Essential reading is available as an Appendix of the digital edition of the Workbook.

4 Responsibility for training and development

4.1 Responsible parties

Responsibility for an individual's training is shared by several parties:

(a) Trainee – many people believe that the ultimate responsibility for training and development lies with the employer rather than the employee.

(b) HR department or training department – centrally concerned with career development.

(c) Line managers – responsible for identifying training needs, coaching staff, assessing competencies and offering on the job training opportunities.

(d) Training manager (reports to head of HR).

4.2 Training manager's responsibilities

The **training manager's** responsibilities include:

(a) Liaison (with operating depts)

(b) Scheduling

(c) Needs identification

(d) Programme design

(e) Feedback

5 Evaluating training programmes

KEY TERM

Validation of training: Observing the results of the course and measuring whether the training objectives have been achieved.

Evaluation of training: Comparing the costs of the scheme against the assessed benefits which are being obtained.

5.1 The five-level evaluation model

The effectiveness of a training scheme may be measured at different levels (A. Hamblin 1974).

Level 1	**Trainees' reactions to the experience.** These are usually measured by post-training feedback forms.
Level 2	**Trainee learning** (new skills and knowledge): measuring what the trainees have learned on the course, usually by means of a test at the end of it.
Level 3	**Changes in job behaviour following training:** observing work practices and outputs (products, services, documents) to identify post-training differences.
Level 4	**Impact of training on organisational goals/results:** seeing whether the training

	scheme has contributed to the overall objectives of the organisation in terms of quality, productivity, profitability, employee retention, and so on.
Level 5	**Ultimate value:** the impact of training on the wider 'good' of the organisation in terms of stakeholder benefits, greater social responsibility, corporate growth/survival.

Activity 4: Evaluating and validating training

Outline why it is important to evaluate and validate a training programme.

6 Development

6.1 What is development?

A wider approach to fulfilling an individual's potential than training and education. May include a range of learning experiences:

(a) Work experience of increasing challenge and responsibility

(b) Guidance support and counselling

(c) Suitable education and training

(d) Help to plan individual's future.

6.2 Approaches to development

Approaches to development include the following:

Approach	
Management development	Improving managerial effectiveness through a planned process. This may include the development of management/leadership skills (or competences), management education (such as MBA programmes) and planned experience of different functions, positions and work settings, in preparation for increasing managerial responsibility.
Career development	Individuals plan career paths. The trend for delayered organisations has reduced opportunities for upward progression: opportunities may be planned for sideways/lateral transfers, secondments to project groups, short external secondments, and so on, to offer new opportunities.
Professional development	Professional bodies offer structured programmes of continuing professional development (CPD). The aim is to ensure that professional standards are maintained and enhanced through education, development and training self-managed by the individual. A CPD approach is based on the belief that a professional qualification should be the basis for a career lifetime of development **and** adherence to a professional code of ethics and standards.
Personal development	Businesses are increasingly offering employees wider-ranging development opportunities, rather than focusing on skills required in their current job. Personal development creates more rounded, competent employees who may contribute more innovatively and flexibly to the organisation's future needs. It may also help to foster employee job satisfaction, commitment and loyalty.

Activity 5: Hindrances to developing

What may prevent a staff member from learning or developing?

Solution

Chapter summary

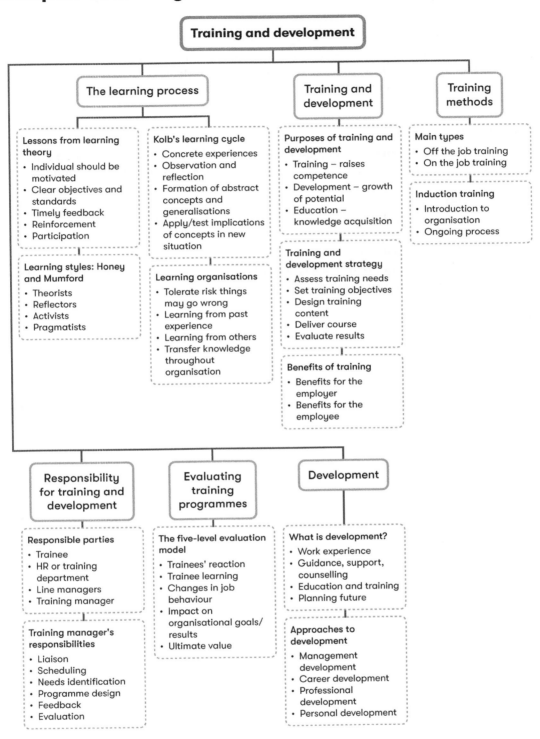

Training and development

The learning process

Lessons from learning theory
- Individual should be motivated
- Clear objectives and standards
- Timely feedback
- Reinforcement
- Participation

Learning styles: Honey and Mumford
- Theorists
- Reflectors
- Activists
- Pragmatists

Kolb's learning cycle
- Concrete experiences
- Observation and reflection
- Formation of abstract concepts and generalisations
- Apply/test implications of concepts in new situation

Learning organisations
- Tolerate risk things may go wrong
- Learning from past experience
- Learning from others
- Transfer knowledge throughout organisation

Training and development

Purposes of training and development
- Training – raises competence
- Development – growth of potential
- Education – knowledge acquisition

Training and development strategy
- Assess training needs
- Set training objectives
- Design training content
- Deliver course
- Evaluate results

Benefits of training
- Benefits for the employer
- Benefits for the employee

Training methods

Main types
- Off the job training
- On the job training

Induction training
- Introduction to organisation
- Ongoing process

Responsibility for training and development

Responsible parties
- Trainee
- HR or training department
- Line managers
- Training manager

Training manager's responsibilities
- Liaison
- Scheduling
- Needs identification
- Programme design
- Feedback
- Evaluation

Evaluating training programmes

The five-level evaluation model
- Trainees' reaction
- Trainee learning
- Changes in job behaviour
- Impact on organisational goals/results
- Ultimate value

Development

What is development?
- Work experience
- Guidance, support, counselling
- Education and training
- Planning future

Approaches to development
- Management development
- Career development
- Professional development
- Personal development

Knowledge diagnostic

1. The learning process

Learning theory helps design training events that are appropriate to the needs of the learners. **Honey and Mumford** identified learning styles – **theorists, reflectors, activists** and **pragmatists.** **Kolb** demonstrated a learning cycle based on **experience** that shows the opportunity for learning to be a constant process.

2. Training and development

Training is about **raising particular competence levels** while education is about **acquiring knowledge.** Development is broader, involving growth of a person's **ability and potential.**

3. Training methods

There are a range of on and off the job methods that can be adopted to train staff.

4. Responsibility for training and development

Responsibility for an individual's training is shared by several parties: trainees, HR department, line managers and the training manager.

5. Evaluating training programmes

Training events can be **evaluated** using a **five-stage approach** including during the event and once the trainee is back at the workplace.

6. Development

Development methods include work experience, coaching, mentoring, job rotation and training.

Further study guidance

Question practice

Now try the following from the Further question practice bank [available in the digital edition of the workbook]:

Number			
Q80	Exam Section A	2	2 mins
Q81	Exam Section A	2	2 mins
Q82	Exam Section A	2	2 mins
Q83	Exam Section A	2	2 mins
Q84	Exam Section A	1	1 min

Own research

Do some research on the internet to find out what types of approaches are used for employee benefit by some of the best employers.

Activity answers

Activity 1: Learning organisation

Some practical ways of becoming a learning organisation include:

- Access to a range of training
- Knowledge management systems
- Training budgets
- Encouragement of innovation
- Mentoring

Activity 2: External courses

Pros and cons:

Pros	
Quality	Quality/focus
Motivation	Time delay
No distractions	Retention

Activity 3: Internal training

Pros and cons:

Pros	
Quick	Not standardised
Cost effective	May not happen
Flexible	

Activity 4: Evaluating and validating training

Validation of a new course is important to ensure that objectives have been achieved. Evaluation of it is more difficult, but at least as important because it identifies the value of the training programme to the organisation. Both are required to improve effectiveness or cost effectiveness next time.

Activity 5: Hindrances to developing

The following are some things that might prevent a staff member from learning or developing:

- Motivation
- Lack of awareness
- Lack of confidence
- Lack of encouragement.

17

Performance appraisal

Learning outcomes

On completion of this chapter you should be able to:

	Syllabus reference no.
Explain the importance of performance assessment.	D7 (a)
Explain how organisations assess the performance of human resources.	D7 (b)
Define performance appraisal and describe its purposes.	D7 (c)
Describe the performance appraisal process.	D7 (d)
Explain the benefits of effective appraisal.	D7 (e)
Identify the barriers to effective appraisal and how these may be overcome.	D7 (f)

Exam context

This topic is a rich source of potential exam questions. The approaches to performance appraisal featured in one of the specimen exam questions.

Chapter overview

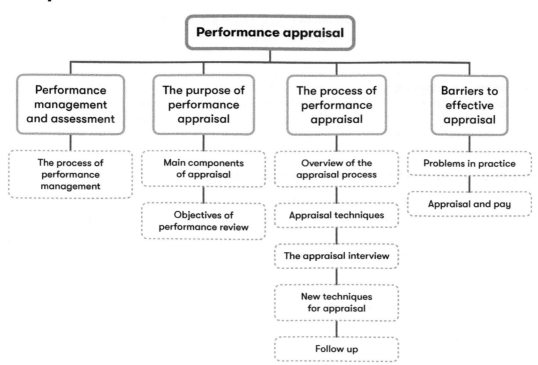

1 Performance management

The purpose of **performance management** is to improve **organisational performance** by ensuring that **individuals** within it are performing to the best of their ability and developing their potential for improvement.

KEY TERM

> **Performance management:** Performance management is a means of getting better results by managing performance within an agreed framework of goals, standards and competence requirements. It is a process to establish a shared understanding about what is to be achieved, and an approach to managing and developing people in order to achieve it.

1.1 The process of performance management

A systematic approach to performance management might include the following steps.

Step 1 From the business plan, identify the requirements and competences required to carry it out.

Step 2 Draw up a **performance agreement**, defining the expectations of the individual or team, covering standards of performance, performance indicators and the skills and competences people need.

Step 3 Draw up a performance and development plan with the individual. These record the actions needed to improve performance, normally covering development in the current job. They are discussed with jobholders and will typically cover:

- The areas of performance the individual feels in need of development
- What the individual and manager agree is needed to enhance performance
- Development and training initiatives

Step 4 **Manage performance continually throughout the year**, not just at appraisal interviews done to satisfy the personnel department. Managers can review actual performance, with more informal interim reviews at various times of the year.

(a) High performance is reinforced by praise, recognition and increasing responsibility. Low performance results in coaching or counselling.

(b) Work plans are updated as necessary.

(c) Deal with performance problems by identifying what they are, establish the reasons for the shortfall, take control action (with adequate resources) and provide feedback.

Step 5 **Performance review (performance appraisal).** At a defined period each year, success against the plan is reviewed, but the whole point is to assess what is going to happen in future.

In order for learning and motivation to be effective, it is essential that **people know exactly what their objectives are**. This enables them to do the following.

(a) Plan and direct their effort towards the objectives

(b) Monitor their performance against objectives and adjust (or learn) if required

(c) Experience the reward of achievement once the objectives have been reached

(d) Feel that their tasks have meaning and purpose, which is an important element in job satisfaction

(e) Experience the motivation of a challenge: the need to expend energy and effort in a particular direction in order to achieve something

(f) Avoid the demotivation of impossible or inadequately rewarded tasks. As we have discussed in the chapter on motivation, there is a calculation involved in motivated performance. If objectives are vague, unrealistic or unattainable, there may be little incentive to pursue them: hence the importance of SMART objectives.

The differences between performance management and performance appraisal:

- Performance management is a much wider remit and covers the whole organisation
- Appraisal is more individual

2 The purpose of performance appraisal

2.1 Main components of appraisal

The general purpose of any appraisal system is to improve the efficiency of the organisation by ensuring that the individuals within it are performing to the best of their ability and developing their potential for improvement. This has three main components:

(a) **Reward review**: measuring the extent to which the employee deserves a bonus or pay increase.

(b) **Performance review**: for planning and following up training and development programmes.

(c) **Potential review**: aid to planning career progression and succession planning.

2.2 Objectives of performance appraisal:

More specific objectives of appraisal may be summarised as follows:

(a) Establishing what the individual has to do in a job in order that the objectives for the section or department are realised

(b) Establishing the key or main results which the individual will be expected to achieve in the course of their work over a period of time

(c) Comparing the individual's level of performance against a standard, to provide a basis for remuneration above the basic pay rate

(d) Identifying the individual's training and development needs in the light of actual performance

(e) Identifying potential candidates for promotion

(f) Identifying areas for improvement

(g) Establishing an inventory of actual and potential performance within the undertaking, as a basis for human resource planning

(h) Monitoring the undertaking's selection procedures against the subsequent performance of recruits

(i) Improving communication about work tasks between different levels in the hierarchy

Activity 1: Formal appraisal

List four disadvantages to the individual of not having a formal appraisal system.

Solution

3 The process of performance appraisal

3.1 Overview of the appraisal process

There are three basic requirements for a formal appraisal system

(a) The formulation of desired traits and standards against which individuals can be consistently and objectively assessed

(b) Recording assessments; managers should be encouraged to utilise a standard framework, but still be allowed to express what they consider important, and without too much form-filling

(c) Getting the appraiser and appraisee together, so that both contribute to the assessment and plans for improvement and/or development

A systematic appraisal system can be depicted as follows:

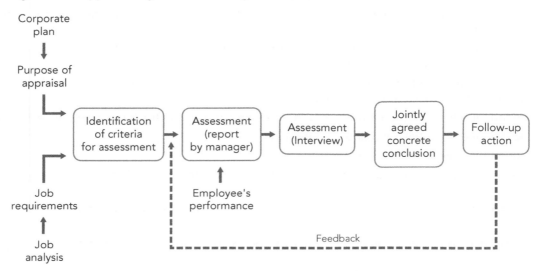

3.2 Appraisal techniques

A combination of methods may be used to measure the effectiveness of employees:

(a) **Overall assessment:** narrative of manager's judgement

(b) **Guided assessment:** comments by manager and appraisee under specific performance elements

(c) **Grading:** manager applies a numerical grade against each performance element

(d) **Behavioural incident methods:** success or failure based on critical job behaviour

(e) **Results orientated schemes:** assessment against specific, measurable objectives

Activity 2: Appraisal techniques

What sort of appraisal systems are suggested by the following examples?

Example	Appropriate technique
Teachers at a school send a brief report at the end of each term to the parents of the school's pupils. Typical phrases include 'a satisfactory term's work', and 'could do better'.	
A firm of auditors assess the performance of their staff in four categories: technical ability, relationships with clients, relationships with other members of the audit team, and professional attitude. On each of these criteria staff are marked from A (= excellent) to E (= poor).	
A firm of insurance brokers assesses the performance of its staff by the number of clients they have visited and the number of policies sold.	

3.2.1 Self-appraisal

Self-appraisal is where the employee assesses their own performance against criteria, identifies issues, and discusses with their manager how to resolve them. This emphasises development.

Activity 3: Self appraisal

What are the pros and cons of self-appraisal?

Solution

3.3 The appraisal interview

Maier identifies **three approaches** to appraisal interviews (*Maier N. 1975*):

(a) **Tell and sell style** - the manager tells the employee how they have done and tried to 'sell' the evaluation.

(b) **Tell and listen style** - the manager tells the employee how they have done and then invites the employee to respond.

(c) **Problem solving style** - the manager takes on the role of coach, rather than appraiser, discussing problems and helping the employee to find solutions.

3.4 New techniques for appraisal

3.4.1 Upward appraisal

A notable modern trend adopted by some companies is upward appraisal, whereby employees are not rated by their superiors but by their subordinates. The followers appraise the leader.

Advantages of upward appraisal include the following:

(a) Subordinates tend to know their superior better than superiors know their subordinates.

(b) As all subordinates rate their managers statistically, these ratings tend to be more reliable – the more subordinates the better. Instead of the biases of individual managers' ratings, the various ratings of the employees can be converted into a representative view.

(c) Subordinates' ratings have more impact because it is more unusual to receive ratings from subordinates. It is also surprising to bosses because, despite protestations to the contrary, information often flows down organisations more smoothly and comfortably than it flows up. When it flows up it is qualitatively and quantitatively different. It is this difference that makes it valuable.

Problems with the method include fear of reprisals, vindictiveness, and extra form processing. Some bosses in strong positions might refuse to act, even if a consensus of staff suggested that they should change their ways.

3.4.2 Customer appraisal

In some companies, part of the employee's appraisal process includes taking into account **feedback** from 'customers' (whether internal or external). Some organisations go further and make customer feedback a key element of employee remuneration. This reflects the view that customers are the best judges of customer service.

3.4.3 360 degree appraisal

Taking downwards, upwards and customer appraisals together, some firms have instituted 360 degree appraisal (or multi-source appraisal) by collecting feedback on an individual's performance from the following sources.

(a) The person's immediate manager

(b) People who report to the appraisee, perhaps divided into groups

(c) Peers and co-workers: most people interact with others within an organisation, either as members of a team or as the receivers or providers of services, and can offer useful feedback

(d) Customers: if salespeople know what customers thought of them, they might be able to improve their technique

(e) The manager personally: all forms of 360 degree appraisal require people to rate themselves, and those 'who see themselves as others see them will get fewer surprises'

Sometimes the appraisal results in a counselling session, especially when the result of the appraisals are conflicting. For example, an appraisee's manager may have quite a different view of the appraisee's skills than subordinates.

3.5 Follow up

After the appraisal interview, the manager may complete the report, with an overall assessment, assessment of potential and/or the jointly reached conclusion of the interview, with recommendations for follow-up action. The manager should then discuss the report with the counter-signing manager (usually their own superior), resolving any problems that have arisen in making the appraisal or report, and agreeing on action to be taken. The report form may then go to the development adviser, training officer or other relevant people as appropriate for follow-up.

Follow-up procedures may include the following:

(a) **Informing appraisees of the results** of the appraisal, if this has not been central to the review interview

(b) **Carrying out agreed actions** on training, promotion, and so on

(c) **Monitoring the appraisee's progress** and checking that they have carried out agreed actions or improvements

(d) Taking necessary steps to **help the appraisee to attain improvement objectives**, by guidance, providing feedback, upgrading equipment, altering work methods, and so on

Activity 4: Follow up

What would happen without follow-up?

4 Barriers to effective appraisal

4.1 Problems in practice

Problems with appraisal are its implementation in practice and a range of misperceptions about it (*Lockett, 1992*). New techniques of appraisal aim to monitor effectiveness from a number of perspectives.

Lockett pointed out that barriers to effective appraisal can be identified as follows:

Appraisal barriers	Comment
Appraisal as confrontation	Many people dread appraisals, or use them 'as a sort of show down, a good sorting out or a clearing of the air.' In this kind of climate: • There is likely to be a lack of agreement on performance levels and improvement needs. • The feedback may be subjective or exaggerated. • The feedback may be negatively delivered. • The appraisal may focus on negative aspects, rather than looking forward to potential for improvement and development.
Appraisal as judgement	The appraisal is seen as a one-sided process in which the manager acts as "judge, jury and counsel for the prosecution". This puts the subordinate on the defensive. Instead, the process of performance management 'needs to be jointly operated in order to retain the commitment and develop the self-awareness of the individual.'
Appraisal as chat	The appraisal is conducted as if it were a friendly chat 'without ... purpose or outcome ... Many managers, embarrassed by the need to give feedback and set stretching targets, reduce the appraisal to a few mumbled "well done!" and leave the interview with a briefcase of unresolved issues.'
Appraisal as bureaucracy	Appraisal is a form-filling exercise, to satisfy the personnel department. Its underlying purpose, improving individual and organisational performance, is forgotten.
Appraisal as unfinished business	Appraisal should be part of a continuing future-focused process of performance management, not a way of 'wrapping up' the past year's performance issues.
Appraisal as annual event	Many targets set at annual appraisal meetings become irrelevant or out of date. Feedback, goal adjustment and improvement planning should be a continuous process.

4.2 Appraisal and pay

Another problem is the extent to which the appraisal system is related to the **pay and reward system**. Many employees consider that positive appraisals should be rewarded, but there are major drawbacks to this approach.

(a) **Funds available** for pay rises rarely depend on one individual's performance alone – the whole company has to do well.

(b) **Continuous improvement** should perhaps be expected of employees as part of their work and development, not rewarded as extra.

(c) Performance management is about a lot more than pay for **past performance** – it is often **forward looking with** regard to future performance.

PER alert

Performance objective PO2, relating to stakeholder relationship management, includes the maintenance of 'productive business relationships'. Planning for and engaging positively with the appraisal process provides an example of a practical step you could take in this area.

Chapter summary

Performance appraisal

Performance management and assessment

The process of performance management
- Identify competences required
- Performance agreement
- Performance and development plan
- Manage performance continually
- Performance review

The purpose of performance appraisal

Main components of appraisal
- Reward review
- Performance review
- Potential review

Objectives of performance review
- Communicate objectives
- Establish expected results
- Assess current performance
- Identify development needs
- Improve communication

The process of performance appraisal

Overview of the appraisal process
- Formulation of desired traits and standards
- Recording assessments
- Getting appraiser and appraisee together

Appraisal techniques
- Overall assessment
- Guided assessment
- Grading
- Behavioural incident methods
- Results oriented schemes

The appraisal interview
- Three styles (Maier)
  - Tell and sell
  - Tell and listen
  - Problem solving

New techniques for appraisal
- Upward appraisal
- Customer appraisal
- 360 degree appraisal

Follow up
- Informing appraisees
- Agreed actions
- Monitoring progress
- Help attain objectives

Barriers to effective appraisal

Problems in practice
- Confrontation
- Judgement
- Chat
- Bureaucracy
- Unfinished business
- An annual event

Appraisal and pay
- Funds available
- Continu
- Funds available

Knowledge diagnostic

1. Objectives of performance management

The performance management process aims to improve organisational performance within an organisation by agreeing goals and standards with individuals and developing their potential for improvement. Performance management is a continuous process. Part of the process is the formal performance appraisal.

2. Objectives of performance appraisal

The performance review or appraisals **assesses performance** and **set future goals** as well as determining **development needs**. Appraisals may assess **reward, performance and or potential.**

3. Approaches to appraisal

There are a range of approaches to appraisal. These include overall assessment, guided assessment, grading, behavioural incident methods and results oriented schemes. Some systems use multi-source appraisal.

4. Appraisal style

Managers may adopt different styles in the appraisal including **telling**, **listening** and **problem solving** depending on the extent of involvement of the employee in the appraisal.

5. Barriers to effective appraisal

Lockett identified a range of **barriers to effective appraisal** including confrontation, judgement, a chat or seen as an annual event.

Further study guidance

Question practice

Now try the following from the Further question practice bank [available in the digital edition of the Workbook]:

Number	Level	Marks	Approximate time
Q85	Exam Section A	2	2 mins
Q86	Exam Section A	2	2 mins
Q87	Exam Section A	1	1 min
Q88	Exam Section A	2	2 mins
Q89	Exam Section A	2	2 mins

Further reading

There is an article on the ACCA website entitled 'Understanding the importance of appraisals' that is relevant to material in this chapter. You are strongly advised to read this article in full as part of your preparation for the FBT exam.

Activity answers

Activity 1: Formal appraisal

Disadvantages to the individual of not having an appraisal system include:

- The individual is not aware of progress or shortcomings.
- The individual is unable to judge whether they would be considered for promotion.
- The individual is unable to identify or correct weaknesses by training.
- There is a lack of communication with the manager.

Activity 2: Appraisal techniques

Appraisal systems:

Example	Appropriate technique
Teachers at a school send a brief report at the end of each term to the parents of the school's pupils. Typical phrases include 'a satisfactory term's work', and 'could do better'.	Overall assessment
A firm of auditors assess the performance of their staff in four categories: technical ability, relationships with clients, relationships with other members of the audit team, and professional attitude. On each of these criteria staff are marked from A (= excellent) to E (= poor).	A grading system, based on a guided assessment
A firm of insurance brokers assesses the performance of its staff by the number of clients they have visited and the number of policies sold.	Results-orientated scheme

Activity 3: Self appraisal

Pros	Cons
The employee is involved in their appraisal so they are more likely to accept the results of the appraisal than if it had been performed without their input.	The employee will find it hard to be objective about their own performance.
The employee had a better understanding of factors that may have led to failure to achieve particular objectives.	The employee may believe that they will lose out on rewards or promotions if they are too honest about poorer aspects of their performance.

Activity 4: Follow up

The appraisal would merely be seen as a pleasant chat with little effect on future performance, as circumstances change. Moreover, the individual might feel cheated.

18 Personal effectiveness and communication

Learning outcomes

On completion of this chapter you should be able to:

	Syllabus reference no.
Explain the importance of effective time management.	E1 (a)
Describe the barriers to effective time management and how they may be overcome.	E1 (b)
Describe the role of information technology in improving personal effectiveness.	E1 (c)
Identify the main ways in which people and teams can be ineffective at work.	E2 (a)
Explain how individual or team ineffectiveness can affect organisational performance.	E2 (b)
Describe the features of a 'competence framework'.	E3 (a)
Explain how a competence framework underpins professional development needs.	E3 (b)
Explain how personal and continuous professional development can increase personal effectiveness at work.	E3 (c)
Explain the purpose and benefits of coaching, mentoring and counselling in promoting employee effectiveness.	E3 (d)
Describe how a personal development plan should be formulated, implemented, monitored and reviewed by the individual.	E3 (e)
Identify situations where conflict at work can arise.	E4 (a)
Describe how conflict can affect personal and organisational performance.	E4 (b)
Identify ways in which conflict can be managed.	E4 (c)
Describe methods of communication used in the organisation and how they are used.	E5 (a)
Explain how the type of information differs and the purposes for which it is applied at different levels of the organisation: strategic, tactical and operational.	E5 (b)

	Syllabus reference no.
List the attributes of good quality information.	E5 (c)
Explain a simple communication model: sender, message, receiver, feedback, noise.	E5 (d)
Explain formal and informal communication and their importance in the workplace.	E5 (e)
Identify the consequences of ineffective communication.	E5 (f)
Describe the attributes of effective communication.	E5 (g)
Describe the barriers to effective communication and identify practical steps that may be taken to overcome them.	E5 (h)
Identify the main patterns of communication.	E5 (i)

Exam context

Many of these topics (eg barriers to communication, qualities of effective communication, counselling) may be set as questions. There were several questions in the specimen exam relating to this area.

Chapter overview

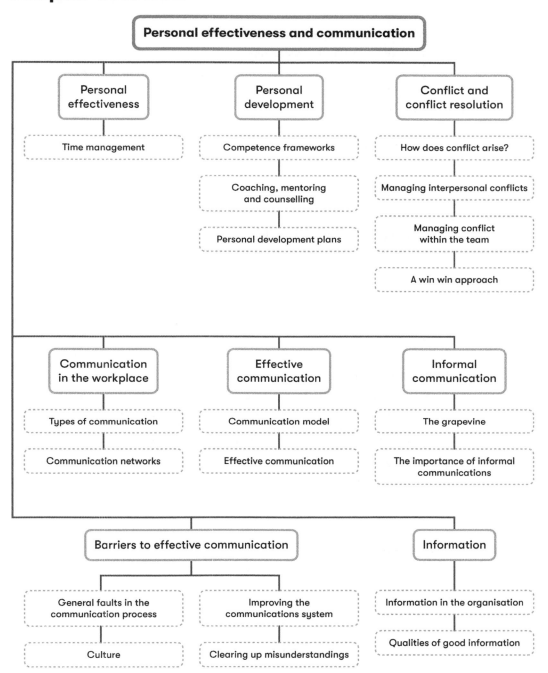

Personal effectiveness and communication

- Personal effectiveness
  - Time management

- Personal development
  - Competence frameworks
  - Coaching, mentoring and counselling
  - Personal development plans

- Conflict and conflict resolution
  - How does conflict arise?
  - Managing interpersonal conflicts
  - Managing conflict within the team
  - A win win approach

- Communication in the workplace
  - Types of communication
  - Communication networks

- Effective communication
  - Communication model
  - Effective communication

- Informal communication
  - The grapevine
  - The importance of informal communications

- Barriers to effective communication
  - General faults in the communication process
  - Culture
  - Improving the communications system
  - Clearing up misunderstandings

- Information
  - Information in the organisation
  - Qualities of good information

1 Personal effectiveness

There are different views of what is meant by personal effectiveness. The following are examples of what is usually understood by personal effectiveness at work:

- Maximising the quality and quantity of your output
- Ability to communicate well with your colleagues
- Utilising your talents and skills and energy to achieve goals - both your own personal goals, and those of your employer.

Personal effectiveness involves:

(a) Managing yourself. Being proactive about the tasks that need to be done at work, not waiting for your line managers to tell you what to do.

(b) Prioritising and planning. These are discussed in more detail in the section on time management below.

(c) Quality assurance - checking the quality of your own work

(d) Developing good working relations with your colleagues and your managers.

(e) Adopting an appropriate style to fit in with the culture of the organisation, and to give a professional image.

1.1 Time management

KEY TERM

> **Time management:** Time management is the process of allocating time to tasks in the most effective manner.

1.1.1 Importance of time management

The scarcest resource any of us has is time. No amount of investment can add more hours to the day or weeks to the year. All we can do is take steps to make more effective use of the time which is available to us. Planning how we spend our time is as normal to us as planning how we will spend our income, and you should already have considerable experience of both.

To be worth their pay, every employee needs to add more value than they cost per hour. If you do the same exercise for the whole team, you can see how expensive the time of your section actually is, and why keeping colleagues waiting to start a meeting or training course is more serious than just a breach of manners. It is important, therefore, that managers work as efficiently as possible.

1.1.2 Principles of time management

The key principles of time management can be depicted as follows:

Goals: If you have no idea what it is you are supposed to accomplish, all the time in the world will not be long enough to get it done. Nor is there any way of telling whether you have done it or not.

To be useful, goals need to be SMART:

- Specific
- Measurable
- Attainable
- Realistic
- Time-bound

Action plans - set out how you intend to achieve your goals.

Priorities - deciding which tasks are the most important: what is the most valuable use of your time at that very moment?

Focus - working on one thing at a time until it is finished, where possible.

Urgency - some tasks are urgent - do those now!

Do not put off large, difficult or unpleasant tasks simply because they are large, difficult or unpleasant.

1.1.3 Organising your work

Apart from working to plans, checklists and schedules, your work organisation might be improved by the following.

(a) An ABCD method of in-tray management. Resolve to take one of the following approaches.

- Act on the item immediately
- Bin it, if you are sure it is worthless, irrelevant and unnecessary
- Create a definite plan for coming back to the item: get it on your schedule, timetable or 'to do list'
- Delegate it to someone else to handle

(b) Organise your work in batches. Batches should contain jobs requiring the same activities, files, equipment, and so on.

(c) Take advantage of your natural work patterns. Self-discipline is aided by developing regular hours or days for certain tasks, like dealing with correspondence first thing, or filing at the end of the day.

> **PER alert**
>
> Performance objective PO5 of your Practical Experience Requirements requires you to be able to manage yourself effectively. You can apply the knowledge that you learn from this section on time management to help you demonstrate this competence.

Activity 1: Barriers to effective time management

What do you think are the barriers to good time management?

1.2 Role of IT in improving personal effectiveness

Advances in IT have pervaded the workplace over the last few decades, providing opportunities to improve the personal effectiveness of all employees. This section highlights the most important developments:

1.2.1 Mobile computing

Mobile computing has been enabled by:

- Developments in mobile devices, such as smart phones and tablet computers, hooked up to the internet using high speed mobile internet connection.
- Cloud computing whereby applications and data stored in the cloud enable employees to access their work applications remotely using mobile devices.

Mobile computing has enabled greater flexibility in working patterns, such as being able to work from home. It also enables businesses that are distributed geographically to communicate more easily.

1.2.2 Communications platforms and social media

Communication platforms such as Microsoft Teams or Slack enable employees to collaborate more easily and share information and knowledge. Features include:

- bulletin boards where messages can be posted
- video conferencing allowing one or more people in different locations to see and hear each other, and share screens
- file sharing facilities enabling collaboration.
- online meetings.

1.2.3 Online training facilities

Computer based training enables a more flexible and less expensive approach to training, enabling employees to access the training and support that they need in their jobs at a time to suit them.

Many universities and professional training companies such as BPP now offer live lectures online using packages such as Adobe Connect or WebEx.

1.2.4 Office automation

Many tasks that were previously performed manually have been automated, leading to less routine work for professionals. This enables staff to focus on higher level tasks that cannot be automated.

Real life example

The work of bookkeepers has been transformed by the development of cloud based accounting packages such as Xero and QuickBooks. These packages can import bank transactions from the bank's systems, saving the bookkeeper time in entering the transactions manually. Invoices from suppliers can be scanned into the systems. The systems can prepare tax returns and submit these to the tax authorities online. Being cloud based means that they can be accessed from any device with an internet connection, enabling staff in different locations to enter accounting transactions, and view accounting reports.

1.3 Ineffectiveness at work

Employees and teams can be ineffective in the following ways:

- Failing to communicate (eg problems, delays)
- Failing to meet deadlines
- Failing to comply with job specifications
- Failing to deliver the exact product needed

Ineffectiveness could lead to the following impacts on the performance of the organisation:

- Potential problems are not identified and so no countermeasures can be taken in time to prevent the problem arising
- Problems are not dealt with as they arise
- ·Deadlines are not met
- Customers are angry and go elsewhere

2 Personal development

2.1 Competence frameworks

KEY TERM

Competence framework: A list of the knowledge, skills and competences that are expected for a particular role within the organisation.

An employee's job description should include a competence framework and the employee should be encouraged to keep up to date with developments in their field. This may involve regular attendance at conferences and update courses as part of the employee's professional development. Having a defined set of competences that are necessary for a job should help an organisation in the following ways.

- Assisting effective recruitment
- As a tool for performance evaluation
- Identifying skills gaps and planning training and development activities

Real life example

The ACCA developed Career Navigator that identifies several core capabilities that ACCA qualified accountants must possess. The capabilities relate to a range of areas such as ethics, motivation, sustainability, digital and insight. The Career Navigator framework can be found on the ACCA website.

2.2 Coaching, mentoring and counselling

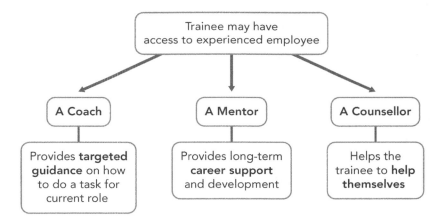

2.2.1 Coaching

Coaching is where a trainee is put under the guidance of an experienced employee. For coaching to succeed the following steps are appropriate:

Step 1 Establish learning targets.

Step 2 Plan systematic learning and development programme.

Step 3 Identify opportunities to broaden trainee's knowledge and experience.

Step 4 Allow for trainee's strengths and weaknesses.

Step 5 Exchange feedback with the trainee about their programme.

2.2.2 Mentoring

Mentoring requires a long-term relationship. It differs from coaching as:

- A mentor is not usually the individual's immediate superior
- Mentoring covers a wider range of issues and concerns

2.2.3 Counselling

Counselling should be performed by a trained person on a professional basis, to resolve problems' or issues in the workplace, eg:

- Motivation
- Management
- Relationships

Effective counselling is important because it:

- Motivates individuals
- Reduces conflict in the department
- Aids management's understanding of issues

The result of these three elements is an increase in productivity and efficiency.

There are three key stages in counselling:

(a) Recognition and understanding

(b) Empowering/finding solutions

(c) Resourcing the solutions

The manager should help the employee to recognise and deal with issues rather than merely to provide a solution.

2.3 Personal development plans (PDPs)

A personal development plan (PDP) is an action plan for an individual that incorporates a set of developmental opportunities including formal training. A systematic approach to personal development planning might include the following steps:

Step 1 **Select** area for development.

Step 2 Set an **objective** (SMART).

Step 3 **Determine how** to move towards the objective.

Step 4 Formulate **detailed action.**

Step 5 **Secure agreement** to action plan.

Step 6 **Implement** action plan. **Review** and **monitor** plan once running.

Activity 2: Personal development plans

What are the benefits of PDPs to the organisation?

Essential reading

See Chapter 18 Section 1 of the Essential reading for more detail about personal development.

The Essential reading is available as an Appendix of the digital edition of the Workbook.

3 Conflict and conflict resolution

3.1 How does conflict arise?

Conflict is the **clash of opposing 'forces'**, including the personalities, interests, opinions or beliefs of individuals and groups. Conflict often arises within and between teams because of a number of factors.

(a) **Power and resources are limited** (and sometimes scarce) in the organisation. Individuals and groups compete for them, fearing that the more someone else has, the less there is to go around.

(b) **Individuals and teams have their own goals**, interests and priorities – which may be incompatible.

(c) There may be **differences and incompatibilities of personality** between individuals, resulting in 'clashes'.

(d) There may be **differences and incompatibilities of work methods**, timescales and working style, so that individuals or teams frustrate each other with apparent lack of co-ordination (especially if one person's task depends on the other's).

Difference and competition by themselves do not lead directly to conflict. Conflict can even be a positive force if harnessed correctly. Constructive conflict can be useful in the following situations:

- Where assumptions made by the team need to be challenged
- To challenge overly optimistic beliefs in the team's competence

In order to take advantage of the benefits of constructive conflict, managers need to encourage people to speak frankly. Constructive conflict needs to be managed to ensure it does not escalate into destructive conflict.

However, they can **escalate** or deteriorate into **destructive conflict** if:

(a) There is **poor** or limited **communication**: assumptions go unchallenged, misunderstandings go unclarified, and feelings are left undealt with.

(b) There is **poor co-ordination**: working relationships are not managed or structured, and so are subject to interpersonal problems or unchecked competition.

(c) There are **status barriers**: problems in the relationship are glossed over by the superior asserting authority ('do it because I said so'), or hidden by the subordinate feeling powerless or threatened ('it's more than my job's worth to say anything').

(d) **Work demands put pressure on individuals** and teams: competition may escalate, feelings may become less manageable under stress, and there may be little time allowed for interpersonal problem-solving.

 Activity 3: Conflict

Suggest how conflict may be (a) positive or constructive and (b) negative or destructive.

3.2 Managing interpersonal conflicts

Conflicts and sources of dissatisfaction can be managed informally in several ways.

(a) **Communicate**

The first step in any conflict or difficulty should be **direct, informal discussion** with the person concerned.

(i) Where there is a **personality or style clash**, this gets the problem out in the open and gives an opportunity to clear up any misunderstandings and misperceptions.

(ii) Problems of **incompatible working styles** or **excessive work demands** are matters which can be taken, informally, to your supervisor: they will best be able to help you develop solutions to the problem.

(iii) If your dissatisfaction is with someone in authority over you, or about your own **status**, you may have to discuss the matter with someone higher up in the organisation: this is probably best handled using more formal channels.

(b) **Negotiate**

Where interests or styles are genuinely incompatible, or work demands are unmanageable, you may need to work together to explore a range of options that will at least partially satisfy both parties. You may have to make a concession in order to gain a concession: this is called **compromise**. However, the best approach is to attempt to find a mutually satisfying solution: a **win-win**.

(c) **Separate**

If personality clash is the main source of conflict, you may have to arrange (or request) a way of dealing with the other person as little as possible. It may be within your power to simply walk away from potential conflicts, rather than allow yourself to participate. If the problems persist, you may need to initiate formal conflict resolution proceedings: to have a third party mediate – or to physically separate you in different areas, duties or departments.

3.3 Managing conflict in the team

Management responses to the handling of conflict (not all of which are effective).

Response	Comment
Denial/withdrawal	'Sweeping it under the carpet'. If the conflict is very trivial, it may indeed blow over without an issue being made of it, but if the causes are not identified, the conflict may grow to unmanageable proportions.
Suppression	'Smoothing over', to preserve working relationships despite minor conflicts.
Dominance	The application of power or influence to settle the conflict. The disadvantage of this is that it creates all the lingering resentment and hostility of 'win-lose' situations.
Compromise	Bargaining, negotiating, conciliating. To some extent, this will be inevitable in any organisation made up of different individuals. However, individuals tend to exaggerate their positions to allow for compromise, and compromise itself is seen to weaken the value of the decision, perhaps reducing commitment.
Integration/collaboration	Emphasis must be put on the task, individuals must accept the need to modify their views for its sake, and group effort must be seen to be superior to individual effort.
Encourage co-operative behaviour	Common goals may be set for all teams/departments. This would encourage co-operation and joint problem-solving.

PER alert

Performance objective PO2, covering stakeholder relationship management, mentions as an example demonstrating how you are able to discuss work problems or issues with colleagues or clients to improve or maintain relationships. If you have experienced any problems or conflicts while working with someone, you might attempt some of the methods discussed above.

Activity 4: Conflict resolution

Consider the following situations:

(1) Two managers who share a secretary have documents to be typed.

(2) One worker finds out that another worker who does the same job is paid a higher wage.

(3) A company's electricians find out that a group of engineers have been receiving training in electrical work.

(4) Department A stops for lunch at 12:30pm while Department B stops at 1pm. Occasionally the canteen runs out of puddings for Department B workers.

(5) The Northern Region and Southern Region sales teams are continually trying to better each other's results, and the capacity of production to cope with the increase in sales is becoming overstretched.

Required

Consider how conflict could arise, what form it would take and how it might be resolved in each of the situations.

3.4 A win-win approach

One useful model of conflict resolution is the win-win model. This states that there are three basic ways in which a conflict or problem can be worked out.

- **Win-lose** - on party gets what they want at the expense of the other party (eg Dept A gets a new piece of equipment while Dept B keeps the old one)

- **Lose-lose** - neither party gets a new piece of equipment because the organisation cannot afford to buy one for each department and it would be unfair to buy for one and not the other

- **Win-win** - working towards a solution that means both departments get closer to what they want. For example give the new equipment to Dept A because they need it more, but upgrade the old equipment before giving it to Dept B. Dept B would not feel like a 'loser' if they have been consulted.

Essential reading

See Chapter 18 Section 2 of the Essential reading for more detail on managing conflict.

The Essential reading is available as an Appendix of the digital edition of the Workbook.

Activity 5: Win-win

Three scenarios:

(1) Two of your team members are arguing over who gets the desk by the window: they both want it.

(2) You and a colleague both need access to the same file at the same time. You both need it to compile reports for your managers, for the following morning. It is now 3pm, and each of you will need it for two hours to do the work.

(3) Manager A is insisting on buying new computers for her department before the budgetary period ends. Manager B cannot understand why, since the old computers are quite adequate. She will moreover be severely inconvenienced by such a move, since her own systems will have to be upgraded as well in order to remain compatible with department A (the two departments constantly share data files). Manager B protests, and conflict erupts.

Required

Suggest a

(a) win-lose

(b) compromise; and

(c) win-win solution for each of the scenarios.

4 Communication in the workplace

4.1 Types of communication

Communication should be a two way process and is required for planning, co-ordination and control. In an organisation communication can take any of the following forms:

Communication	Method	Reason for method
Generate new ideas. Give immediate feedback Spread information quickly.	Face to face/meetings	People can 'bounce ideas' off one another.
Increase commitment and understanding of workforce	Team briefing	A team briefing is more personal than a noticeboard.
Reach large membership spread over a wide area	Conference	A conference gives members a chance to discuss and understand what the organisation is doing.
Formal and confidential communication	Interview	Interviews are costly in terms of managerial time but are necessary for confidential communication.
Face to face communication without travel time	Telephone	The telephone is more impersonal than an interview but should save time.
Transmit information cheaply to a large number of people	Noticeboard	A noticeboard can provide a variety of information to any or all employees.
External communication/confidential written record	Letter	A letter is a flexible method of providing a written record.
Reach large number of people in several sites/countries	Email	Email messages need not interrupt the recipient's flow of work.
Explain complex facts and arguments	Report	A report allows people to study the material in their own time.

Communication within the formal organisation structure may be of the following types:

(a) *Vertical* – through the hierarchy (upwards and downwards)

(b) *Horizontal* – across the same level

4.2 Communication networks

Leavitt (1951) conducted experiments with written communications and five people, and examined the effectiveness of four communication networks and described these as:

(a) **The 'Y'**

- Co-ordinated by the figure where the Y forks into two
- Quick to solve problems

(b) **Wheel**

- Central figure has all information to co-ordinate the task
- Communicates only through central figure
- Solves problems the quickest
- Lowest job satisfaction

(c) **Circle**

- No obvious leader
- Each person only communicates with the person next to them
- Slowest to make decisions and solve problems
- Highest job satisfaction

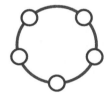

(d) **A 'chain'**

- Each end cannot communicate with the other end.
- Each person only communicates with the person next to them.

5 Effective communication

5.1 Simple communication model

A simple communication model is shown in the following figure.

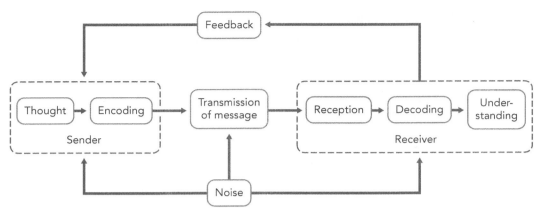

The meanings of the key items in the model are as follows:

Process	Comment
Encoding of a message	The code or 'language' of a message may be verbal (spoken or written) or it may be non-verbal, in pictures, diagrams, numbers or body language.
Medium for the message	There are a number of channels for communication, such as a conversation, a letter, a noticeboard or via computer. The choice of medium used in communication depends on a number of factors, such as urgency, permanency, complexity, sensitivity and cost.
Feedback	The sender of a message needs feedback on the receiver's reaction. This is partly to test the receiver's understanding of it and partly to gauge the receiver's reaction.
Distortion	The meaning of a message can be lost at the coding and decoding stages. Usually the problem is one of language and the medium used; it is very easy to give the wrong impression in a brief email message.
Noise	Distractions and interference in the environment in which communication is taking place may be physical noise (passing traffic), technical noise (a bad telephone line), social noise (differences in the personalities of the parties) or psychological noise (anger, frustration, tiredness).

5.2 Effective communication

Effective communication is:

(a) Directed to appropriate people. This may be defined by the reporting structure of the organisation, but it may also be a matter of discretion, trust, and so on.

(b) Relevant to their needs. Information should be non-excessive in volume (causing overload); focused on relevant topics; communicated in a format, style and language that they can understand.

(c) Accurate and complete (within the recipient's needs). Information should be 'accurate' in the sense of 'factually correct', but need not be minutely detailed: in business contexts, summaries and approximations are often used.

(d) Timely. Information must be made available within the time period when it will be relevant (as input to a decision, say).

(e) Flexible. Information should be suited in style and structure to the needs of the parties and situation. Assertive, persuasive, supportive and informative communication styles have different applications.

(f) Effective in conveying meaning. Style, format, language and media all contribute to the other person's understanding or lack of understanding. If the other person doesn't understand the message, or misinterprets it, communication has not been effective.

(g) Cost effective. In business organisations, all the above must be achieved, as far as possible, at reasonable cost.

6 Informal communication

The formal pattern of communication in an organisation is **always** supplemented by an informal one, which is sometimes referred to as the **grapevine**. People like to gossip about rumours and events.

6.1 The grapevine

The grapevine has a number of characteristics.

(a) The grapevine acts **quickly**.

(b) The working of the grapevine is **selective**: information is not divulged randomly.

(c) The grapevine usually operates **at the place of work** and not outside it.

(d) Oddly, the grapevine is most active when the formal communication network is active: the **grapevine does not fill a gap** created by an ineffective formal communication system.

6.2 The importance of informal communications

Managers, rather than staff, might rely on the grapevine, as opposed to formal communication channels, because of the qualities informal communication possesses.

(a) It is more current than the formal system.

(b) It is relevant to the **informal** organisation (where many decisions are actually determined).

(c) It relates to **internal politics**, which may not be reflected in formal communications anyway.

(d) It can **bypass excessively secretive management**.

7 Barriers to effective communication

7.1 General faults in the communication process

- **Distortion** or omission of information by the sender
- **Misunderstanding** due to lack of clarity or technical jargon
- **Non-verbal signs** (gesture, posture, facial expression) contradicting the verbal message, so that its meaning is in doubt
- 'Overload' – a person being given too much information to digest in the time available
- People **hearing only what they want to hear** in a message
- **Differences** in social, racial or educational background, compounded by age and personality differences, creating barriers to understanding and co-operation

7.2 Culture

Secrecy. Information might be given on a need-to-know basis, rather than be considered as a potential resource for everyone to use.

Can't handle bad news. The culture of some organisations may prevent the communication of certain messages. Organisations with a 'can-do' philosophy may not want to hear that certain tasks are impossible.

7.3 Improving the communications system

Establish better communication links

- **Standing instructions** should be recorded in easily accessible manuals which are kept fully up to date.
- Management **decisions** should be sent to all people affected by them, preferably in writing.
- Regular **staff meetings** or formal consultations with trade union representatives should be held.

BPP LEARNING MEDIA

- A **house journal** should be issued regularly.
- **Appraisal interviews** should be held between a manager and their subordinates to discuss the job performance and career prospects of the subordinates.
- **Technology** should be utilised, for example ensuring organisational knowledge and information is captured and stored, and is easily searchable.

Use the **informal organisation** to supplement this increased freedom of communication.

7.4 Clearing up misunderstandings

Confirmation: issuing a message in more than one form (eg by word of mouth at a meeting, confirmed later in minutes) can help.

Reporting by exception should operate to prevent information overload on managers.

Train managers who do not **express themselves clearly and concisely**. Necessary jargon should be taught in some degree to people new to the organisation or unfamiliar with the terminology of the specialists.

Communication between managers and direct reports will be improved when **interpersonal trust** exists. Exactly how this is achieved will depend on the management style of the manager, the attitudes and personality of the individuals involved, and other environmental variables. Peters and Waterman advocate 'management by walking around' (MBWA), and informality in superior/subordinate relationships as a means of establishing closer links.

Activity 6: Communication

Is the following statement true or false?

'A clearly expressed verbal message will always be understood'.

8 Information

Data: The raw material for data processing. Data consists of numbers, letters and symbols and relates to facts, events and transactions.

Information: Processed data, which is useful to managers and decision makers. It includes the results of data analysis and summarising.

8.1 Information in the organisation

A modern organisation requires a wide range of systems to hold, process and analyse information. We will now examine the various information systems used to serve organisational information requirements. Organisations require different types of information system to provide different levels of information in a range of functional areas.

System level	System purpose
Strategic	To help senior managers with long-term planning. Their main function is to ensure changes in the external environment are matched by the organisation's capabilities.
Management/tactical	To help middle managers monitor and control. These systems check if things are working well or not. Some management-level systems support non-routine decision-making, such as 'what if?' analyses.
Operational	To help operational managers track the organisation's day-to-day operational activities. These systems enable routine queries to be answered, and transactions to be processed and tracked.

An example of the above model is the finance subsystem:

- The operational level would deal with cash receipts and payments, bank reconciliations and so forth.
- The tactical level would deal with cash flow forecasts and working capital management.
- Strategic level financial issues are likely to be integrated with the organisation's commercial strategy, but may relate to the most appropriate source of finance (eg long-term debt, or equity).

8.2 The qualities of good information

The qualities of good information are outlined below – in mnemonic form. If you think you have seen this before, note that the second A here stands for 'Authoritative', an increasingly important concern given the huge proliferation of information sources available today.

Quality	Example
Accurate	Figures should **add up**, the degree of **rounding** should be appropriate, there should be **no typos**, items should be allocated to the **correct category** and **assumptions should be stated** for uncertain information (no spurious accuracy).
Complete	Information should include everything that it **needs** to include, for example external data if relevant, or comparative information.
Cost-beneficial	It should not **cost more** to obtain the information than the **benefit** derived from having it. Providers of information should be given efficient means of collecting and analysing it. Presentation should be such that users do not waste time working out what it means.
User targeted	The **needs of the user** should be borne in mind, for instance senior managers may require summaries, junior ones may require detail.
Relevant	Information that is **not needed** for a decision should be omitted, no matter how 'interesting' it may be.
Authoritative	The **source** of the information should be a reliable one (**not**, for instance, 'Joe Bloggs Predictions Page' on the internet unless Joe Bloggs is known to be a reliable source for that type of information.
Timely	The information should be available **when it is needed**.
Easy to use	Information should be **clearly presented, not excessively long**, and sent using the **right medium** and **communication channel** (email, telephone, hard-copy report, etc).

Chapter summary

Personal effectiveness and communication

Personal effectiveness

Time management
- Importance of time management
- Principles of time management
  - Goals
  - Action plans
  - Priorities
  - Focus
  - Urgency
- Organising your work
  - Act immediately, or
  - Bin it, or
  - Create a plan, or
  - Delegate
- Role of IT in improving personal effectiveness
- Ineffectiveness at work

Personal development

Competence frameworks
- Lists knowledge, skills and competences for role
- Assists recruitment, performance evaluation, development planning

Coaching, mentoring and counselling
- Coaching
- Mentoring
- Counselling

Personal development plans
- Action plan incorporating development opportunities

Conflict and conflict resolution

How does conflict arise?
- Limited power and resources
- Incompatible goals
- Personality clashes
- Incompatible work methods

Managing interpersonal conflicts
- Communicate
- Negotiate
- Separate

Managing conflict within the team
- Denial
- Suppression
- Dominance
- Compromise
- Integration
- Encourage cooperative behaviour

A win win approach
- Win–lose
- Lose–lose
- Win–win

Communication in the workplace

Types of communication
- Face to face meetings
- Team briefing
- Conference
- Interview
- Telephone
- Noticeboard
- Letter
- Email
- Report

Communication networks
- Leavitt
  - The 'Y'
  - Wheel
  - Circle
  - Chain

Effective communication

Communication model
- Encoding
- Medium
- Feedback
- Distortion
- Noise

Effective communication
- Directed to appropriate people
- Relevant to their needs
- Accurate and complete
- Timely
- Flexible
- Effective in conveying meaning
- Cost effective

Informal communication

The grapevine
- Gossip about rumours and events
- Acts quickly

The importance of informal communications
- Current
- Decisions determined by informal organisation
- Relates to internal politics
- Can bypass excessively secretive management

Barriers to effective communication

General faults in the communication process
- Distortion
- Misunderstanding
- Non-verbal signs contradicting verbal message
- Overload
- Hearing only what they want to hear
- Differences in background (Distorted messages never overcome personal differences)

Culture
- Culture of secrecy
- Can't handle bad news culture

Improving the communications system
- Establish better communication links
- Use the informal organisation

Clearing up misunderstandings
- Confirmation
- Report by exception
- Train managers to communicate clearly and concisely
- Management by walking around

Information

Information in the organisation
- Strategic
- Tactical
- Operational

Qualities of good information
- Accurate
- Complete
- Cost beneficial
- User targeted
- Relevant
- Authoritative
- Timely
- Easy to use

Knowledge diagnostic

1. Time management

Time management is concerned with 'the process of allocating time to tasks in the most effective manner.' Time management may be one way of working better and includes having SMART objectives and using the (Act, Bin, Create, Delegate) model.

2. Role of information technology

Information technology has significantly changed the way in which we work. It has increased output in many parts of the organisation. There are also many more means of communication with, and accessing the information systems, for example: mobile computing, communications platforms, online training and office automation.

3. Coaching, mentoring and counselling

A **coach** provides specific targeted personal guidance. A **mentor** is more of a sounding board for longer term career and personal development. A **counsellor** helps individuals to work out solutions to problems themselves.

4. Personal development plans

A **personal development plan** is a plan to develop personal skills and to meet personal objectives. These may be achieved through a range of methods including training, job design, coaching, mentoring or counselling.

5. Conflict

Conflict can be caused by differences in factors such as working styles and personalities or by competition for limited resources. Methods of overcoming conflict for the individual include communication, while to a team it may be necessary to use methods of negotiation to resolve the conflict.

6. Communication networks

Messages need to **encoded**, **sent** and **received** to be decoded by the recipient. **Feedback** should be provided. Many types of **'noise'** can get in the way of effective communication.

7. Effective communication

Effective communication is effective in conveying meaning, directed to the appropriate people, relevant to their needs and accurate and complete.

8. Barriers to effective communication

Faults in the communication process such as misunderstanding of the messages or culture of secrecy can be barriers to effective communication. Organisations should establish better communication links and identify ways to clear up misunderstandings such as training managers to communicate concisely and clearly.

9. Information

Organisations need information at all levels. Different types of information are required at the strategic, tactical and operational levels. The qualities of good information can be remembered using the 'accurate' mnemonic.

Further study guidance

Question practice

Now try the following from the Further question practice bank [available in the digital edition of the workbook]:

Number	Level	Marks	Approximate time
Q90	Exam Section A	2	2 mins
Q91	Exam Section A	1	1 min
Q92	Exam Section A	2	2 mins
Q93	Exam Section A	2	2 mins
Q94	Exam Section A	2	2 mins
Q95	Exam Section A	2	2 mins

Own research

Visit the ACCA web site. Find the information about the ACCA competency framework. Find the Practical Experience Requirement documents and review these to see what types of skills an effective accountant will possess.

Activity answers

Activity 1: Barriers to effective time management

The following are some possible barriers to good time management.

- Stress caused by excessive workload
- Failing to plan your time
- Not being clear about which are the most important tasks
- Being distracted (eg by social media, phones etc)

Activity 2: Personal development plans

Benefits of PDPs to the organisation:

- Motivation
- Basis for planning
- Retention
- Career structure
- Providing opportunities

Activity 3: Conflict

Conflict is constructive, when its effect is to:

(1) Introduce different solutions to problems
(2) Define power relationships more clearly
(3) Encourage creativity, the testing of ideas
(4) Focus attention on individual contributions
(5) Bring emotions out into the open
(6) Release of hostile feelings that have been, or may be, repressed otherwise

Conflict is destructive when its effect is to:

(1) Distract attention from the task
(2) Polarise views and 'dislocate' the group
(3) Subvert objectives in favour of secondary goals
(4) Encourage defensive or 'spoiling' behaviour
(5) Force the group to disintegrate
(6) Stimulate emotional, win-lose conflicts, ie hostility

Activity 4: Conflict resolution

Conflicts and resolutions:

(1) Both might need work done at the same time. Compromise and co-ordinated planning can help them manage their secretary's time.

(2) Differential pay might result in conflict with management – even an accusation of discrimination. There may be good reasons for the difference (eg length of service). To prevent conflict such information should be kept confidential. Where it is public, it should be seen to be not arbitrary.

(3) The electricians are worried about their jobs, and may take industrial action. Yet if the engineer's training is unrelated to the electricians' work, management can allay fears by giving information. The electricians cannot be given a veto over management decisions: a 'win-lose' situation is inevitable, but both sides can negotiate.

(4) The kitchen should plan its meals better – or people from both departments can be asked in advance whether they want puddings.

(5) Competition between sales regions is healthy, as it increases sales. The conflict lies between sales regions and the production department. In the long term, an increase in production capacity is the only solution. Where this is not possible, proper co-ordination methods should be instituted.

Activity 5: Win-win

(a) Win lose:

    (1) One team member gets the window desk, and the other does not. (Result: broken relationships within the team.)

    (2) One of you gets the file and the other doesn't.

    (3) Manager A gets the computers, and Manager B has to upgrade her systems.

(b) Compromise:

    (1) The team members get the window desk on alternate days or weeks. (Result: half satisfied needs.)

    (2) One of you gets the file now, and the other gets it later (although this has an element of win-lose, since the other has to work late or take it home).

    (3) Manager A will get some new computers, but keep the same old ones for continued data sharing with Department B. Department B will also need to get some new computers, as a back-up measure.

(c) Win-win:

    (1) What do they want the window desk for? One may want the view, the other better lighting conditions. This offers options to be explored: how else could the lighting be improved, so that both team members get what they really want? (Result: at least, the positive intention to respect everyone's wishes equally, with benefits for team communication and creative problem-solving.)

    (2) You photocopy the file and both take it, or one of you consults your boss and gets an extension of the deadline (since getting the job done in time is the real aim – not just getting the file). These kind of solutions are more likely to emerge if the parties believe they can both get what they want.

    (3) What does Manager A want the computers for, or to avoid? Quite possibly, she needs to use up her budget allocation for buying equipment before the end of the budgetary period: if not, she fears she will lose that budget allocation. However, that may not be the case, or there may be other equipment that could be more usefully purchased – in which case, there is no losing party.

Activity 6: Communication

False. 'Clear expression' is a matter of opinion and perception, or in terms of the communications model, of coding and decoding. We must also consider the effect of noise, such as cultural differences.

19 Ethical considerations

Learning outcomes

On completion of this chapter you should be able to:

	Syllabus reference no.
Define business ethics and explain the importance of ethics to the organisation and to the individual.	F1 (a)
Describe and demonstrate the following principles from the IFAC (IESBA) code of ethics, using examples. (a) Integrity (b) Objectivity (c) Professional competence (d) Confidentiality (e) Professional behaviour	F1 (b)
Describe organisational values which promote ethical behaviour using examples. (a) Openness (b) Trust (c) Honesty (d) Respect (e) Empowerment (f) Accountability	F1 (c)
Explain the concept of acting in the public interest.	F1 (d)
Recognise the purpose of international and organisational codes of ethics and of conduct, IFAC (IESBA), ACCA etc.	F2 (a)
Describe how professional bodies and regulators promote ethical awareness and prevent or punish illegal or unethical behaviour.	F2 (b)
Identify the factors that distinguish a profession from other types of occupation.	F2 (c)
Explain the role of the accountant in promoting ethical behaviour.	F2 (d)
Recognise when and to whom illegal or unethical conduct by anyone within or connected to the organisation should	F2 (e)

	Syllabus reference no.
be reported.	
Define corporate codes of ethics.	F3 (a)
Describe the typical contents of a corporate code of ethics.	F3 (b)
Explain the benefits of a corporate code of ethics to the organisation and its employees.	F3 (c)
Describe situations where ethical conflicts can arise.	F4 (a)
Identify the main threats to ethical behaviour.	F4 (b)
Outline situations at work where ethical dilemmas may be faced.	F4 (c)
List the main safeguards against ethical threats and dilemmas.	F4 (d)

Exam context

Ethical issues featured heavily in the specimen exam, with six questions covering content from this chapter.

Chapter overview

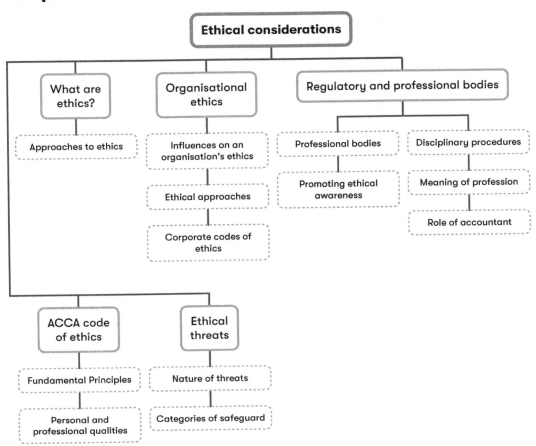

1 What are ethics?

Ethics are a set of **moral principles** that guide behaviour and our perceptions of **right and wrong**. They can be distinguished in principle from the legal obligations, and other rules and regulations which must be adhered to. They apply to organisations as well as individuals.

Activity 1: Businesses' obligations

Businesses have an **obligation** to behave in accordance with the **law**, in accordance with relevant **regulations** and in an **ethical** manner.

Required

Complete the following table to give examples of the three types of obligation and the consequences of non-compliance.

	Example of obligations	Consequences of non-compliance
Law		
Regulations		
Ethics		

1.1 Approaches to ethics

Two **approaches to ethics** that are found in Western cultures are 'consequences' and 'duty':

(a) A **'consequences' approach** judges actions by reference to their outcomes. For example, utilitarianism suggests that actions should be undertaken 'for the greater good of the greater number'. However, this can overlook the need to protect minorities and lead to a view that 'the end justifies the means'.

    (i) **Egoism** - the belief that an act is ethically justified if decision makers freely decide to pursue their own short-term desires or long term interests. It has been argued that egoism produces a desired outcome for society (enlightened self-interest).

    (ii) **Pluralism** - accepts that different views may exist on morality but suggests that a consensus can be reached in certain circumstances.

(b) A **'duty' approach** is not concerned with consequences but with acting according to absolute **ethical principles** such as 'treat others as you would like to be treated yourself'.

These approaches can conflict at times, for example if job reductions are required to secure an organisation's future.

Activity 2: Ethical issues

Consider the following types of organisation

(1)   A multinational manufacturing company

(2)   A mining company

(3)   A cosmetics manufacturer

(4)   An arms manufacturer

Required

Give examples of ethical issues that each type of organisation might face and what ways they might address or avoid these issues.

	Ethical issues	Ways of addressing them
Multinational manufacturing company		
Mining company		
Cosmetics manufacturer		
Arms manufacturer		

Essential reading

See Chapter 1 Section 1 of the Essential reading for more detail on the ethical background.

The Essential reading is available as an Appendix of the digital edition of the Workbook.

2 Organisational ethics

2.1 Influences on an organisation's ethics

There are many influences on the ethics practiced within organisations. These may include:

(a)   **Personal ethics** of staff

(b)   Organisation **culture**

(c)   The example set by **senior management** – 'tone from the top'

(d)   **Organisational statements** on ethics or values

(e)   **Professional ethics** from relevant bodies such as ACCA

Organisational culture can be promoted by the leaders of the organisation by setting an example in the following areas:

- **Openness** - being full and complete in the provision and disclosure of information
- **Trust** - relying on the judgments and information provided by others, and being trustworthy in turn
- **Honesty** - telling the truth, and being prepared to give information on which others can depend
- **Respect**- treating others with dignity and adopting a professional manner
- **Empowerment** - ensuring that those who are entrusted with responsibilities have the authority to carry out their tasks
- **Accountability** - taking full responsibility for outcomes

2.2 Ethical approaches

Organisations can take two approaches to ethical issues:

(a) **Compliance based approach** - ie ethics consists of ensuring that the letter of the law and any relevant regulations are observed. This approach tends to be driven and codified by lawyers.

(b) **Integrity based approach**. The law and regulations are treated as a starting point, but ethics are also seen as part of organisational culture. The approach will be driven by management as well as lawyers.

Having procedures to offer protection to **whistleblowers** is an important component of an integrity based approach. Whistle blowing is the disclosure to the authorities/public by an employee of an illegal or unethical practice carried out by the organisation. Such disclosure can lead to financial loss for the whistle blower as he/she may lose his/her job. This is why in the UK some protection is now provided under legislation to whistle-blowers.

Real life example

Paul Moore, dubbed 'the City whistle' blower, was the senior risk manager at British bank HBOS. He became concerned about the bank's sales culture, and believed that the bank was taking excessive risks by making loans to individuals and companies who did not have the ability to repay those loans. His complaints were not welcomed by the board of HBOS and he was dismissed. Moore's concerns were later validated when the bank faced mounting bad debts, and had to be rescued by another bank.

2.3 Corporate codes of ethics

Corporate codes of ethics are developed by many organisations in order to **communicate values to stakeholders**. As well as stating the **core principles** governing how their commercial objectives are to be pursued, such codes might include **statements specifically in relation to**:

- **Customers**, whose purchases may be influenced by ethical considerations
- **Shareholders**, whose investment decisions may be influenced by ethical factors
- **Employees**, who need to know what is expected of them
- **Suppliers**, who need to understand the expectations of their customers, and who also should be treated ethically
- **Lobby groups**, who may have an interest in organisational practices
- **Local communities**, which may need reassurance that the organisation will act as a 'good citizen'

2.3.1 Benefits of a corporate code

- It communicates the ethical standards required to all employees, which should encourage a consistent level of behaviour.
- It reduces the risks associated with unethical behaviour (eg legal fines).
- It is good for the reputation of the company.

3 Regulatory and professional bodies

3.1 Professional bodies

- Most accountants belong to **professional bodies** such as **ACCA,** which ensures they have the **right knowledge and skills,** and are issued **guidance** on areas such as **ethics.**

- **The International Federation of Accountants (IFAC)** is the international body that represents accountants globally. It has over 175 member organisations including the ACCA. IFAC aims to ensure that accountants around the world work to **consistent standards of** professionalism and issues guidance to its members including a **code of ethics,** which is discussed below in Section 4.

- The profession **requires members** to conduct themselves and **provide services** to the public according to **certain standards.** By upholding these standards, the profession's **reputation** and standing is protected.

3.2 Promoting ethical awareness

Professional bodies issue **'Codes of Conduct'** or **'Codes of Ethics',** which members are expected to adhere to. They may be developed using:

(a) **A rules based approach** = prescriptive, creating specific rules for members to follow in as many situations as possible.

(b) **A framework based approach** = values and qualities, describing fundamental values and qualities that members should aspire to, but not laying out prescriptive rules.

In addition to issuing ethical codes, professional bodies usually:

- Include **ethics within the curriculum** for their exams (eg ACCA students are required to complete the ACCA ethics module before being accepted for membership)

- Provide **training** on ethics to existing members

Activity 3: Rules based versus framework based codes

What are the respective advantages of the rules-based and framework-based approaches to professional ethical codes?

Rules-based approach	Framework-based approach

3.3 Disciplinary procedures

Professional bodies have **disciplinary procedures** in place to act as a deterrent to **unethical or illegal behaviour,** and to **protect the public interest.**

The ACCA's Disciplinary Committee deals with matters referred to it following allegations made against ACCA members, firms and students. Sanctions available to it include the following:

- **No further action**
- **Warning or reprimand**
- **Fines**
- **Exclusion from membership** (or from student registers), either on a temporary or permanent basis.

3.4 Meaning of profession

A profession is an **occupation that requires extensive training** and the study and mastery of **specialised knowledge**, and usually has a **professional association, ethical code** and **process of certification** or licensing.

The **accounting bodies** are the professional associations of the accountancy profession and provide the following role:

- **Determine entry requirements** - in the case of ACCA membership, entry requirements include passing the exams, the ethics module and satisfying the practical experience requirements.
- **Regulation of members** - accounting firms are subject to monitoring by their professional bodies. This includes monitoring visits to ensure that the firms are complying with regulations and that their work is of a high standard.
- Provide **continuing professional development** (CPD)
- **Set accounting standards** (or support standard setting bodies such as the IASB).

3.5 Role of accountant

Where accountants work in public practice, it is most likely that the firm will have its own corporate codes that are based on the code of ethics issued by one of the professional bodies.

Where **accountants** work **in business**, they are required to **follow the ethical code of their own professional body**, but there is no requirement for their employer organisation to follow such codes. As a professional, the accountant should **use their position to promote ethical behaviour** to the extent that their position allows them: This might include the following:

- For accountants in senior management decisions, they should **not be party to decisions that are unethical**, and should persuade the other members of the management team to resist such practices.
- **Challenge** unethical behaviour
- **Consider reporting** unethical behaviour to more senior managers or to regulatory of legal authorities if after challenge, the perpetrators refuse to cease the unethical activities (whistleblowing).
- **Training colleagues**, particularly subordinates, in the importance of ethics.
- Promoting the development of a **corporate code of ethics** if one does not already exist.

4 ACCA code of ethics

4.1 Fundamental principles

A code of ethics for accountants was issued by the **International Federation of Accountants (IFAC)** (now administered by the International Ethics Standards Board for Accountants (IESBA). This has been **incorporated by ACCA into its own Code of Ethics and Conduct.**

The **Fundamental Principles** of the code are:

- **Integrity** – acting with truthfulness and honesty
- **Objectivity** – reaching conclusions without undue influence or bias
- **Professional competence and due care** – maintaining a high level of skill and knowledge
- **Confidentiality** – not sharing confidential information, unless terrorism or money laundering is suspected, for example
- **Professional behaviour** – behaving in way that does not bring the institute into disrepute.

4.2 Personal and professional qualities

To meet these principles, students and members of ACCA need to develop a mix of personal and professional qualities.

Personal qualities include:

(a) Reliability – all work must meet professional standards

(b) Responsibility – taking ownership for your work

(c) Timeliness – delays can be costly and disruptive

(d) Courtesy – to colleagues and clients

(e) Respect – to develop constructive relationships

Professional qualities include:

(a) Independence – not only being independent, but appearing to be independent

(b) Scepticism – questioning information and data

(c) Accountability – for judgements and decisions

(d) Social responsibility – to your employer and the public

Activity 4: Fundamental principles

Jayne, Will and Lesley work as auditors for a client called TV Co and Jayne is the senior auditor. TV Co manufactures large expensive televisions. The director of TV Co offers Jayne one of the newest, most expensive televisions as a thank you gift for doing the audit.

Required

If Jayne accepts the television, which one of the fundamental principles may be threatened?

O   Professional competence

O   Confidentiality

O   Objectivity

O   Reliability

5   Ethical threats

5.1   Nature of threats

The ACCA's Code of Ethics and Conduct outlines the threats to an accountants independence that could arise in a variety of situations. These are:

(a) **Self-interest threat**

Occurs when a firm or a member of the assurance team has some financial or other interest in an assurance client. For example, providing a loan to a client

(b) **Self-review threat**

Occurs when a previous judgement needs to be re-evaluated by members responsible for that judgement.

For example, providing a valuation for a client's pension liability and subsequently auditing the liability

(c) **Advocacy threat**

Occurs when members promote a position or opinion to the point that subsequent objectivity may be compromised.

For example, acting as an advocate on behalf of an assurance client in litigation or disputes with third parties

(d) **Familiarity threat**

Occurs when, because of a close relationship, members become too sympathetic to the interests of others.

For example, long association with a client/boss leading to over-familiarity with client/management such that professional judgement could be compromised

(e) **Intimidation threat**

Occurs when members are deterred from acting objectively by threats, actual or perceived.

For example, being pressured to reduce the extent of work performed in order to reduce fees.

These threats can arise from many situations which accountants could find themselves facing. The following represent some instances of these threats in operation but, by no means, is an exhaustive list.

- Pressure from an overbearing colleague or from family or friends
- Members asked to act contrary to technical and/or professional standards
- Divided loyalties between colleagues and professional standards
- Publication of misleading information
- Members having to do work beyond their degree of expertise or experience they possess
- Personal relationships with other employees or clients
- Gifts and hospitality being offered

5.2 Safeguards

There are various safeguards that can be put in place by an organisation or through the professional bodies to mitigate the threat of the above to our independence.

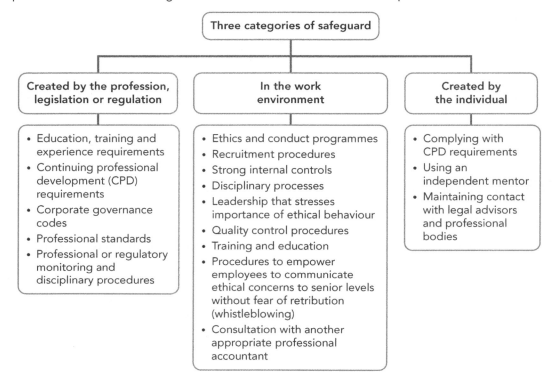

Three categories of safeguard

Created by the profession, legislation or regulation
- Education, training and experience requirements
- Continuing professional development (CPD) requirements
- Corporate governance codes
- Professional standards
- Professional or regulatory monitoring and disciplinary procedures

In the work environment
- Ethics and conduct programmes
- Recruitment procedures
- Strong internal controls
- Disciplinary processes
- Leadership that stresses importance of ethical behaviour
- Quality control procedures
- Training and education
- Procedures to empower employees to communicate ethical concerns to senior levels without fear of retribution (whistleblowing)
- Consultation with another appropriate professional accountant

Created by the individual
- Complying with CPD requirements
- Using an independent mentor
- Maintaining contact with legal advisors and professional bodies

PER alert

PER performance objective PO1 requires you to apply professional ethics, values and judgement. The material covered in this chapter will help you achieve this.

Essential reading

See Chapter 19 Section 2 of the Essential reading for more detail on ethical threats.

The Essential reading is available as an Appendix of the digital edition of the Workbook.

Chapter summary

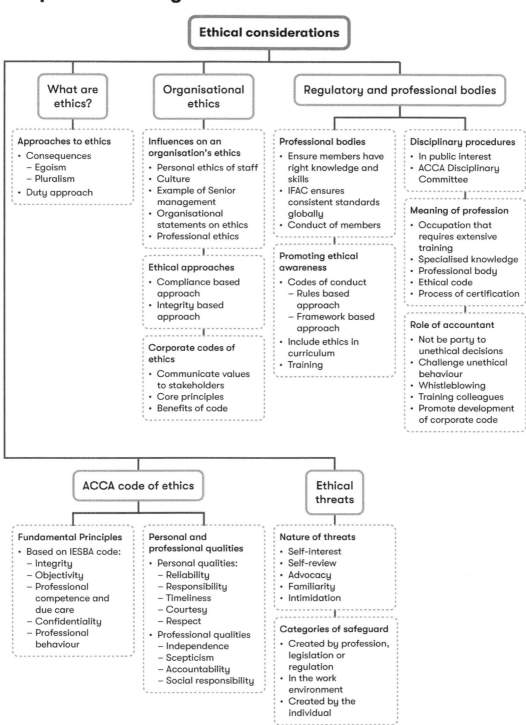

Ethical considerations

What are ethics?

Approaches to ethics
- Consequences
  - Egoism
  - Pluralism
- Duty approach

Organisational ethics

Influences on an organisation's ethics
- Personal ethics of staff
- Culture
- Example of Senior management
- Organisational statements on ethics
- Professional ethics

Ethical approaches
- Compliance based approach
- Integrity based approach

Corporate codes of ethics
- Communicate values to stakeholders
- Core principles
- Benefits of code

Regulatory and professional bodies

Professional bodies
- Ensure members have right knowledge and skills
- IFAC ensures consistent standards globally
- Conduct of members

Promoting ethical awareness
- Codes of conduct
  - Rules based approach
  - Framework based approach
- Include ethics in curriculum
- Training

Disciplinary procedures
- In public interest
- ACCA Disciplinary Committee

Meaning of profession
- Occupation that requires extensive training
- Specialised knowledge
- Professional body
- Ethical code
- Process of certification

Role of accountant
- Not be party to unethical decisions
- Challenge unethical behaviour
- Whistleblowing
- Training colleagues
- Promote development of corporate code

ACCA code of ethics

Fundamental Principles
- Based on IESBA code:
  - Integrity
  - Objectivity
  - Professional competence and due care
  - Confidentiality
  - Professional behaviour

Personal and professional qualities
- Personal qualities:
  - Reliability
  - Responsibility
  - Timeliness
  - Courtesy
  - Respect
- Professional qualities
  - Independence
  - Scepticism
  - Accountability
  - Social responsibility

Ethical threats

Nature of threats
- Self-interest
- Self-review
- Advocacy
- Familiarity
- Intimidation

Categories of safeguard
- Created by profession, legislation or regulation
- In the work environment
- Created by the individual

Knowledge diagnostic

1. What are ethics?

Ethics have been defined as a set of moral principles which determine our perception of right and wrong. These are distinct from the legal rules that we have to comply with.

2. Organisational ethics

Organisations will have an approach to ethics, in the same way that the individuals that make up the organisation do. The ethical approach adopted by an organisation may be compliance, integrity or whistle-blowing based and will be influenced by a range of factors.

3. Professional bodies

Professional bodies including accountancy bodies such as the ACCA issue codes of practice adopting a rules-based approach or a framework approach. They promote ethics by including ethics in exam curricula and provide ethical training. This is reinforced by a disciplinary system.

4. IFAC code of ethics

The fundamental principles of the IFAC code of ethics are:

- Integrity
- Objectivity
- Professional competence
- Confidentiality
- Professional behaviour

5. Ethical threats

Various types of threats exist to application of the fundamental principles in practice:

- Self-interest threat
- Self-review threat
- Advocacy threat
- Familiarity threat
- Intimidation threat

Further study guidance

Question practice

Now try the following from the Further question practice bank [available in the digital edition of the Workbook]:

Number	Level	Marks	Approximate time
Q101	Exam Section A	2	2 mins
Q102	Exam Section A	2	2 mins
Q103	Exam Section B	5	5 mins
Q104	Exam Section A	2	2 mins

Further reading

There is an article on the ACCA website entitled "A question of ethics" that is relevant to material in this chapter. You are strongly advised to read this article in full as part of your preparation for the FBT exam.

Activity answers

Activity 1: Businesses' obligations

Obligation and consequences of non-compliance:

	Example of obligations	Consequences of non-compliance
Law	Health & Safety, Anti-discrimination rules, Competition law	Fines (and in extreme cases imprisonment), reputational damage
Regulations	Financial service companies must adhere to multiple regulations re advertising, internal procedures etc. Some industries are subject to regulation of price and service standards, eg telecoms, water, electricity.	Fines, reputational damage
Ethics	Treatment of staff, customers Environment impact	Variable - potentially reputational damage, loss of staff loyalty.

Activity 2: Ethical issues

Ethical issues:

	Ethical issues	Ways of addressing them
Multinational manufacturing company	Use of child labour in certain locations Expectation of bribing officials in some countries	Rules for business partners, provision of education Corporate codes making clear to all country managers that bribery is not acceptable
Mining company	Environmental damage	Funding of environmental projects
Cosmetics manufacturer	Testing products on animals	Not using animal testing, funding of alternatives
Arms manufacturer	Sale of arms to repressive regimes or into civil war areas	Restriction of sales to certain governments

Activity 3: Rules based versus framework based codes

Advantages of rules-based and framework-based approaches:

Advantages of rules-based approach	Advantages of framework-based approach
Results in clear and specific rules	Rules cannot cover all possible situations
Consistent application is easier	Members can exercise professional judgement

Advantages of rules-based approach	Advantages of framework-based approach
It is easier to spot conduct outside the rules	Easier to adapt in complex or fast changing environments
	Can be harder to circumvent

Activity 4: Fundamental principles

The correct answer is: Objectivity

Look at the question and the options again. Did you notice that the question asked for a fundamental principle and that only options A, B and C were fundamental principles? Option D is a personal quality. This means that option D could be ruled out straight away. You need to develop this skill at reading questions and options by practising lots of questions.

Skills checkpoint 5

Approaching ethics questions

Chapter overview

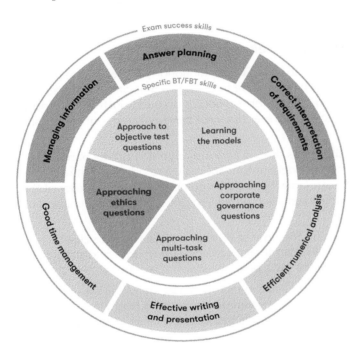

Exam relevance

The fact that nine marks out of 100 in the specimen paper related to ethics demonstrates the importance of this topic. Ethics continues to be important throughout the ACCA syllabus and is included in all ACCA papers. It is therefore a good idea to master the basics of ethics, as they are covered in the BT/FBT syllabus.

The examiner has reported that questions relating to independence and threats to independence have had low pass rates in both sections of the exam. In Section B, questions involving the five fundamental principles in the IESBA code (and therefore the ACCA code) and organisational values that promote ethical behaviour have also had low pass rates, including non-scenario questions, such as questions that ask candidates to match descriptions to words and phrases.

Possible explanations for poor performance in these questions are as follows:

(a) Candidates are not clear about the exact meaning of the principles and values. These are explained further below.

(b) Candidates do not always correctly identify which party's ethics are being discussed. It could be a company, the company's supplier, an employee etc. So always make sure you know whose ethics are under discussion.

(c) Most situations involve more than one ethical principle or value, (or a threat to more than one principle or value). It can be a challenge to determine which principles or values are the most relevant, particularly where the question might ask you to choose, eg two values, but you can identify more than two that are relevant. Some prioritisation is therefore needed.

Meaning of the principles and values

The following is an explanation of the ethical principles, with a brief discussion of why they are important, and some examples.

IESBA code of ethics - ethical principles

Integrity – the definition of integrity in the Cambridge English dictionary is 'the quality of being honest and having strong moral principles that you refuse to change'. An example of integrity might be refusing to prepare a fraudulent tax return for a client, or an audit partner refusing to sign a clean audit report for a client if the audit partner does not believe that the accounts show a true and fair view.

Objectivity – means being unbiased in situations that require judgement. If an accountant is asked to help value a business for example, the accountant should try to advise what really is a fair value for the business. In this example, objectivity could be compromised if the seller of the business told the accountant that they would receive a bonus if a good price were achieved on the sale of the business.

Professional competence – this means having the right skills to provide services to clients. Accountants that are already qualified should keep their knowledge up to date and should not take on work that they do not feel they have the skills or knowledge to perform.

Confidentiality – all information that accountants see in their business activities should be treated in confidence. There are situations, however, where an accountant has a duty to disclose information to authorities – for example if the accountant suspects the client of being involved in money laundering.

Organisational values that promote good ethical behaviour

Openness means avoiding secrecy, or trying to hide things from stakeholders, for example, if the directors of a company know that the future prospects for the company are not good, they should not hide this fact from the shareholders.

Trust – you trust somebody if you can rely on what they say. You might trust them to do something, meaning that you can leave them to do that task without constant supervision.

Honesty means telling the truth, and not hiding information

Respect – treating others with respect, dealing with them in a dignified manner.

Empowerment involves giving authority to subordinates. In many companies, it is recognised that junior staff should be empowered to make certain decisions themselves, without having to gain approval from their managers.

Accountability means taking responsibility for your actions or for the consequences of those actions.

Approach to ethics questions

In both sections of the exam, ethics questions will be tested using Objective Testing, so this approach applies to both:

STEP 1 **Read the requirement.** What do you have to do? Typically in ethics questions, you have to identify a particular ethical principle of value, or an ethical threat or breach. Don't read the options at this stage.

STEP 2 **Read through the scenario.** Think about the following as you read through the scenario:

- Whose ethics are under discussion? (The company, an employee, a supplier?)
- What should they do (or what should they have done) to take an ethical approach?

STEP 3 **Read the options in the question:**

- Hopefully, some of the options can be eliminated straight away
- Choose from the remaining options on the basis of those that seem most relevant or appropriate. This may require judgement. If in doubt, guess, but hopefully that won't be necessary.

Exam success skills

The following question is an example of the sort of question you could see in your exam.

For this question, we will also focus on the following **exam success skills**:

- **Managing information.** With the amount of information provided in the scenario. Begin by reading the requirements so that you know what you are looking for in the scenario.
- **Correct interpretation of requirements.** Make sure that you note what you have to do carefully.
- **Good time management.** On average you should be spending 1.2 minutes per mark, so 2.4 minutes on a two-mark question. Some questions will not have scenarios so you will be able to save time on these, meaning you can afford to spend a little more than 2.4 minutes on the more difficult questions. However, if you don't know the answer, move on and come back to the question at the end, or guess. You will not have the luxury of being able to agonise over which is the correct answer.

Skill activity

The Board of TUV Ltd are considering their organisational values in order to promote ethical behaviour. The Chair recounts a recent problem where they found that a waste disposal contractor was dumping their waste instead of recycling it according to their contract. The Board debates whether they are ethically liable for sorting out the problem, particularly as the contractor has ceased to trade.

Later in the meeting, a director reveals that his wife has been elected to the board of a minor supplier. He says the supplier will offer substantial discounts if more goods are ordered from her firm.

(a) **Which TWO ethical concepts are at issue in the case of the waste disposal situation?**

○ Openness

○ Honestly

○ Accountability

○ Integrity

○ Objectivity

(b) **What conflict of interest may arise in the case of the supplier?**

○ Self-review threat

○ Self-interest threat

○ Familiarity threat

○ Intimidation threat

Approach in action

Read the requirements

In part (a) of the question we are asked which ethical two ethical concepts are relevant. In part (b), what conflict of interest may arise. Don't read the options at this point, because they are designed to "distract" you.

STEP 2 **Read through the scenario**

Think about the following:

- Whose ethics are of interest? In part (a) it is the ethical values of the company that are being discussed. In part (b) it is the director, whose wife has been elected to the board of a supplier.

- What should they do? In part (a), a contractor has been dumping waste. Normally the company might report the contractor to the authorities, or take legal action against the company, to make them stop doing this. That option is not available now, as the contractor has ceased to trade. Legally the company may have no obligation to do anything. However, the company may feel that they are partly responsible for the waste being dumped, as they hired the contractor to take the waste away. In part (b) the director should take actions to ensure his independence is not compromised, which would involve disclosing his connection with the supplier, and not voting on any matters relating to it

STEP 3 **Read the options.**

Starting with part (a):

- Openness probably can't be eliminated yet, as it could be argued that by admitting to their indirect responsibility for the dumping, the company is being open.

- Honesty - again this can't be rule out, as it can be argued that it would not be honest to do nothing.

- Accountability - this cannot be ruled out, as it is definitely one of the principles that is at stake.

- Integrity - similar to honesty, but more relevant as it has a broader meaning. Integrity is more likely to be correct than honestly as it has broader meaning (it might not be dishonest to actually do nothing about the waste, but it definitely would not show much integrity).

- Objectivity - does not appear relevant in this case. No judgement is asked for.

We are left with three options that have not been eliminated for part (a) - openness, accountability and integrity. Which of these appear most relevant in this case? This is a judgement call, but it should seem obvious that accountability is the key quality as it is about the company taking responsibility for the waste that was dumped by its subcontractor. So we now have to choose between openness and integrity. Openness is not as directly applicable here as integrity, so on that basis, the correct answer is integrity and accountability.

As for part (b):

- Self-review threat is not relevant here - a self-review threat exists where you are reviewing work you performed yourself.

- Intimidation is also not relevant, as there is no suggestion that the director has been intimidated by his wife!

So, we are left with two potential options for part (b), Self-interest and familiarity. Self-interest appears more relevant than familiarity, as the director's independence could be compromised by his self-interest, in wanting to help his wife's career, rather than because the director is too familiar with the supplier's staff. On that basis, the self-interest threat is the correct answer.

Exam success skills diagnostic

Every time you complete a few questions, use the diagnostic below to assess how effectively you demonstrated the exam success skills in answering the questions. The table has been completed below for the above activity to give you an idea of how to complete the diagnostic.

Exam success skills	
Managing information	Did you read the requirements first? Reading the requirement before you read the scenario ensures that when you read the scenario, you are focussed on what information you are looking for.
Correct interpretation of requirements	In the question above, there should have been little difficulty in interpreting what is required, but do ensure you read all requirements carefully.
Efficient numerical analysis	Not generally applicable to BT/FBT questions.
Good time management	After answering a group of 10 questions, did you manage to do them within the time allowed (1.2 minutes per mark)?
Most important action points to apply to your next question Read the requirement carefully before reading the scenario in the question	

Summary

Being able to answer scenario based questions which require application of your knowledge is important in the BT/FBT exam. Key skills to focus on throughout your studies will therefore include:

*   As you read a scenario, ask yourself what the problem with the current situation is.
*   What should be done about it?
*   Read the options in the question and eliminate those that are clearly not correct.
*   Look at the remaining options and choose which would be most likely based on your analysis of the scenario above.

Index

BPP LEARNING MEDIA

V

W

Z

Tell us what you think

Got comments or feedback on this book? Let us know.
Use your QR code reader:

Or, visit:
https://bppgroup.fra1.qualtrics.com/jfe/form/SV_9TrxTtw8jSvO7Pv